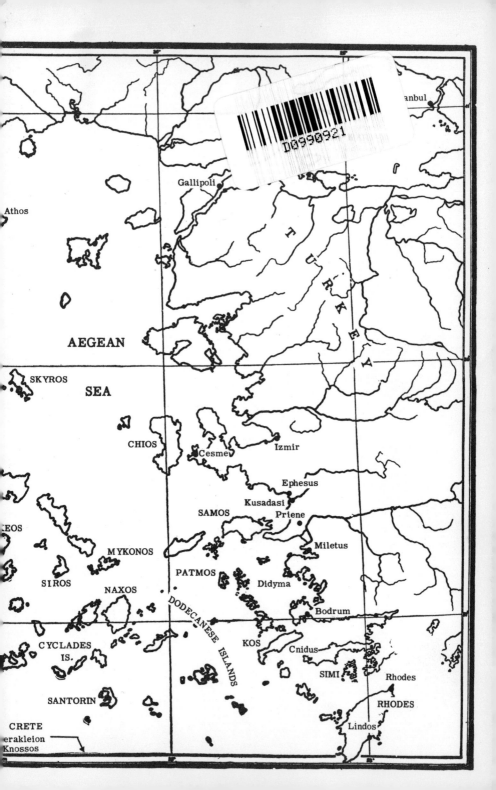

anbul

Gallipoli

Athos

T
U
R
K
E
Y

AEGEAN

SKYROS

SEA

CHIOS

Cesme

Izmir

Ephesus

Kusadasi

SAMOS

Priene

KEOS

Miletus

MYKONOS

PATMOS

Didyma

SIROS

Bodrum

NAXOS

DODECANESE ISLANDS

CYCLADES
IS.

KOS

Cnidus

SIMI

Rhodes

SANTORIN

RHODES

CRETE
erakleion
Knossos

Lindos

Landfalls Remembered

Anne Hyde Choate

Oct. 1963 —

Rara Avis in Aegean waters, 1960

Landfalls
Remembered

Susan S. Hammond

New York: A. S. Barnes and Company, Inc.
London: Thomas Yoseloff Ltd.

To
Mnemosyne
Goddess of Memory
and to the
People of Greece
Their Past and Their Future

Preface

Due to the whirlwind speed at which the face of earth, sky, and sea are changing nowadays, this volume can hardly offer itself as a dependable guide to travel. The days when it was the custom to carry an up-to-date Baedeker instead of a passport are over. However, during our six Mediterranean cruises, I was able to note along the way some of the amenities of travel, such as attractive restaurants, comfortable hotels, and a few unsung islands with safe harbors—all of which factors added greatly to our convenience and pleasure. My hope is that these pages may perhaps act as steppingstones from which other travelers will want to do their own exploring.

The orthography in this book is not entirely consistent. The Greek alphabet does not translate itself letter for letter into English or European alphabets, and due to the antiquity of the region, time has gradually applied a variety of spellings to Greek geographical names. For instance, the island of Keos, in the Aegean Sea, is very often spelled Kea, because Italian archaeologists have been working there for a number of years and it came to acquire an Italian ending through this association. Though Corfu is Kerkira to the Greeks, you would never hear an American say, "I am going to Greece next summer and hope to spend a week in Kerkira." On the other hand, Kos is to everyone the commonest way of spelling the island of

Hippocrates. Though you find "Sunion" in Hachette's *World Guide,* and "Sounion" in other reference books, how could I quote, "Place me on Sunium's marbled steep," in any but Byron's own way of writing it?

It wasn't until this volume began to take shape that I fully realized how true it is that we are continually being helped in the most unlikely ways, while we build on the influences of a lifetime. It is possible, therefore, only to offer thanks to those who have been visibly helpful, and trust that no obvious indebtedness has been overlooked.

My deep gratitude is due first to my husband Paul Hammond, without whose imagination, ability, and steadfastness I would have had no story to tell. My daughters Lucy Swann Schwartz and Lily Swann Saarinen have cheered me warmly from the beginning. My friend Mrs. Franz Schneider gave me wise criticisms and suggestions. Rear Admiral Samuel E. Morison, Professor Carl W. Blegen, Dr. Karl Vogel, Mrs. Walter H. Page, Jr., and my cousins Roxane and Alexander C. Sedgwick kindly read and corrected parts of the manuscript and gave me encouragement.

To the following authors I am indebted for being allowed to quote from their writings; Dr. Arnold J. Toynbee, Mr. Göran Schildt, Lord Kinross, Mr. Wilmarth S. Lewis, Dr. E. V. Rieu.

For two delightful contributions to this volume, the youthful diaries of Richard Delano, kept on our Cruise in 1934, and Jane Nichols Page, in 1937, I am very grateful.

To my secretary Miss Margaret J. Martin, I owe endless thanks for tact, patience, accuracy, and interest.

Lastly, I am indebted to my young friend, Franz Schneider, Jr., for his apt suggestion of the title.

S. S. H.

Prologue

After several years of preparation and anticipation, my husband and I began our cruises in the eastern Mediterranean in the summer of 1934 on our Ketch, *Landfall*, and repeated them in 1935, 1936, and 1937. During that time, her winter berth was for the most part in Malta, through the courtesy of the Royal Navy. Then after a lapse of a quarter of a century, we resumed our summer cruises in the Mediterranean in 1959, and 1960 on our Thames sailing barge, *Rara Avis*.

Each year, in our afterguard we have taken along a variety of family and friends. They were not all the same on either *Landfall* or *Rara Avis*, but as shipmates they differed only in the kind of individuals that they were— all won our hearts, and we were, on each cruise, a happy ship.

Our adventures have brought us enriching experiences of persons, places, archaeology, and history. Of these we have had an endless golden chain, leaving behind links of precious memories that in turn stir up fireside thoughts of new charts to plot. We traveled from place to place in a great free world of antiquity and returned to our own busy life of today, more than ever aware of the Hippocratic aphorism, "Art is long and life is short."

We had no accidents, no illnesses, and no narrow
escapes worthy of those terms, partly, no doubt, due to
Paul's indefatigable attention to the details of preparation, and it might well be asked why such uneventful
voyages are of sufficient interest to warrant adding them
to the weight of travel stories. My only excuse for this
summing up is that we have had not just one cruise among
the Greek Islands, like so many other fellow voyagers, but
six, over a span of a quarter of a century. During these
fateful years, the world changed with a threatening rapid-
ity, for man finally contrived to split the atom and enter
space. Pressed by the danger of defeat in World War II
we chose to challenge forces beyond our control while
neglecting the Delphian warning, pronounced over 2,500
years ago and repeated again and again, "Know thyself."

As we sailed among the Aegean Islands in 1960, I kept
asking myself why we Anglo-Saxons are so especially
touched by the incomparable beauty of these sun-soaked
isles of Greece. What is it about this past that quickens
our joy of life today and warns us of tomorrow? Without
even understanding their language, why are we able to
communicate so easily with the natives and recognize their
characteristics?

The answer came, vividly expressed, from the pen of
the historian Arnold J. Toynbee, who had had like cruises
in the Mediterranean over a comparable span of time:

What light have we that we can project upon the darkness of the future? We have the precious light of experience, which has always been Mankind's guide to action in
public, as in private, affairs. . . .

The experience of the Hellenic society—the Graeco-
Roman world—is particularly illuminating from this point
of view, because the Greeks' and Romans' experience is

now over—their world is now dead—and, in consequence, we know the plot of that play from beginning to end, in sharp contrast to our ignorance of what lies before ourselves in a play which is still being acted, and in which we living actors have all the time to improvise our parts.

For this reason, Greek and Roman history is perpetually gaining in interest for us as it is receding in time. Every passing year of our own history that makes Greek and Roman history chronologically more remote brings it closer to us psychologically. If there is any key to the riddle of our destiny, that key lies here, I believe; and, believing this, I find the fascination of Greek and Roman history always growing greater for me as I live through one decade after another of the formidable contemporary history of the Modern world.*

Enjoying the rapturous conditions of being lightly dressed, comfortably stowed in the lee of our broad and beamy deck, surrounded by my books, and afloat on the favorite element of Greek life, my eyes strayed from these arresting pages to the lovely world about me. It was with keen pleasure that I felt the delicious sunshine and the tempering breeze on my hot skin. The sapphire sea sparkled, the mountains looked on Marathon. I sensed the common ties with our forerunners in Attica. I thought of the beauty of their temples, remembered the charming simplicity of the natives, and knew that the joy of sharing these delights with friends was the best of all.

There are many autobiographical accounts of adventurous cruises in the Mediterranean Seas, undertaken by lone, independent sailors or courageous young couples who pull their weight in their own craft. Such adven-

* Arnold J. Toynbee, *Greek Civilization and Character* (New York: Mentor, 1953), p. xii. Reprinted by permission of J. M. Dent & Sons, Ltd., London.

turers often act as captain, engineer, navigator, mate, cook, and able-bodied seaman at the same time. A pioneer voyage among these was made in 1930 by one of our foremost authors and yachtsmen, Alfred F. Loomis, and his wife. As I remember it, their sporting little ship was hoisted on the deck of the American Export steamer *Excelsior* in New York, fully equipped with water, canned food, and lubricating oil, and her mast was stepped after her arrival in Athens. The success of the cruise that followed was the inspiration for many that came after, and *Hotspur's Cruise in the Aegean** reads today with as much zest and gaiety as it did thirty years ago.

Another quite beautiful story, called *In the Wake of Odysseus*, written by a Swedish scholar and sailor, Göran Schildt, gives a unique and vivid glimpse of life along the shores of the Greek islands. Schildt's windwise remarks in the early pages, concerning travel by sail in these waters, are a candid confession from a genuine lover of sail:

An ironic fate has willed that the majority of the Mediterranean yachts frequent waters which are least fitted for sailing. . . . Dead calm and squalls make the motor-boat by far the most suitable means of transport in these parts, but this hardly fulfills the dream of cruising out to sea through foaming waves. The result is that people have sailing-boats with auxiliary engines, used in practice as motor-boats with auxiliary sails.†

I quote one of the fraternity rather than lay myself open to such awful heresy. Not from me will you hear

* Alfred F. Loomis, *Hotspur's Cruise in the Aegean* (New York: Jonathan Cape & Harrison Smith, 1931).

† Göran Schildt, *In the Wake of Odysseus* (London: Staples Press, 1953), p. 33.

that we "boiled along for several hours with a spanking westerly"; nor shall I say that we carried a spinnaker for a thousand miles—something that Olin and Rod Stephens actually did accomplish when they won the race from Newport, Rhode Island, to Plymouth, England, in their famous little yawl *Dorade* in the summer of 1931. Those conditions do not often arise in the eastern Mediterranean, as you must have realized when you read the *Iliad* and the *Odyssey*.

No, almost everyone with experience will acknowledge that the summer wind in these waters is either nonexistent or dead ahead; or it is a Levanter or a Meltemi or a Boreas, or some other kind of a strong northerly—all too violent to permit more than a minimum of sail.

There is a lovely passage at the end of Schildt's book that touches an echoing chord. "Delphi, Delos, and Festos," he exclaims, "nothing has taught me as you have done, that the present is a place in the landscape of eternity, from which one has a view over both the past and future."* It is to the archaeologists of all nations that we owe a deep sense of gratitude for the light and understanding that they have brought to these two vistas of history.

* *Ibid.*, p. 285.

Contents

Illustrations appear as a group following page 134

Landfalls Remembered

The next thing most like living
one's life over again seems to be
a recollection of that life, and to
make that recollection as durable as
possible by putting it down in writing.

—Benjamin Franklin, *Autobiography*

PART I

*Rara Avis—Summers of 1959
and 1960*

The 1959 Cruise

R ara Avis is what her name implies, because she is by Will Everard's largest Thames sailing barge, out of an 1840 three-masted Bermuda schooner, and launched in the heyday of technological gadgets. The model and rig of the Thames sailing barges have been developing along the coast of England and across the channel for commercial purposes for over two hundred years. Their annual race in the Thames Estuary is one of the great sporting events in England. Many people have converted them into sailing yachts, but my husband is probably the first one to build a new hull and rig. She was designed in New York by Philip Rhodes. Paul's ways of expressing himself include roller furlers on the square sails, brails on the fore and aft sails, and endless wire-reel winches. Another unique feature is the drop-blade inside the steel rudder, adjustable from the deck, to suit the long ocean waves or other seas. There are also two centerboards in tandem, copied by Paul from a system successfully tried out by Seward Johnson on his last two craft, *Sea Goose* and *Ocean Pearl*. They help in going to windward and the after centerboard eases the steering in a heavy sea. The deck is clear of hazards; no deck leads to stub your toe on and no steps up or down any deck to stumble over. Thus you can walk fifty times around the roomy deck for your constitutional mile. One of our prize features, secured

3

to the foremast, is an antique ship's bell on which is engraved "From *Drumbeat* to *Rara Avis*," a gift from Max Aitkin who is one of Great Britain's finest sailormen and a keen exponent of ocean racing.

Rara Avis is, I trust, the final accomplishment of a series of seven previous sailing craft largely dreamed up and designed by my husband during a long life in which sailing has been his passionate interest. Just under 100 feet on deck, with a broad beam of 23 feet, and a shoal draft of 4½ feet, she can easily enter tempting harbors that deny themselves to any other craft so long and beamy. The working sail-area is 3,500 square feet, and a variety of lightweight sails permit changing the melody in moderate winds. When running or reaching we set the dramatic trade twins that Paul christened the "Gish Sisters," in competition with an attenuated jib known as "Greta Garbo," and a billowy spinnaker called "Mae West."

The design (started directly after World War II) was to utilize the roomy, cargo-carrying space of the Thames sailing barges for especially comfortable cabins. There are three large double cabins, each having its own bathroom, and king-sized stowage lockers. Our cabin has a cozy, Delft-tiled Dutch stove, its own gangway, and includes a set of the *Encyclopædia Britannica,* that acts as our Oracle, and serves as arbiter in our arguments.

The deckhouse is the center of all our activities. The large windows are so placed that no shift of wind or weather, no sight of beauty or interest, can escape the notice of anyone. Here we eat our meals on a secured table large enough for eight, and in one corner there is a tiny enclosed galley with a small ever-ready refrigerator. After a night watch at sea, a tired navigator may stretch himself out on the long settee and be undisturbed. There can be entertainment here too. One gala evening we had a song-and-dance show, staged by the dramatic John Lodge family. 'Cesca's beautiful hands snapped castanets and her lithe figure swayed, pirouetted and glided, Spanish style, while John and Beatrice sang accompaniments, and the rapt audience clapped in rhythm.

The interior trim is as simple as it could possibly be made. There is a sky-blue ceiling with a blue-leather couch along one side, and the walls are paneled in Bermuda cedar. In the spring of 1939 Paul and I had gone to Bermuda with Jane and George Nichols, Paul to crew on their famous six-meter *Goose* in a team race against the Trimingham brothers and other Bermudians. At that time, many magnificent cedars had been chopped down in an effort to save still-healthy trees from extinction caused by a devastating blight. Paul immediately took steps to have some of the most massive logs shipped to our red barn in Syosset, the birthplace of his cutter *Barnswallow* built ten years earlier. There they lay, for seventeen years, a constant reminder of his future deckhouse, till he shipped them over to Holland in 1957 to be sawed up for the paneling.

The wardroom is large, with one half devoted to dining-room space and the other half to reading, writing and conversation. The walls are painted white and the deck beams are exposed, as in all the living quarters, because a ship should look like a ship. All other woodwork, either of mahogany or teak, are of natural finish, and a massive plank of teak, in one corner, forms a desk. Along one bulkhead there is a settee, which can occasionally be used as a bunk, and two comfortable armchairs.

In this cabin we have a sentimental attachment to the main piece of furniture—the mantelpiece over the Dutch stove. There we have placed four colored tiles that once decorated the interior of the deckhouse of *Aloha*—the bark designed by Clinton Crane, that was the dream-ship of the late Commodore Arthur Curtis James. On September 15, 1921, the Commodore, his wife, and several guests, among them our friend Dr. Karl W. Vogel, set out from the East River on their longest and crowning voyage, during which they circled the world, and returned to Newport Harbor two years later. In the thirties, times changed so rapidly and to such a degree that Commodore James was forced to make the choice between selling or destroying his beloved ship. He chose the latter alternative. *Aloha* was dismantled in a Fall River salvage yard in 1938, and the following year Paul seized the opportunity of buying yards, square sails, and many essential fittings to be used on *Capitana*, the craft that he later converted to a barkentine for the Harvard Columbus Expedition.* At the same time the Commodore made a present of the tiles to Karl, who afterwards gave them to us. The two inner tiles depict, under sail and power, symbolic ships of the Royal Navy and Merchant Marine which Kipling described in his "Coastwise Lights," written during the days when the sun never set on the British Empire. Inscribed on the two outer tiles are four of Kipling's lines:†

> Come up, come in from Eastward,
>   from the guardports of the Morn!
> Beat up, beat in from Southerly,
>   O gypsies of the Horn!

* The Harvard Columbus Expedition is described in Part III of this book.
† *Rudyard Kipling's Verse, 1885–1932.* (New York: Doubleday Doran, 1934).

Swift shuttles of an Empire's loom
that weave us main to main,
The Coastwise Lights of England
give you welcome back again!

Now that Karl Vogel has entered on the scene, I have an opportunity to speak of the many works of art that he creates with keen imagination, clever hands, and endless industry. Most notable of these is, of course, his widely known scale model of the *Constitution*, familiarly known as "Old Ironsides." If the world suddenly shrank to smaller proportions than even Alice's rabbit hole, you could hoist her sails and weigh anchor with every bit of canvas drawing and every sheet in place, and pace the quarter-deck on a U.S. frigate, thirty-six inches over-all in length, with a beam of six inches. For many years Karl burned his midnight oil making such masterpieces as this model, while his daylight hours were occupied with his work in clinical and pathological medicine in connection with St. Luke's Hospital.

Our sailing master, Jariilo Walter, is now an American citizen, but he was born in a small Estonian fishing village, Henste, on the shores of the Baltic Sea. Jay is a do-it-yourself man. He can do anything that helps to make a ship safe, seaworthy, efficient, and comfortable. He never spares himself in the performance of any duty, and won a distinguished war record when he commanded merchant vessels and tankers of every tonnage.

Jay and his three brothers are famous sailors who have never known life except by the sea or on it. Their mother's father had been a sea captain, and their own father, who had run away from home to follow the sea, taught his sons to be sailors of the old school. They are experts at marlin-spike seamanship and used to think nothing of going aloft hand over hand, up the shrouds, using their feet for additional support. Jariilo was born in the early part of this century when Estonia belonged to Imperial Russia and he still remembers the resentment against the intolerable rule of the czars.

Baptism was required in those days by church law, but the names that their father insisted on giving his sons were from the pagan Finnish gods of mythology and taboo in the orthodox service. When the belated day for an over-all baptism finally arrived, there was a somewhat heated disagreement between the parents and the priest, which was finally settled by a compromise of having the service held in the home instead of in church. The four boys were christened together. The oldest was named Kou for the god of thunder and lightning; Jariilo for the god of wisdom; Uku for the king of gods; and Ahto for the god of the seas.

Ahto, the younger, co-authored a book in 1932, when he was twenty-three years old, which he called *Racing the Seas*. At eighteen he was determined that he must have a command of his own, and for that purpose he would use his savings, already made in the United States, to buy a double-ended sloop, 31 feet long, that lay in the mud a few miles from his home, and belonged to an old smuggler who had been caught so many times that he had renounced the profession. Ahto bought the little sloop for $72.00, procured a mast for $1.00 and sails for $2.50, and with that outfit, he and Kou and two friends sailed across the Atlantic from Tallin, Estonia, to Miami, Florida. In 1930, he and Jay made a similar passage alone in a 26-foot sloop called *Ahto*, still extant and afloat in Long Island Sound.

Our long-awaited first cruise on *Rara Avis* was scheduled to start from Gibraltar on May 26, 1959. Jay had sailed her from Cowes, on the Isle of Wight, early that month, with a crew of mixed nationality—British, Dutch, Swedish and German. As it was early in the season, they had quite a dusting in the Bay of Biscay, and all of them but Jay were seasick. When Paul asked him later if he had found any of them useful, his answer was a laconic bit of Nordic humor: "Yes, when anchoring."

Paul and I had sailed from New York on board the American Export liner S.S. *Constitution* on May 16 and had enjoyed a smooth and comfortable voyage. Had we made the crossing on a British ship our landing would have been in Gibraltar, but being on an American steamer, our destination was the Spanish city of Algeciras, with the attendant delays of putting in at a foreign-language port. After a conventional landing we would have faced the further delays of two customs clearances and a long twenty-five-mile overland trip, which would have involved changing from a Spanish to a British car en route.

Actually, we confronted no problems with Spanish customs since the gear and stores for a ship in transit are duty-free in all world ports. Thus, we were able to undertake a little plan of our own, which saved us time and trouble. Paul is a past master at tourism as well as seamanship, and that talent, added to his fetish for killing two birds with one stone, led to a somewhat novel manner of disembarking from our steamer.

"The Rock" lies east of Algeciras, and as we passed it we looked through our glasses and could see *Rara Avis* moored in Admiralty Harbor. In Gibraltar we had been given the courtesy of an advance introduction from Lord Mountbatten to the Admiral in command of Her

Majesty's Dock Yard. We were also being accorded a courteous leniency on the part of the Spanish immigration officials through the attention of our embassy in Madrid, where a friend John Lodge was our ambassador.

Beside these two concessions, we had the good will of the American officers on the S.S. *Constitution*. So, at the end of the voyage, after presenting our passports to the Spanish immigration officials in the lounge, we were told to follow our leader and descend to the entrails of the ship. Once there, we were gently guided by the officers of the S.S. *Constitution* through one of the massive iron cargo hatches of a water-tight compartment into the friendly arms of Royal Naval officers on a large Admiralty power craft. They, in turn, conducted us and our luggage, without further ado, alongside *Rara Avis*. It was a neat transfer.

Paul had been on duty in Gibraltar in 1941–42 studying U-boat warfare, but for me it was the first real visit.

History records this famous fortress of Gibraltar as the visual symbol of permanence and durability in Europe. Prehistory, which deemed it the end of the inhabited world, called the Rock one of the Pillars of Hercules.

Considering its importance in the world, Gibraltar is absurdly small. If it were set down in New York City it would almost fit inside of Central Park. Although it has always been the smallest of the British crown colonies, it has its own autonomous government. Within this tiny member of the British Commonwealth, the population of 25,000 inhabitants falls into three distinct categories: Spanish, English, and Gibraltarian. This year they were celebrating the first Commonwealth Day after fifty-six years of Empire Day; but even Commonwealth Day is anathema to nationalist-minded Spain.

Gibraltar has been a free port, with short exceptions, since 1705, but we were not particularly interested in duty-free shopping. Our only needs were certain items for *Rara Avis*, and our traffic was chiefly with the vittling stores. We had already provided the crew with warm blankets, but we needed some for ourselves. As the Royal Navy was cutting down in every department, they let us buy, among other useful gear, twelve superbly thick white wool officer's blankets. We have been using them ever since. Two per person, per night, was not too many throughout the western part of the Mediterranean in June. A sailing craft is always colder than you expect it to be, especially at night.

On May 25, 1959, Mary and Henry Sears flew in and joined us at Gibraltar. Harry had, the summer before, as organizer, navigator and half-owner, successfully defended the America's Cup with his Sparkman & Stephens–designed *Columbia*, having first defeated three superlative contestants. He is the son of the late Dr. Henry Francis Sears, who was born in Boston in 1860. After receiving degrees at Harvard University, Dr. Sears was connected with Boston City Hospital and became a distinguished pathologist. Early in his career, the latter joined a pioneer research committee that went to Europe to study a number-one killer, Yellow Fever, then known as Yellow Jack. The fight against Yellow Jack in those days was a challenge to many self-sacrificing scientists. It culminated in the victory, won by the brave army of doctors, engineers, and members of allied professions, who worked for its destruction under our Army Surgeon General William C. Gorgas, at the scene of the Panama Canal early in the twentieth century. Ever since then, the sailor's nickname for the yellow quarantine flag has been Yellow Jack.

Harry began his sailing career in 1921 with a Swampscott dory. Having been a sufferer from asthma during the short nine years of his life on land, he persuaded his father, who was not himself a sailor, that the hope of a cure lay in leaving his allergies behind him and taking to the sea. This experiment was agreed to and the family stood by while he cut sails out of the white summer slip covers protecting the household's handsome upholstered furniture and fitted them to his first dory *Actaea*.

From Swampscott dory, Harry graduated to the racing classes of Brutal Beast, O Boat, R Boat, and then to a series of cruising and ocean-racing craft.

For over a hundred years there has been a Sears dynasty of *Actaea*'s, beginning with one that was built for Harry's grandfather David Sears in 1836. Harry himself owned and sailed eight of these, and they are the ships that relate his life history in terms of sail. He was extremely helpful to us on board in every way, and he stood a night watch whenever it was necessary. He would naturally be a great addition on any ship in any sea, and so would Mary. They are both past masters in the art of cruising, and, I might add, the art of living anywhere.

While waiting for the Searses to fly in, the Governor of Gibraltar, General Sir Charles Keightley, and his wife, very kindly invited us to lunch in the Governor's Palace, which has been the home of the British rulers ever since 1728, when it was converted from a monastery.

We lunched in the magnificent vaulted banquet hall, which must be thirty feet in height. The cornices of the ceiling are so contrived that the coat-of-arms, flags, mottoes, and like symbols of each successive governor are part of an elaborate and splendid scheme of decoration, and the whole room echoes with British tradition.

At the end of the satiny, mahogany table, in front of the Governor's chair, was placed a flat, crimson velvet cushion on which lay four colossal, polished silver keys. I had never before seen huge shiny silver keys lying cushioned on a dining-room table, where ordinarily you would expect a cut-glass or china bonbonnière to be placed. They were the keys to the four Gates of Gibraltar when they came into the possession of Great Britain in 1704. "Two of them," said Sir Charles firmly, "still fit." I realized then that, as the Rock is the symbol of defense, so those shiny keys are the symbol of possession.

During a beautiful drive on the Rock that afternoon, I had my first glimpse of the famous Barbary apes, whose presence insure the permanence of the British administration. With the death of these apes, so the story goes, dies the British rule in Gibraltar.

They are the last of the tailless monkeys in Europe and are destructive little creatures whose greatest joy is the ripping to shreds of prized upholstery, reached through the open window of a parked car.

It wasn't until 1856 that the British Government decided to restrict the bad habits of these valued delinquents. The homes of the apes were then confined to a certain area, and the inhabitants of this dominion were placed under the protection and direction of the British Military in the person of a sergeant—the Keeper of the Apes. Nowadays they have an official allowance of six pence a day for rations, and their governing body consists of a major, a sergeant, and a private.

During the Second World War, Sir Winston Churchill became alarmed because the number of apes had dwin-

dled to six. Thereafter, it was decreed that the number
never fall below twenty-four, and sixty additional individuals were imported from their native habitats, Algeria
and Morocco.

The following day we departed Admiralty Harbor,
rounded Europa Point, and cruised along the *Costa del
Sol,* bound for Malaga (Picasso's birthplace). De luxe
cruise ships like to call Malaga "the grandstand of the
Mediterranean," for if your itinerary takes you along that
beautiful coast, you find yourself witnessing the long historical pageant of the Mediterranean Sea, with relics and
traces of Phoenicians, Greeks, Carthaginians, Romans,
Byzantines, Moors, and Spaniards, from the luxurious
vantage point of present-day comfort. Attractive modern
Spanish resorts such as Malaga, Alméria, Cartagena, and
Alicanti have all of this to offer.

We made Malaga easily and were enchanted with the
beauty of the panorama: the sapphire sea, the beaches, the
beautiful Moorish *alcazaba,* the foothills of the Sierra
Nevada Mountains in the background, with snow still lying on many of them. It was the sunniest and serenest of
days—one of those that make you expect it to repeat itself
every day thereafter, ad infinitum; but you learn with
experience that, especially in the Mediterranean, weather
changes come suddenly and without warning.

We had arranged to meet our friends Amanda and
Keith Kane in Alicanti on May 28, but the easterly wind
gathered force, and we could go no farther than Cartagena. We made fast, stern to, using our twenty-foot Mediterranean gangplank as usual, and drove to Alicanti by car
in a torrential downpour. There we picked up the Kanes
and all returned to *Rara Avis* for a rainy night.

Our next landfall was Iviza, the smallest of the three important Balearics. Iviza is unspoiled and not yet tourist-ridden, and it has great charm. Behind the simple little quay and waterfront rises a steep hill, and on the upper fortifications of the hill are not only a tiny archaeological museum, but a delightful hotel and restaurant, El Corsario. The attractive and capable proprietress provided us with a delicious meal on a pretty terrace, open to the sky, with lovely views of the sea. No restaurant that we later sampled ever outdid that well-designed and imaginative layout.

Here we first saw the picturesque Talayots that one soon begins to look for as the characteristic profile of the Balearics. They are the Catalan watchtowers, round or square, about forty feet high and built of rugged blocks of sand-colored stone. They are indigenous to the skyline of these hills and are related to the Nuraghes of Sardinia; both served as fortified dwelling places or shelters in prehistoric times.

It was great fun taking Amanda and Keith Kane along, not only on account of their irreplaceable companionship but because they contributed a quest for us to pursue. Not so far and wide a quest as the one for the Golden Fleece but a search for an ancestor.

In February, 1959, when the Kanes decided that they would be able to join us on *Rara Avis* from May 28 to June 10, Keith began looking up facts about the Balearic Islands. It was then that he discovered the ancestor.

We were to meet on the east coast of Spain so that we could circle the Balearics, something none of us had ever done before.

I quote from Keith's notes in our log book:

Just before we received the welcome invitation of Supaul [a shorthand nickname our friends use for Paul and me] to cruise with them among the Balearic Isles, I had been looking through some family memoirs. Mention of Minorca reminded me that an uncle of my ancestor, John Kane, who settled in New York early in the Seventeenth Century, had become Governor of Minorca in 1713, when the island was secured to the British by the Treaty of Utrecht. We were intrigued by the opportunity of discovering more about this early kinsman.

During our visit we learned that Sir Richard had busied himself building the first highway from Mahón, which the British had captured and made the capital, to the former capital of Ciudadela. The Islanders apparently considered this quite an achievement for they built a monument to him at the roadside on the outskirts of Mahón.

The island is a most peaceful place. There are few automobiles or other mechanical contrivances of any sort. There are a number of flourishing farms where almonds, olives, figs and apricots abound in season and grain seems to prosper despite the rocky soil. The industrious natives make their delicious cheeses and other products in their own houses.

Fishing is one of the principal industries. When we put in at the picturesque little harbor of Fornells, we were able to enjoy *langouste* lifted by Señor Caules, proprietor of the Hotel Burdo, directly from the water and served with delicious *salsa mahonesa*. This is the progenitor of our mayonnaise and was first served to admirals of the Royal and French Navies in honor of a victory in the early eighteenth century.

We visited the Manor House, where Lord Nelson is said to have stayed after the battle of Aboukir. It has a commanding view overlooking the imposing harbor and the old port of Mahón. The house contains much contemporary furniture and many fine pictures and mirrors.

We drove to Ciudadela in an ancient taxi, but the trip was worthwhile, as there we were invited to see a charming century-old residence which gave evidence of prosperity and taste. . . .

The little port of the town lies at the head of a long steep-sided inlet. The island is certainly not spoiled by modern tourists however many visitors and settlers there may have been, in ages past, who left their marks. It gave us a delightful feeling of isolation although soldiers and sailors were much in evidence. The spectacular coast line has now disappeared and we keep only the happiest memories. We can understand why others have remained to live. . . .

Keith was too modest to describe the twenty-foot, white marble column with an admiring inscription to "Sir Ric. Kane," and too proud to admit that we soon abandoned the Kane Highway for a more comfortable byway.

The ancestor-worship having been successfully accomplished, we set our course to find one of the most exciting of modern houses.

The northeasterly headland of Majorca is a long, narrow, rocky promontory that Poseidon will undoubtedly choose for his *sans souci* when he finally retires. The northers that sweep down on Cape Formentor are quite fierce enough and sudden enough to remind him of Sunium.

We sailed in under the lee of this arm of granite land and let go our anchor about a hundred yards from a forbidding rock-bound landing. We took the starboard launch and approached the shore. Looking back at the receding *Rara Avis*, she made an unforgettable picture. She floated head on between a sea of aquamarine and a sky of turquoise. Two of her lifeboats hung outboard on their davits, one on either side. Her three bare masts, tall against the sky, told the tale of the treacherous winds; it would have been unsafe to carry sail rounding that rocky northerly coast even on so calm a sea and in so sunny an hour as this. She looked very tiny and courageous flanked by two huge rocks that were mighty enough to crush her like an eggshell. We were glad to wave her a safe passage to the harbor of Sóller, on the west coast; she could make that quiet haven in two hours and we would drive overland and meet her there.

The attractive Hotel San Vincente had already cropped up in this remote setting and it was lucky for us, because we needed the kind of a big car provided by a hotel, to hold the Kanes, Searses and ourselves. The proprietor greeted us with, "It is a surprise to see a yacht anchored off Calle San Vincente, storms sweep up so unexpectedly here that few attempt it." We asked him if he knew where Whitney Straight lived and he answered that he knew him very well and would be glad to let us use his bus to drive there. Presently, it drew up bringing some tourists from the airport.

We settled ourselves comfortably and proceeded on a long, tortuous climb; hairpin curve followed hairpin curve for about ten miles. The higher we rose, the more dramatic became the views. Finally we rounded the last curve and the house became a reality. As we stepped out of the car, we had a strange feeling that we had reached the end of the rainbow. The sun shone with such brilliance that every color of the spectrum was ablaze.

Unfortunately we missed the Straights as they were in England, but we were made to feel very much at home by their hospitable representatives who run the ménage. Behind the house there is a rose garden, a cutting garden, and garden walks. A tennis court is near at hand, and from the little terrace about one hundred stone steps

take you down to bathe in the limpid waters. The out-
look is of majestic opalescent promontories, that vie with
the Pillars of Hercules in precipitousness and cut down
through the sparkling aquamarine sea, raising their great
shoulders to the shining June sky.

The white stucco house was ingeniously designed by
Don Pepe Alcover, in collaboration with Sir Hugh Cas-
son, and gives the impression of being cut out of the
mountainous rock and of overhanging the sea. It has the
charm of something indigenous, in the way that the Talayots are indigenous to the landscape. It seems to belong
where it stands.

As we drove away from this scene of so much natural
beauty, someone mentioned the poignant novel published
in 1937 by Elliot Paul, called *The Life and Death of a
Spanish Town*. It was a brooding tale of the town of Santa
Eulalia situated on the Island of Iviza, and it foreboded
the heavy clouds of World War II. Having visited that
very island only a few days ago, we were happy in the
thought that though it may have fallen on evil days, it had
since then entered on a new life. As is the way with Mediterranean islands, it had seen good times as well as bad,
for upwards of three thousand years, but the inhabitants
can yet boast of a rich ancestry in which strains of all the
cultures of Europe still endure. It has undergone a resurrection, and is now benefiting through increasing travel
lanes that widen its horizon.

For those who are old enough to remember, it was
World War I, not World War II, that first warned us
harshly of the shape of things to come. That was the war
that seems now to have been in vain because it was fought
"to end all wars." Whitney's own father, Willard D.
Straight, died in Paris in 1918, just as the first World

War came to an end; his useful and brilliant career was cut short in its prime. The night before his departure for the front, he left a letter to his oldest son, then four years old, a touching and beautiful letter that might have been written to many sons, by many fathers: "You may never see this letter, I hope you never will," it began, "but should anything happen to me, . . . I trust for your sake, and all three of you, your mother will be there to guide you." And it closed with the wisest of admonitions, "Hold your head high, and keep your mind open. You can always learn."*

We were soon driving in a southwesterly direction, through the lovely hilly country, toward the Harbor of Sóller, where *Rara Avis* would be awaiting us. We had heard of the beauty of this harbor from John Hallowell.

In the summer of 1933 Alexander Forbes had taken a number of boys and girls, including John Hallowell, on a wonderful cruise in the Mediterranean in his ninety-foot fisherman-type schooner, *Ramah*. She had originally been built by Columbus Iselin in Shelburne, Nova Scotia, for oceanographic work. John had remembered Sóller for her beautiful mountainous coast and had on that cruise been able to take a remarkable picture of *Ramah* under full sail, which now hangs in his office in Western Reserve Academy, Ohio. When *Ramah* left Majorca in late July, and sailed easterly to Naples about five hundred miles distant, they had a fine reaching breeze all the way, a rare break in these waters.

Sóller is only a short distance from Puerto Adraitx. Our enjoyment of this attractive harbor was abruptly inter-

---

* Herbert Croly, *Willard Straight* (New York: Macmillan, 1924), p. 568.

rupted by customs regulations as we had no go-between
to pick up the fragments of our broken Spanish and put
them together persuasively for the officers in authority.
Our irregularity consisted in trying to put some ship stores
and spare gear ashore for the winter; this was objected to
by watchful customs officers and our patience and powers
of persuasion wore thin as precious hours passed by.

These complications, in one form or another, are occasionally bound to arise when an American craft enters
foreign ports, but fortunately somebody's sense of humor
is sure to come to the rescue and you move on waving
cheerful farewells to an audience of smiling and friendly
faces.

The night of June 5 Paul and I spent at the Hotel Ben-
dinat—Majorcan for "good dining." It did indeed offer
delicious food. It is a most attractive and comfortable hotel, about three miles outside of Palma. Inviting rooms
give on the sea, and you walk from your pretty bedroom,
along a parapet of rocks, to the ladder where you enter
the deep water for a swim. A native craft will sail you and
your friends with a picnic lunch off for the day, if you so
wish, or you can enjoy a few quiet hours right there,
dipping in the transparent sea and eating snacks in the
excellent restaurant.

We wound up our idyllic week of sailing around the
Balearics and made fast, stern to, at the Club Nautica in
Palma. There we enjoyed a dish of *langoustina* that was
out of this world. It was lunch time when we arrived, and
Paul made a visit to the kitchen. He came back to report
that the whole top of the immense stove had been cleared
for action and that clouds of smoke were rising from a

succulent mass of cooking-in-oil *langoustina* which was being sprinkled with lemon juice. It was soon served to us, piping hot, *en casserole,* and never did any dish taste better—until it was repeated the following day! Many other delicious meals in Palma were later enjoyed at the excellent Hotel Maricel.

The time had now come to look up the haunts of the famous couple who first turned the spotlight of an inquisitive world on the island of Majorca. The sophisticated in Palma seem to avoid the subject of their visitation and one hears little of it there. We found in a book shop a paperback copy of *A Winter in Majorca* by George Sand, recently translated by a famous resident, Robert Graves.

It is a strange book, this curious story of an ill-starred little group of tourists: George Sand and her children, Maurice and Solange, a maid, and Chopin. The authoress never once mentions the name of Chopin throughout her book, speaking only occasionally of a "sufferer" or "invalid." It is a tale in which you sense the kindly Majorcans eagerly anticipating the arrival of the notorious French novelist and the world-renowned Polish musician, anxious to lavish them with invitations to the 1840 counterparts of cocktail parties. George Sand, already overlionized, jealously sought only privacy and peace for her beloved invalid and refused to be drawn into endless hours of well-intentioned but unwanted conviviality. Her ill-concealed excuses or out-and-out indifference were soon met with hostility; quarrels reared their ugly heads; the rain continued; and the unendurable cold of every room was tempered only occasionally by the coals in a small bronze brazier. The high spirits of the children and the low spirits of the adults were intensified, and the dream of a sunny idyl found defeat.

The cold drizzle of early June reminded us that a pilgrimage was now on the schedule, and Mary, Amanda, and I took a taxi that slowly climbed the slippery seventeen miles through a drenched countryside to the beautifully situated monastery of Valldemosa. We saw the cells of the monks which the travelers inhabited, the garden walks alive with flowers that must have been enchanting on the rare occasions when the sun shone; we touched the little piano that Chopin had played on, and read the manuscript of his Raindrop prelude, inspired by the drip, drip, drip of the relentless rain.

The torrential downpour on the day the Kanes joined us in Alicanti was repeated on the day of their departure from Palma. They took off from a field several inches deep in mud and so clogged up with planes that passengers had difficulty in differentiating between those that were warming up preparatory to departing and those that were just temporarily grounded. While the Kanes were contemplating a sea of mud on one airfield, the John Lodges and their daughter Beatrice were flying in from Madrid to a sea of mud at the military airport on the opposite side of the island.

John had been our Ambassador to Madrid since 1955. He has many talents, and among them are a great facility for language and an easy friendliness for all. When he resigned his post, at the end of six years of service, after our change of administration in 1961, the right-wing Spanish newspaper *Arriba* had this to say of him: "Gentlemanly, frank and generous, he has penetrated the mysterious stronghold into which not all are able to enter: the soul of the Spanish people." His wife had also penetrated that mysterious stronghold, and came on board fresh from a great adventure in horsemanship that deserves recognition.

Under the auspices of both the Spanish and Portuguese governments, and organized by the Ministers of Agriculture of both countries, a group of Spanish and Portuguese horse breeders and cavalry officers take part in a yearly, cross-country ride from Lisbon to Madrid. This has been a spring project for many years, in which about sixty-five men participate, to test both the endurance, resistance, and speed of horse and rider.

Francesca Lodge, well known as a rider and horse lover, had been invited to take part in the yearly *Raid.* (The word means "ride" and is pronounced that way.) It takes ten to eleven days, riding eight to ten hours per day in the tropical heat of Extremadura, stopping each night in a different place, and roughing it with little comfort. It is a race, and neither protocol nor "manners" is expected on the road. Each day's run is clocked, and the rider who makes the best average per hour wins. No woman had ever before participated, let alone an ambassador's wife. This would present difficulties, and when Mrs. Lodge was invited, she hesitated because it seemed to her a gracious gesture from her Spanish hosts rather than a formal invitation.

Ever since Ambassador Lodge's arrival in Spain in 1955, he had been implementing the Lodge people-to-people program all over the country, and to permit his own wife to ride to remote villages, making new friends among Spaniards, and accepting their proffered hospitality would, he knew, seal the program with his highest approval; he had confidence in his wife's horsemanship

and was sure she would greatly enjoy the experience, so
he gave his consent.

The *Raid* called for following many *cañadas,* which is
the word for the shepherds' paths that abound in Spain
and Portugal. In fact, they are the only countries of Europe where you can still cross from one end to the other
along these trails. One day, when breaking for lunch in
the tiny village of Navalmoral de la Mata, high in the
mountains, a group of twenty children and half a dozen
adults came into view from the nearby mountain. They
had been walking several hours in the midday sun and
the little bunches of flowers that the girls were carrying
in their hands had fallen like vines around their wrists
and arms. They came to bring thanks for the milk and
cheese that they had been receiving under our agricultural
surplus program, through the Catholic Welfare Confer-
ence and *Caritas* in Spain. In costume, they sang their
thanks and ended with a joyful "Viva la mujer! Viva los
Estados Unidos."

At the end of each day, Mrs. Lodge and her companion
Mrs. Richard Hawkins, the wife of the counsellor at our
Embassy in Madrid, went to the stables, and with the
assistance of the groom, made sure that their mounts were
rubbed down, and their legs bandaged, before they satisfied themselves that their horses were well cared for.
With a parting "good night" and a crunchy carrot, the
tired animals were left to take their rest after a job well
done. The wives of our envoys would then change their
riding-habits for evening clothes, and attend a ceremony
given by a local reception committee. Pretty girls in peasant costume would present Mrs. Lodge with a bouquet
of flowers, and officials would offer her every considera-

tion while proudly showing her the charms of their village. Often she would be interviewed by representatives of the press, and it was a long day, but a happy one, before it was over.

The twenty-nine kilometers from Navalcarnero to Madrid was the last lap of the *Raid,* and by that time only twenty-nine of the original sixty-five competitors were still in the running. The distance was covered at a fast walk. In the large stadium of the "Feria de Campo," or big country Fair, four thousand enthusiasts were waiting to greet the twenty-nine survivors of the Lisbon-Madrid marathon with thundering applause, and again the shout went up: "Viva la mujer! Viva los Estados Unidos!"

The Lodges are now the American grandparents of a little Spanish Señorita, Matilde, born to Beatrice and her husband Don Antonio de Oyarzabal y Marchesi in April, 1962. Her sporting grandmother plans a return to Spain and a repeat of the *Raid* in 1963.

It was a long stretch from Majorca to Sicily. There were clear skies, but there were also head winds and heavy sea swells. It was thirty hours before we could anchor on the south side of Sardinia, off Punta del Aliza in the Golfo di Palmas. Just before reaching this point, we were challenged by an Italian naval craft—reason unknown—and then allowed to proceed. We were all glad to make a quiet harbor for the night after a rough passage, but we had to continue on our way the next morning because the Searses had an engagement to keep and we had a new clutch arriving from Germany that would have to be installed in Palermo. When we reached Palermo, the clutch couldn't be located and this led to endless communications with

customs officials and necessitated working late into the
night to speed completion.

Except for Paul and Jay, none of us suffered from this
engine trouble. We simply abandoned the pleasures of
being afloat for the luxurious life of the Villa Igea. This
comfortable hotel could well be described as a grounded
ocean liner, with its broad beam giving on the sea. To
complete the analogy, the hotel has numerous beautifully
appointed salons on many different levels, and a main
deck in the form of an enchanting terrace of flowered
walks.

We parted regretfully with the Lodges and Searses soon
after arriving in Palermo. They were replaced by the
Wallace Harrisons who revealed to us the beauties of Sicily through their fund of knowledge and experience.

Ellen and Wally Harrison were constant and valued
friends even before Wally designed the Trylon and Peri-
sphere for the World's Fair of 1938–39. Since then the
colorful dome and the Director's Residence of the Rocke-
feller Institute have taken shape on New York's East
River. Two notable examples of Wallace's work, one of
glass and one of aluminum, are the Corning Glass Works
building on Fifty-fifth Street and Fifth Avenue and, farther afield, the Alcoa Headquarters in Pittsburgh, Pennsylvania. Imaginative in conception and successful in exe-
cution as are these chefs-d'oeuvres, they became realities
without his having to draw on certain fundamental qualities of mind and heart that are, perhaps, the *summum
bonum* of his character. It was when Wallace headed up
the United Nations Committee of eleven architects from
eleven different countries that his qualities of leadership
and persuasion came most conspicuously to the fore. Who
but Wallace Harrison could have effected a meeting of

minds between Australia, Belgium, Brazil, Canada, China, France, Sweden, Russia, Great Britain, and Uruguay? Yet that is what he accomplished in 1950.

Sicily is the largest island in the Mediterranean and is a sightseer's Mecca. Its highest point is the snow-covered active volcano of Mt. Etna, over ten thousand feet; its history reaches into the dimmest years of antiquity. Beautiful temples from the fifth century B.C. are numerous, and the Byzantine mosaics of Mon Reale and Cefalu vie with those of Ravenna. The island can boast of an importance not only in prehistoric times, but in Graeco-Roman, Byzantine, medieval, and modern history as well. Today, she continues to cherish and cultivate much of the traditional and local color that belongs to the Sicilian landscape. She is still sufficiently removed from European highways to have preserved many a pretty painted donkey-cart carrying people with the appropriate peasant costumes, and her roads are still more like country roads than parkways or expressways. It is fair to say that no other one thousand square miles in the world, except the neighborhood of Attica, can boast of such a rich display of showmanship. Many of her villas have been converted into modest hotels for the comfort of travelers and offer warm hospitality with excellent food and service. These villas in Sicily are ghostlike forms of "the stately homes of England." They are to be found in every stage of well-preserved perfection and every condition of sad decay, but they always have nostalgic charm and traces of nobility. One surprising exception in Palermo jolts you roughly out of your dreamy mood, when you come upon the villa Palagonia with its garden wall carrying on high a comic frieze of grotesquely ugly creatures.

At the turn of the nineteenth century, Sicily still belonged to the kingdom of Naples, and one of these villas was occupied by the British envoy, Sir William Hamilton and his wife, the fascinating Emma. Not far away was Lord Nelson on his flagship *Victory*.

A few days before we left, Wally and Ellen took us to call on their friends Prince and Princess Nisciemi, whose beautiful villa, surrounded by a grove of orange trees, is a veritable museum. On another occasion we were received in two palaces, hidden away in the old section of the town. They were vast, and seventeenth-century, and built around square courtyards. Both of the piano nobiles had been rebuilt in baroque style, and both held magnificent collections of china and porcelain from many parts of the world—Europe, the Near East, Persia, and China. In order to show off these treasures to their best advantage, the architects of Sicily have developed an elaborate decoration peculiar to the villas of Sicily. They design innumerable niches to hold each superb ceramic treasure, and the effect is that of great richness and variety.

The sailors of antiquity were brave men and had few fears, but they quailed before the approach of the Straits of Messina. Here the main current runs from north to south and the subsidiary one in the opposite direction. These currents usually alternate every six hours, but they are affected by sun, moon, and wind. The fiercest wind is a Boreas from the north. Even migrating fish find a challenge in these waters and are often spewed high in the air and sucked under the roiling waters much as the hapless mariners of old were wrenched from the open decks of their vessels and tossed to the waves. The wily arms of Scylla and the whirlpool of Charybdis were nightmares to the fishermen and galley slaves of ancient triremes. Steam and science have long since curbed their antics, and nowadays the racy little hydrofoil, speeding its way on struts, shuttles hourly between Reggio Di Calabria in the toe of Italy, and Messina, where it disgorges its passengers on the quay of the excellent Jolly Hotel.

Needless to say, *Rara Avis* had easily taken the Straits in her stride, and it was here on the quay at the hotel that my daughter Lily Swann Saarinen and her daughter Susie joined the Harrisons and ourselves on June 22.

Lily and Susie had flown from Cambridge, Massachusetts, to Rome for three wonderful days of sight-seeing, and they had been rewarded by the privilege of spending a few hours with our great classical scholar Miss Gisela Richter and the gifted artist Miss Maude Robinson. Lily had been a pupil in one of the latter's classes when she was six years old and owes much of her technique in ceramics to her. Miss Robinson was always ready understandingly to permit her to transform an embryo vase into a lizard or a sacred ram or a hippopotamus while the other children were occupied with vases built up in coils of clay. These were not satisfactory to Lily, for she wanted only to create the animals that she so dearly loved.

After lunch at the Jolly Hotel and a stroll through the town, we weighed anchor. With the benefit of a calm sea and a few hours of fair wind during the overnight passage, we glided through the narrow entrance to the port of ancient Pylos the following morning. A long, thin needlelike island called Sphacteria lies across the entrance to the harbor. It guards the Bay of Navarino, the famous scene of the sinking of the Turkish fleet in Greece's struggle for independence. We landed in the clean white town of modern Pylos and lunched there under a green canopy of vines at the edge of the water. Wallace later painted a water color of that view of Sphacteria, which we treasure in our logbook.

In 1936 we had had the privilege of being conducted over the ruins of the nine cities of Troy by Dr. Carl Blegen. We were now approaching one of the high spots of this cruise because we had his promise that he would this year show us over his present dig, the palace of King Nestor.

To give some idea of the importance of these excavations, I must go back to 1939 when Dr. K. Kourouniotis, Director of the Greek Archaeological Service, invited Dr. Blegen to join him in a Greek-American expedition to explore this area on the western coast of the Peloponnesus.* Some vaulted tombs of the Mycenaean period had been accidentally discovered and the likelihood that these tombs belonged to kings and ruling families indicated the possibility that a palace lay near by. After two weeks of systematic exploration, they selected the site of a flat-topped hill, now called Épano Engliános, four miles from the Ionian seacoast.

Their very first day's work was richly rewarded: they unearthed several thick stone walls badly damaged by fire, traces of delicate frescoes, stuccoed floors, hundreds of pieces of broken Mycenaean pottery, and, *mirabile dictu,* several clay tablets in the ancient Linear Script B,

---

* *See* Dr. Carl W. Blegen, "King Nestor's Palace," *Scientific American.* May 1958, Vol. 198, No. 5.

which till then had been found only on the Island of Crete.

Soon after this exciting beginning the war intervened and it was not until 1952 that they were able to resume the work on the site of the excavation. Dr. Kourouniotis had died in 1945, and Professor Spyridon Marinatos was appointed in his place. The whole undertaking was made financially possible by the generosity of Professor and Mrs. W. T. Semple in the name of the University of Cincinnati. Many other students and scholars, of course, unselfishly assisted in this great enterprise, and much has been published, but lack of space restricts me to a few names and a brief story.

The significance of the finding of the Linear Script B tablets in ancient Pylos takes us back sixty years, to the time when Sir Arthur Evans was digging in the great palace of Minos at Knossus in Crete. Sir Arthur then found over nineteen hundred clay tablets inscribed in two strange, unknown scripts. One he named Linear Script A, the other Linear Script B. He devoted many years of intensive investigation in attempting to break the codes, but died with the secrets still hidden. The puzzle of Script A has not yet been solved, but Linear Script B was cracked in 1952 by the late Michael Ventriss, a brilliant young British architect (*not* an archaeologist) who had a flair for cryptology. That year will go down in history as the red-letter year when the language of Homer's heroes became decipherable. That language was at last proved to be a pre-Homeric form of Greek.

We dropped our anchor on a Sunday, but we had too much consideration for the work-weary archaeologists to interrupt their day of rest, so we did no more than drive the long miles of rough, dusty road to the royal site. There we found Dr. and Mrs. Blegen, paid our respects, and received the hoped-for invitation to return the following morning.

The next day, the sun shone in all its glory, and when we arrived it was our good fortune that our small group of Harrisons, Saarinens and Hammonds found itself alone with Dr. Blegen as he led us from one point of interest to another. "If there ever was a King Nestor," he began in his slow, gentle cadence, "and archaeologists have recently found much evidence that the *Iliad* and the *Odyssey* are based on historical facts, then we can confidently say that his palace stood here."

He pointed out the wide spread of the central structure with its two wings. The central unit contains the apartments of state, leading up, as in the palaces of Mycenae and Tiryns, to the climax of the throne room. Next to the doorway is a slightly elevated stand reminiscent of the gatekeeper's vigil at the lion-gate of Mycenae.

Dr. Blegen showed us the two small rooms near the front gateway where over a thousand clay tablets in Linear B were found; also the various utilitarian rooms and the Queen's elegant suite, including her private walled court, her boudoir, and the "powder-room."

Finally we came to the pretty terra-cotta bathtub on its clay base—the very one in which the tired Telemachus, searching for news of his long-lost father Odysseus and finding his way to Pylos, had been bathed by the tender hands of Polycasta, the youngest daughter of King Nestor. In touching and vivid terms, Dr. Blegen reminded us of the King's warm welcome to the son of his old friend. No, Nestor regretted, he had seen nothing of

Odysseus since the victorious fleet had left the shores of Troy, but Telemachus must spend the night in the palace and be wined and dined after a refreshing bath. He promised to speed him on his quest the following morning.

After this vivid presentation, we drove with dreamy memories of Odysseus to the little village of Khora. There the Blegens have a temporary home, and in a nearby studio we were shown hundreds of beautiful goblets, vessels and urns of all sizes and shapes that had been miraculously preserved from the flames of destruction. Dr. Blegen says that so many millions of fragments of goblets have been found in or near the banquet hall that there is reason to believe that our custom of dashing the emptied glass against the wall after drinking a toast may have originated among the Achaeans—not Harvard's heroes, but Homer's heroes are responsible for that fashion.

It is only a short sail from Pylos to Katakolon and the latter is a convenient port from which to see both Olympia and the Temple of Apollo at Bassae.

We devoted the first day to Olympia and were fortunate to find ourselves almost alone in that calm and peaceful valley that is watered by the river Alpheus and enriched with many fallen drums, ruins of temples, and numberless fragments of votive offerings.

There is an indescribable atmosphere of holiness about Olympia. As the wind soughs through the evergreens, it whispers that this is the Grave of the Gods, the scene of the immortal contests, and that here is contained the studio-workshop of Phidias. Perhaps the fact that the ancient competitions once staged here have been revived with so much fanfare, creates the strange sense of contrast between life and death. Whatever the cause, though Olympia is not the most spectacular of the shrines of Greece, it is one of the most moving.

Twenty-five years earlier, we had made the first of our pilgrimages to Olympia. At that time the asphodel, wild hollyhocks, and uncut grass were growing thickly over the lines of marble toe-marks from which the runners made their start, and Lily and I searched long and hard before we finally penetrated the thick growth and found what we were looking for. Lily's glimpse of the Olympic past must have been an omen, for two years later, in 1936, she was at the winter games in Parten-Kirchen, a member of the F.I.S., the first American girl's ski team to race in the Olympics.

Since that first visit to Olympia, the hotel had grown, and what was then a tiny museum had increased enormously in importance and stature—it had come of age. An understanding curator recognized our enthusiasm and, guiding us into an unfinished room, showed us the bronze helmet of Miltiades, the victor of Marathon. The color is a deep, rich green; the texture is rough and unpolished; the shape is long, narrow, and graceful; and it is engraved in the bold Greek letters, that spell his immortal name.

The second day of sight-seeing was a long one. We drove the slow climb up the well-engineered, but not quite completed, road to Bassae. Until very recently this was the most inaccessible of the Temples, for reaching it meant many hours, uphill and downhill, seated on the back of a little four-footed beast of burden, and this could not be accomplished in a day.

At one point along the road we were checked by a stopgate at a railroad crossing. After quite a long wait, during which we heard the distant toot-toot coming nearer and nearer and getting louder and louder, the gate was raised as the little train crossed our bow. Imagine our surprise, when the gate was in an upright position, to find our chauffeur turning ninety degrees to the left and pursuing the train along the railroad tracks and over a trestle bridge. A mile or so beyond, we found our wheels off the tracks and on the main highroad once more.

Somewhat farther along and higher up on a sharp shoulder, our road suddenly ceased to exist. We had to wait a half hour while two massive road-making machines came to our rescue by constructing the missing roadbed. When this impromptu engineering feat was accomplished, we were waved along on our way.

The Temple of Apollo at Bassae was designed by Ictinus, the chief architect of the Parthenon. It owes its poetry to the Arcadian countryside, the light delicacy of its proportions, and to solitude. It is personified by grace rather than majesty; and there is an ethereal effect in the quality of the local gray limestone. Fortunately, it has withstood the ravages of time better than any other temple, except that of Hephaistos. And Time, the destroyer of all good things, hurried us away long before we were ready to leave.

The Sword of Damocles was now hanging over our heads, for the day had come when the Harrisons were to leave us. In fact, the rest of us—the Hammonds and Saarinens—had only a few days left before we would have to sail back to Athens and turn *Rara Avis* over to Gretchen and Merrill Stubbs, who had chartered her from July 15 to August 31. Monday, June 29, we spent at Patras, where flags and bunting were flying in celebration of St. Peter and St. Paul's Day and, therefore, the nameday of the King of Greece.

The next day we returned, after a lapse of twenty-five years, to the enchanting little harbor of Lepanto. During our first visit in 1934, we had been able to take *Landfall,* with her eighteen-foot beam, inside the inner harbor, which was denied to *Rara Avis* with her twenty-three-foot beam. She therefore anchored outside while we revisited the miniature harbor in our starboard launch and rediscovered the picturesque town with its Venetian walls.

Lepanto was a battlefield in the fifth century B.C. and again when it became an important Venetian stronghold in the fifteenth century. The great Battle of Lepanto in 1751 was fought between the Turks (then in possession) and the Holy League of the pontifical galleys of Venice, Spain, Genoa, Savoy, and the Knights of Malta, under the command of Don Juan of Austria. This battle is celebrated for its heavy casualties and for being the last great fight in which both sides used oar-propelled vessels. It was also the engagement in which Cervantes lost an arm. The medieval ghost of this battlemented, roughly cobbled, fortress-like little townlet still walks its streets.

As these grim thoughts passed through our minds, we were seeking signs of the Lepanto of today, and we hadn't far to look. Suddenly we beheld, walking toward us, down the roughly cobbled pavement, two slim feminine figures that might have stepped out of the pages of *Vogue.* They were wearing the latest fashion prescribed by Saks Fifth Avenue and had Charles-of-the-Ritz hairdos. Each wore a creaseless, sleeveless linen sheath, one white and one beige, and the highest of stiletto-heeled slippers. The blonde was wearing Duchess of Windsor starfish earrings, while the brunette had large gold rings in her ears. No, they were not American debutantes, not friends of my children or grandchildren, not friends of friends. We couldn't claim them in any possible way. They were two natives of Lepanto, and their names turned out later to be Thalia and Katarina Papachristos.

While Lily whispered to me, "We have always heard that Greek women dress very well," Paul was already plying our fashionable manikins with many questions and receiving ready answers in perfect English. We soon had acquired two charming guides to show us the intimate sights of Lepanto, and we ended the day with a delicious dinner at an attractive restaurant overlooking the harbor, drinking our only toast—"To the United Nations!"

Their story was along familiar lines. As children, in the early thirties, their parents had taken them to Salt Lake City. In 1939 they had returned and were caught by World War II. For a few years they shared a life of privation and hardship with their war-torn compatriots. When the war was over the family returned to America, this time to Chicago, and now the girls had returned to their native land for their first home holiday since the war. Being Greeks, they knew their way around among small simple inns, and their expenses sometimes amounted to $2.50 a night for both of them. They were seeing their old friends and living comfortably on what would be to any other travelers an impossible budget.

When we parted, Paul assured Thalia that one of the customs of sailors was to wear one hoop earring. At this she presented him gaily with one of hers. "To be returned," said he, "when we all lunch together at the

United Nations,"—a meeting that took place the following winter in New York.

Every return to Delphi is a breath-taking delight. The fact that we were approaching it for the fifth time only enhanced our anticipation. The high mountains, the overhanging rocks, the deep abyss, the low-lying plains where the chariot races took place, the history-telling ruins, all combine to make it the most spectacular and exciting of natural shrines.

For centuries before the Oracle held sway, the Castalian fountain had gushed forth out of the side of Mount Parnassus, forming a perpetual spring of life-giving waters. And only about seven miles north, in a deep gorge of the high Parnassian Cliff, was the famous Corcyrian Cave where three thousand Delphians could take refuge from an enemy invasion. Small wonder that the Greeks considered Delphi the center, or navel, of the world.

Though the approaches are now often clogged with a dense tourist population, and though hotels along the route are omnipresent, the shrines that have been there for twenty-five hundred years are little changed in a lifetime and their pristine beauty has even survived being buried under modern Delphi for many centuries.

On an earlier occasion, when we had been standing near the Temple of Apollo, we had heard the notes of a peasant's flute being wafted down from the mountain top. My granddaughter Susie had remembered this when we told her about it years ago and had brought along her flute. While we were approaching the Temple, she darted up the mountainside and hid herself among the rocks and ruins.

We had the luck to find no busloads of tourists; only two young Greek students who were absorbed in identi-

fying the site of the Oracle. Presently the clear notes of a
flute in classic rhythm and melody came floating down to
us and both of the young men reacted with instant recognition and attention. Both expressed intense pleasure and
some surprise, and one of them bounded up to the point
from which the liquid notes came, and disappeared
among the shrubs and underbrush. When the music was
over and our little musician returned, she described the
student's surprise at finding an American girl acting the
goatherd with the flute. She was thrilled that he had pat-
ted her shoulder with an approving, "Good, good."

On the drive back from Delphi to the port of Itea
where there are many excellent shops, we bought some
things that later turned out to be very satisfactory and
that included the purchase of some white goatskin rugs.
It was a painless procedure (usually I hate shopping while
traveling), because we managed to save ourselves endless
bother with extra bulk and, later on, United States customs regulations. We paid cash, left our addresses, and
kept the receipt to show the customs officers on our return
to the United States. Soon after our arrival at home there
came a notification from the U.S. Post Office, followed by
well-done-up packages that might have come from Santa
Claus.

Once again, as on earlier cruises, we sailed through the
impressive Corinth Canal, and on July 3 we anchored in
Phaleron Bay. I spent most of that day at the National
Archaeological Museum greedily devouring with my eyes
the endless beauty that is so successfully shown there.
Now that the Schliemann treasures are on display, this

archaeological museum cannot be matched in richness and variety anywhere in the world.

That evening we lay moored in crowded Tourkolimano, and we were happy to have Audrey and Peter Lucy, cousins of Whitney Straight, dine on board with us.

The following day we sailed around the Poros Peninsula and anchored in the Bay of Nauplia where *Rara Avis* remained while we went sight-seeing by means of other conveyances. That evening we boarded the little ferry, run by a father and son, that plies between the mainland and the Venetian fifteenth-century fortress that once was the executioner's island. It now bears the title of "Bourzi," and is a charming hotel. The terraces or ramparts are ablaze with flowers and shrubs, and the fort, being circular, has a dozen pie-shaped bedrooms that are appropriately and attractively furnished.

After dining there, we drove to the ancient theater of Epidaurus to see "Oedipus at Kolonos." Every summer from June 15 to August 15, a series of magnificent revivals of Greek plays are given in the ancient theater on the site of the sanctuary of Aesculapius. It is the best preserved of all the Greek theaters and has amazing acoustics. The acting, the directing of the choruses, the design and colors of the costumes are a delight to the eye, and if the untutored ear fails to understand the words, the drama is deeply felt nonetheless.

The following day we renewed our acquaintance with the "Wall-girt Tiryns" of Homer and drove north to Mycenae by way of the plains of Argos. After an absence of twenty-five years we again returned to a tiny inn, described then in the *Guide Bleu* of the early thirties as *"rustic mais propre"* and then called "La Belle Hélène de Menelaus." We had spent the night there on that occasion and rejoiced to find our own Orestes and Agamemnon prepared to give us a good meal as before. We recognized them at once, in spite of the lapse of twenty-five years, and we identified our signatures in the now-discarded hotel register of 1934. I could not help noticing that, if our Greek had not improved during this interruption, neither had their English.

On that first visit, our frame of mind was such a haze of blissful ignorance that we readily accepted the fact that this family of Sophoclean names—Orestes, who waited on us at table; Agamemnon, who cooked a delicious dinner; Helen, who made our beds; and Electra, who answered to that name as she hung up the laundry when we arrived; were the direct descendants of the House of Atreus. In a later and calmer mood we realized that this minute hostel must have sprung into being even since the pioneer era of Heinrich Schliemann, to accommodate his many classical progenitors in historic, architectural, and archaeological fields.

In the days of Schliemann, he and his beautiful young Greek wife must have been boarded and lodged by the more affluent natives of the village. He no doubt won friends and influenced people by officiating at baptisms and treating the ills of his human bulldozers with whatever knowledge of medicine his extensive experience had equipped him. The christenings were irresistible opportunities to bless future generations of Greeks with the Homeric names that occupied his every waking hour.

The late Professor A. J. Wace was one of those to inherit the mantle of Schliemann, and his photograph, with a grateful dedication to Agamemnon, hangs on the wall in a place of honor and is proudly pointed out.

It did not take us long to realize that it was the

Acropolis of Mycenae that had dug its way farther into the deeps of the past than all other sites during our absence of twenty-five years. In the early fifties, important excavations were made by Professor Wace and his British colleagues. And these were enhanced and furthered by the miraculous discovery on the part of Dr. John Papadimitriou of a second Grave Circle, the first one having been discovered by Schliemann in 1876. Seventy-five years from Shaft Grave Circle I to Shaft Grave Circle II, both within a small circumference, only goes to show what rewarding surprises lie in wait at the next step for the patient and scholarly "pioneers to the past."

Our Cruise of 1959 was rapidly drawing to a close. Within a few days we had turned the beloved *Rara Avis* over to our friends Gretchen and Merrill Stubbs in Athens and were on our way home on the American Export liner *Constitution*.

The 1960 Cruise

In 1960 our start was from Syracuse, once the chief Greek city of ancient Sicily, and one of the earliest Greek settlements on the island. According to Thucydides, it was founded in 734 B.C. Syracuse is more than half way down the eastern coast, far enough south to be well out of reach of the whirlpool of Charybdis, and the ship-wrecking arms of Scylla. It is also a good point of departure for crossing the Ionian Sea to Corfu.

Jariilo Walter, accompanied by two friends, G. Anderson and A. F. G. Moss, had brought *Rara Avis* up from her winter berth in Valletta, Malta. My husband and I crossed the Atlantic on the American export liner, S.S. *Independence,* on April 23, disembarked at Naples, and joined the others in Syracuse on May 5. We were also joined by another friend and keen sailing enthusiast, Moune Labey.

We made our usual early start at 4:00 A.M. the following morning, and that first day was a bad one. For thirteen hours a following wind blew in gusts up to sixty miles an hour. We suffered no damage worse than the threat of losing our starboard launch overboard, but knowing that Valletta harbor in Malta would be closed in such a gale, we sailed downwind ten miles and took refuge in the westerly harbor of Gozo. Though Gozo was not on our schedule, Jay, with his never-failing forethought, had

44

brought along a large-scale chart of this little wonder harbor called Cala Dueira. It is circular and spectacular and is surrounded by high protecting limestone cliffs. It is a thousand feet in circumference, and entered by a channel about fifty feet wide, which was just wide enough to permit the cautious entrance, under power and in the teeth of a gale, of our twenty-three-foot beam.

Admiral Barney Sieglaff was at that time the Deputy Chief of Staff for Intelligence in the Headquarters of the Allied Forces in the Mediterranean, HAFMED for short.* Two days later, in Malta, when he came on board to "inspect the ship," he wrote in our logbook, "My hat's off to the sailing Hammonds who made Gozo when our NATO Ships were chased to sea."

Gozo is the second largest of the Maltese group, and is identified with Ogygia, the island where the nymph Calypso, who wished to marry Odysseus, kept him in her vaulted cave for seven long years. This identification was news to us when we first heard of it, but it seems to be accepted by several authorities. Gozo is about eight miles in length, and four miles wide. Its chief town, Victoria, near the center, stands on one of a little cluster of steep conical hills. Though tiny, the island rivals Malta in having a prehistoric temple, called Gigantia, of the same vintage as Hagiar Kim.

As suddenly as the violent Levanter had attacked us in the early hours of the morning, we found ourselves lying in the proverbial millpond. No more rolling, no more

* France, Greece, Italy, Turkey, the United Kingdom and the United States were included in this organization.

pounding, no more noise from our powerful engines, no more rushing of waves, nor howling of wind. Just the heavenly calm of the lap-lapping of gentle waves against the hull in the oncoming twilight.

There were no houses or habitations of any kind in sight. Not a sign of life except the circling of a gull-like bird. We could just make out a tiny gray shelving beach, near which was anchored a small fisherman's dory, the Greek equivalent of a Cape Cod dory.

A sense of quiet and well-being stole over us, and I for one (after a cup of hot tea, the first food or drink that I had thought of all day) began wondering whether this was the particular harbor into which Odysseus had drifted, naked and alone, astride the keel of his ship, to the overwhelming joy of the waiting nymph Calypso.

Like many of the Greek deities, Calypso was both human and divine, and by promising him immortality she had hoped to keep him as her lover forever. He, however, after accepting her flattery for seven long years, became disenchanted. He loved his wife Penelope, he had been away from her and their son Telemachus for ten years, and he was homesick.

The translation of the *Odyssey* that I find the most readable and persuasive is the one by Dr. E. V. Rieu. It lay close at hand on my desk, and I soon was enthralled by descriptive passages of the island of Ogygia, written by one of the greatest story-tellers of the ages.

Athene, who had at first connived with Calypso in detaining Odysseus, and had steadily ignored Penelope's fears for her son's life at the hands of the Suitors, was now being pricked by qualms of conscience and was moved to assist him in his heart's desire. At one of the conclaves of the Gods, on Mount Olympus, she said

'Father Zeus, . . . Look at Odysseus, that admirable
king! To-day, not one of the people he once ruled like a
loving father gives him a single thought. No, he is left to
languish on an island in misery. He is in the Nymph Calypso's clutches; and she sees that he stays there. Not that
he could reach Ithaca in any case, for he has neither galley
nor crew to carry him so far across the sea. Meanwhile, his
beloved son has gone to sacred Pylos and blessed Lacedae-
mon for news of his father, and they mean to murder him
on his way back.'

'My child,' replied the Gatherer of the Clouds, 'I never
thought to hear such words from you. Did you not plan the
whole affair yourself? Was it not your idea that Odysseus
should return and settle accounts with these men? As for
Telemachus, you are well able to look after him: use your
own skill to bring him back to Ithaca safe and sound, and
let the Suitors sail home again in their ship with nothing
accomplished.'

Zeus now turned to Hermes, his son. 'Hermes,' he said,
'in your capacity as our Envoy, convey our final decision to
that dainty Nymph. Odysseus has borne enough and must
now set out for home. On the journey he shall have neither
gods nor men to help him. He shall make it in a boat put
together by his own hands; and on the twentieth day he
should reach Scherie [Corfu], the rich country of the
Phaeacians, our kinsmen, who will take him to their hearts
and treat him like a god. . . .'

Hermes obeyed his father, "the thunderer," as he always must. Picking up his magic wand and fastening on
the golden sandals that would convey him over land or
sea, he skimmed the treacherous waves till he arrived at
the far-away island of Ogygia.

In her sheltering cavern . . .

He found the lady of the lovely locks at home. A big fire
was blazing on the hearth and the scent from burning logs

of split juniper and cedar was wafted far across the island.
Inside, Calypso was singing in a beautiful voice as she wove
at the loom and moved her golden shuttle to and fro. The
cave was sheltered by a verdant copse of alders, aspens, and
fragrant cypresses, which was the roosting-place of feathered
creatures, horned owls and falcons and garrulous choughs,
birds of the coast, whose daily business takes them down to
the sea. Trailing round the very mouth of the cavern, a
garden vine ran riot, with great bunches of ripe grapes;
while from four separate but neighbouring springs four
crystal rivulets were trained to run this way and that; and
in soft meadows on either side the iris and the parsley
flourished. It was indeed a spot where even an immortal
visitor must pause to gaze in wonder and delight.

The nymph Calypso hearkened to her immortal visitor
in fear, and when he had finished with his severe repri-
mand from the god of gods, she defended herself by the
common device of casting aspersions on others:

'A cruel folk you are, unmatched for jealousy, you gods who
cannot bear to let a goddess sleep with a man, even if it is
done without concealment and she has chosen him as her
lawful consort. You were the same when Rose-fingered
Dawn fell in love with Orion. Easy livers yourselves, you
were outraged at her conduct, and in the end chaste
Artemis rose from her golden throne, attacked him in
Ortygia with her gentle darts and left him dead. And so
again, when the lovely Demeter gave way to her passion
and lay in the arms of her beloved Iasion in the thrice-
ploughed fallow field, Zeus heard of it quickly enough and
struck him dead with his blinding thunderbolt. And now it
is my turn to incur that same divine displeasure for living
with a mortal man—a man whom I rescued from death as
he was drifting alone astride the keel of his ship, when Zeus
had shattered it with his lightning bolt out on the wine-
dark sea, and all his men were lost, but he was driven to

this island by the wind and waves. I welcomed him with open arms; I tended him; I even hoped to give him immortality and ageless youth. But now, goodbye to him, since no god can evade or thwart the will of Zeus. If Zeus insists that he should leave, let him be gone across the barren water. But he must not expect *me* to transport him. I have no ship, no oars, no crew to carry him so far across the seas. Yet I do promise with a good grace and unreservedly to give him such directions as will bring him safe and sound to Ithaca. . . .'

Having given her promise, Calypso proceeded to carry it through. She sought out her lover and with a gentle rebuke, she reproached him for his faithlessness and warned him of the dangerous seas he would encounter on this last long voyage to Ithaca.

By now the sun had set and it grew dark. So the two retired to a recess in the cavern and there in each other's arms they spent a night of love.

But the new Dawn had scarcely touched the East with red before Odysseus put his cloak and tunic on. The Nymph dressed herself too in a long silvery mantle of a light material charming to the eye, with a splendid golden belt round her waist, and a veil over her head. Then she turned her thoughts to the problem of her noble guest's departure. First she gave him a great axe of bronze. Its double blade was sharpened well, and the shapely handle of olive-wood fixed firmly in its head was fitted to his grip. Next she handed him an adze of polished metal; and then led the way for him to the farthest part of the island, where the trees grew tall, alders and poplars and firs that shot up to the sky, all withered timber that had long since lost its sap and would make buoyant material for his boat. When she had shown him the place where the trees were tallest the gracious goddess left for home, and Odysseus began to cut the timber down. He made short work of the task. Twenty trees in all he felled, and lopped their branches with his axe; then trimmed them in workmanlike manner and trued them to the line. Presently Calypso brought him augers. With these he drilled through all his planks, cut them to fit across each other, and fixed this flooring together by means of dowels driven through the interlocking joints, giving the same width to his boat as a skilled shipwright would choose in designing the hull for a broad-bottomed trading vessel. He next put up the decking, which he fitted to ribs at short intervals, finishing off with long gunwales down the sides. He made a mast to go in the boat, with a yard fitted to it; and a steering-oar too, to keep her on her course. And from stem to stern he fenced her sides with plaited osier twigs and a plentiful backing of brushwood, as some protection against the heavy seas. Meanwhile the goddess Calypso had brought him cloth with which to make the sail. This he manufactured too; and then lashed the braces, halyards, and sheets in their places on board. Finally he dragged her down on rollers into the tranquil sea.*

Yes, that was it. That was our harbor of Cala Dueira, a thousand feet across, and protected by high rocks, with a fifty-foot-wide channel—a spring-board to the open sea.

And it may be noted in passing that Odysseus was not the only man who thought that a wide, flat-bottomed freight-carrying hull was a good design for sailing the Mediterranean seas.

The following day we completed our sail to Valletta. The name immortalizes the first Grand Master of the Knights of St. John after they were driven from Rhodes by the Turks. Jean Parisot de La Valette commanded the

* Homer *Odyssey*. v. Trans. by E. V. Rieu (Baltimore: Penguin, 1959), pp. 88–94.

Maltese and the Knights. Fighting side by side, they hero-
ically resisted one of the great sieges of history. Here is
one of the most magnificent examples of a fortification in
the world, and the British fleet has used it as one of their
unconquerable bases. Even in World War II when Malta
literally suffered daily bomber raids, it emerged with flying colors. Not only were individual heroes decorated
with medals of honor, but the island of Malta itself was
awarded the George Cross by the British government.

Malta has many charms and anomalies. The native taxi
is a picturesque little boat called *djhaisa*, with a high
stem at either end and is a cousin to the Venetian gondola.

There is also to be seen (though rarely now) the graceful black *faldetta*, a broad hood of heavy, rich corded silk
that protects both the mother and babe from the broiling
sun.

There are districts, where tier upon tier of tiny homes
are cut into the sandstone, and it is said that they are
some of the most overpopulated spots in the world.

The day after our arrival, we were driven to the famous
Bay of St. Paul, where the Saint was shipwrecked in about
60 A.D., and from whence he walked, hungry and ex-
hausted, to the home of Publius, the "chief man" of the
island.

Then we saw the strange prehistoric hypogeum at Hal
Salfieni and the temple structures at Hal Tarxien. Here
there are rather charming little neolithic bas-reliefs of
sheep, goats, and pigs, dating from about 2200 B.C. There
are also odd shapes of obese females, far from beautiful,
and one oversized lady in a flounced skirt.

It was during this drive that we first encountered with
a jolt the fire of nationalism that is spreading so fast every-

where. We were so wrapped up in the past that we had temporarily forgotten the troubled world of today. Our taxi driver was a swarthy, middle-aged Maltese who spoke good English. He was very talkative and after telling us much about Malta, past and present, he took up the theme of "We want our independence; we want to be free."

Sitting beside him was Tom Cabot, economist, engineer, Trustee of M.I.T., and Overseer of Harvard University. He is also an important and integral part of the Boston family firm known as Cabot Corporation. For eighty years it has dealt with huge quantities of carbon black, but is now adding color to itself by entering the fields of pigments and plastics. We had begun to discover that Tom could take over the job of guidebooks. His memory is such that, in what seemed like a few minutes of reading, he would brief us on all the sites that awaited us, as well as sketch in the long history that led up to them.

Tom let our taxi driver talk for some time and then he said, "The Maltese are dependent on trade; all nations, both great and small, live largely on trade. The British Navy has been making trade possible for you for many, many years. They have helped, not only with trade but with food. Their ships brought the first rich earth to your shores to enable you to plant wheat along these little terraces of a limestone island. A small nation without trade and with a meager grain supply will starve." But still, like a faulty phonograph record, the phrase was repeated and repeated, "We want to be free. We want to be free. We want to be free."

Early in March, 1960, we had made a date with our

friend Bobby Somerset to meet in Malta on May 5, but due to the heavy gale that developed we were both belated. *Rara Avis* was already tied up in her former winter berth in Siliema Creek, when Bobby's yawl *Thanet* moored on the eighth in Valletta Harbor.

He had three companions with him: James Mackie, Richard Beaumont, and a little black miniature poodle who wrote in our logbook, "Jessica Somerset, who would like to come along." She, no doubt, enjoyed our clear, beamy deck. They were on their way from Majorca to Istanbul to pick up three friends and sail them back.

Bobby is one of the most web-footed friends we have, and one of the most experienced of yachtsmen. He bought the famous cutter *Jolie Brise* from George Martin shortly after George won the Fastnet Cup with her. Bobby sailed her to victory himself in 1929 and 1930. He and his wife now live in their pretty Casa Caromandel, overlooking Puerto Adraitx, Majorca, which is the winter berth for his floating home. He, his ship, and his lovely wife have a sort of working arrangement that resembles the life of a naval couple—duty afloat and shore duty.

During our last evening in Malta, Bobby and his guests dined with the Cabots, Perkinses and ourselves, at the large and impressive Phoenician hotel, and that was our opportunity to profit by Bobby's vast experience in Mediterranean waters and to get his advice for our itinerary.

The following day we were starting on our way to Greece, but before crossing the Ionian Sea we were irresistibly drawn back to the island of Gozo. The scene of the seven year tryst of Calypso and Odysseus had cast a spell over us, so we spent one more night of enchantment in the harbor of Cala Dueira (Qala Tad-Dwejra).

The next morning, May 10, we were under way at 4:00 A.M. with the lightest of fair winds, and after another night spent at Syracuse, we had a delicious thirty-hour sail across the Ionian Sea to Corfu under perfect conditions. Though later we returned for a longer stay, this time we remained in Corfu only overnight. On the morning of the fourteenth, we steamed through a narrow entrance to the pretty harbor of Gayo, on the island of Paxoi, but failing time for more than a tantalizing glimpse, turned on a dime, withdrew, and proceeded in a southeasterly direction. This was one of the attractive harbors that Bobby Somerset had marked on our chart.

The night of May 14 was spent in the harbor of Vliko on Levkas Island. After an early start and a look at Sivota Bay, everyone was on deck at 5:00 A.M., seeking for the height from which Sappho may have met her death, and from which accused persons were required to dive as the test of a "Judgment of God" in later centuries. A sheer wall of terrifying height and steepness hung above us menacingly as we steamed through the early morning quiet on an even keel.

Presently we knew that we had arrived. The rocky promontory on our right rose steeply and to a great height, along the full length of Cape Doukatos. The easterly wind was blowing great swirls of smokelike mist, obliterating sky, precipice and sea, just as it may have done when the beckoning hands from Hades were raised for death or deliverance.

The Levkadian Leap was the only site in the whole sun-soaked Greek waters where we ever saw the faintest suggestion of fog.

Of the three Ithacan ports we next entered, Kioni on

the Northeast coast came first. Like Odysseus we were on
the long voyage from Gozo (Ogygia) to Ithaca, searching
for his home port. Not quite satisfied with Kioni, we
sailed downwind about ten miles, and, as we entered the
natural semicircular shell, surrounded by hills, that forms
the harbor of Vathi, it was beautiful enough to satisfy our
highest hopes, and we were ready to believe, with Schliemann and Dörpfelt, that this was the scene of Odysseus'
homecoming.

Our companions since our arrival in Malta were Vir-
ginia and Tom Cabot, and Marian and Jim Perkins, shipmates who couldn't be improved upon. They are great
skiers, mountain climbers, riders, and sailors, and love
every form of outdoor life. They are keen observers and
tireless travelers and sight-seers. These four explored the
hinterland from the port of Vathi with an enthusiastic
following of assorted juveniles. They carried on a lively
interchange of Graeco-English, and the quartet returned
with their Greek vocabulary noticeably increased.

In the meantime the Hammonds had gone ashore to
arrange a lunch on the quay for the returning pedestrians,
and had fallen in with a nice round-faced Greek school-
teacher, who offered himself as the necessary dictionary.
He turned out to be an itinerant teacher, in primary education—a "Civil servant," moving from island to island,
at two- or three-year intervals. "In that way, I have my
traveling expenses paid for," said he.

That afternoon we left Vathi for Port St. Andreas, a
lovely little cove on the southern end of Ithaca. This harbor was so tiny and narrow that there was no room
to swing on our anchor. Bobby Somerset had described
this harbor to us in Malta with a light in his eye: "You
can really secure your stern to a two hundred year olive

tree." Diving overboard, Tom picked up a lightweight mooring-line and swam ashore, holding it in his teeth as a sailor does when both hands are occupied. He hauled enough slack on shore around the tree trunk to enable him to take the free end back to the ship. There we spent the night, with neither sight nor sound of human being, and the next morning all we had to do was let go the line on deck.

Patras came our way on May 16. Though one of the larger ports of Greece, it has little to offer the tourist, and its ruins are insignificant. The train rumbles through the flat town, picks up produce brought in by the many ships tied along the lengthy quay, and carries it back to Athens so that it can be redistributed. One of our U.S. destroyers was docked there, and we were grateful to two skillfull young U.S.N. electric technicians who repaired our Sperry Automatic Pilot, making the required parts by hand and doing a smart temporary job. Well-cared-for fishing nets dry themselves in the sun, lying along the full length of the quay; and if you want a swim, a little native boat will sail you to a rocky beach where cleaner water can be found. Patras connects the main highways to Olympia, providing an opportunity that the Cabots and Perkinses did not miss, and they secured an excellent English-speaking chauffeur, called Alexopouros. While there, they fell in with the head of the Archaeological Service in Olympia, Dr. Nicholas F. Yalouris, and were happy to give him a lift back to Patras, as he was on his way to Athens. It was a lucky encounter for our guests as they learned much from him along the way.

The next day we looked in at the narrow entrance to the tiny battle-scarred port of Lepanto—too small for our broad beam—and we left it unvisited this time. Instead, we stopped in at one of Bobby's tiny islands, Trizonia, at the western end of the Gulf of Corinth, to which we hoped to return later for a longer stay. A little east of Trizonia we spoke *Thanet* in the flattest of flat calms and tactlessly offered Bobby a tow, which he declined.

Arriving at the port of Itea in the early afternoon, we had time for a few hours of glorious Delphi. Threatening thunderclouds hung over us as we explored the ruins and climbed to the stadium, where two young Greek soccer teams were carrying on the contests of old. I found the familiar base of the Plataean Column solidly buried near the Temple of Apollo and filled as ever with memories of courage and greed. When we reached the museum we discovered that it had grown from a small and simple embryo to a large and handsome building. A piece of sculpture, a symbol of the "navel of the world," is given a place of honor near the entrance, and the walls are hung with the exquisite small fragments of metopes and friezes from the sixth century treasuries of Sicyon, Siphos and Cnidus.

We returned to our ship, the clouds still lowering but not breaking, to find *Thanet* in the offing, just before sundown. The best anchorage in Itea for small craft, according to Jay, is the landing pier, preferably on the west side. There is one drawback for light sleepers, however. A local ferryboat, plying regularly in and out, lowers its ramp on the stone pier every night with a big bang. The next day saw us through the Corinth Canal to Piraeus, where we anchored in Phaleron Bay.

On May 19, at 6:00 A.M., we departed for the Island of Aegina and anchored off the town of that name. This means a long drive up to the well-preserved Temple of Aphaia. Though on higher ground than Olympia, it is well-wooded and gives the same quiet, peaceful impres-

sion. Aegina is the only small island that offers the
intimacy of a great and beautiful fifth-century B.C. temple
with many of the features of a miniature summer resort.
It can be reached by frequent steamers and sailboats, and
should be allowed as much time as can be spared.

The Poros Channel is deep and safe and so we chose
that way to reach Hydra. Its shore is full of activity and
city life; ships of all kinds—yachts, and naval and commercial vessels—carry on a daily traffic, and the tourist
trade is endless. The next day, having spent the night in
Hydra harbor, we stopped to have a look at the island of
Spetsai, in the Gulf of Argolis.

Drayton Cochran, a friend, and one of the keenest and
ablest of offshore sailormen, had kept his *Little Vigilant*
there every winter for several years and had recom-
mended it to us for a winter berth for *Rara Avis*. Spetsai
has shared with Hydra, only twenty miles away, a long
history of a seafaring people that prospered during the
Napoleonic era and distinguished themselves for bravery
and patriotism in the Greek war of independence. There
are many attractive houses to be seen, giving evidence of
taste and refinement, and there is a hotel with the appropriate name of Grand Hotel Poseidon. One of the advan-
tages that Spetsai enjoys is that when the Meltemi blows
in other quarters of the Cyclades, it bypasses her harbors.
On the mainland, near Spetsai is another well sheltered
harbor, Port Heli, where tiny fingerling coves with shelving beaches and olive trees shading them tempt you for
a swim.

Turning there, on our proverbial dime, we arrived at
Nauplia at noon. This was a chance to show the Cabots
and Perkinses the sanctuary of Aesculapius, and after
lunching on board, we all drove to Epidaurus and once

again enjoyed the grandeur of the theater and the interesting museum. This year we were too early for the theatrical season so we contented ourselves with another visit to the executioner's island. Again we took the little ferry, manned by father and son and were welcomed on our arrival by the proprietor accompanied by four little girls dressed in neat black uniforms, who were very attentive and later served us a good dinner of red snapper and a light native wine. The old fortress was a handsome mass of gray stone in the fading light, and splendidly dressed up by the gay flowering shrubs of hibiscus, geranium, bleeding heart, and oleander, tastefully planted among the ramparts and against the massive walls.

We departed Nauplia at 6:00 A.M. on May 22 with Crete our distant objective, about two hundred miles to the southeast. We hadn't gone more than a short distance, when what to our wondering eyes appeared, but a colossal and magnificent three-masted schooner anchored off the tiny island of Spetsopoulo; the yacht, *Creole*, quite dwarfed the little island. Both yacht and island turned out to be the possessions of Mr. Stavros Niarchus. This splendid apparition took us quite by surprise, and we were silenced in awe for several miles. What would the wooden horse of Troy have had in common with this steel thoroughbred, we were asking ourselves; what indeed, but the Eternal Quest?

This was to be the last lap of our cruise with the Cabots and Perkinses, and, though very light, the winds were favorable. Incidentally, the Cabots' yawl *Avelinda* has been for many years a familiar sight along the coast of Maine. With children and friends, they have carried on the adventurous spirit of the early explorers along that foggy and rock-bound coast, and Jim Perkins came by his sailing know-how in the strictest of yachting schools, that of his cousin Charles Francis Adams, our one-time Secretary of the Navy. The first day of our new lap was a glorious day of sail with two outstanding sailormen.

They set the jib, port trade twin, main staysail, overlapping mainsail, and mizzen in a light northeasterly wind, and we made a good seven knots, though we expected to do no more than four in the excessively light winds. Toward the end of the afternoon they became lighter and lighter and by sundown the sails were all lowered. That day and during our return cruise north to Santorin were the only times when we were able to carry so many sails.

The following day, we of the afterguard did not know, as we headed for a day of sight-seeing, that our seemingly satisfied and satisfactory mixed crew had staged one of those mild mutinies that are a concomitant to all marine activities where crews are concerned. They asked for a raise of $50 a month and complained to Jay that we were too continuously on the go. Actually we were spending many hours, and having many meals ashore in order to see more of the natives and islands that we had come to see, as well as to give the crew time off, and it seemed to us surprising that they thought we were moving too fast. According to Jay, the men had, at the beginning of the voyage, accepted a reasonable offer for a certain term of service, and the code of the sea does not permit defaulting in this accept-our-new-terms-or-we-leave way. However, there were too many factors involved to risk losing them entirely, so our part had to be that of surrender. To Jay, who always leaned over backwards to do more than his duty, this behavior on the part of the crew was a great disappointment.

Don't let anyone minimize the importance of the island of Crete and hurry you through too quickly. It is not a steppingstone en route to other places, but a world in itself, and once you are there, you will find it rewarding to devote to it as much of your time as possible. It is the largest island in the Greek archipelago, and twice as large as New York's Long Island. The palaces of Achaean kings, the castles of Achaean noblemen, and several small towns, such as Gournia, have been excavated with painstaking care by archaeologists from many countries in collaboration with Greek authorities.

As hotels are few and far between and transportation still meagre, short stays are advisable for those who love their creature comforts, but for the young and adventurous, the fascinations of Crete are endless. A delightful and fairly recent book, to be read before you go, as well as taken with you, is Leonard Cottrell's *The Bull of Minos.**

The legendary birthplace and cradle of Zeus is high on the rugged shoulder of Mount Ida, and the long, irregular coast line has been the scene of countless mythological and historic landfalls and departures throughout the ages, beginning with the time when the Pythian Apollo turned himself into a dolphin and swam from Delphi to Crete.

Crete achieved an amazing degree of civilization and culture through her sea lanes to Egypt, to the islands and mainland of Greece, and to parts of Asia Minor. This intercourse and influence can be traced back to the pre-dy-

* Published in New York by Holt, Rinehart, & Winston, Inc., 1959.

nastic period of Egypt in the latter half of the fourth millennium B.C., and the great flowering came about almost contemporaneously with the New Empire of Egypt. The New Empire is dated from about 1555 to 1350 B.C., and, as you will remember, includes the reigns of Thutmosis I, II, and III, and the notable reign of Queen Hatshepsut, half-sister and wife of Thutmosis II. She was on the throne in 1492 B.C. It may seem a long hop from that year to 1492 A.D., but that kind of comparison is my way of remembering dates.

The traditional site of Knossos was the mound of Kephala, a few miles from Herakleion. There, in 1877, the Spanish Consul sunk some shafts which established the existence of at least one large building at a great depth under the ground.

By 1873 Heinrich Schliemann had had the delight of slashing successfully through the great mound at Hissarlik, Turkey, and finding gold as well as going far toward revealing the nine cities of Troy. This work soon began to arouse the disapproval of the Ottoman government and Schliemann betook himself, with his devoted wife, to Mycenae, where in 1876 he proceeded to dig near the Lion Gate. There he discovered five shaft-graves with a double ring of slabs, as well as an immense treasure of gold, silver, bronze, and ivory. After such a triumphant success, he was in the mood for new fields to conquer. He next applied to the Greek government for permission to dig in Crete, but by this time he was *persona non grata* in Greece as well as Turkey, and was refused.

A few years later Schliemann made an effort to buy the site of the Spanish Consul's embryo dig. The negotiations were complicated and fell through because the landowner insisted on selling his entire estate with not only the excavations, but also many thousands of olive trees, for all of which he demanded 100,000 francs. After this failure Schliemann made two trips to Egypt, which no doubt further whetted his appetite for the Egyptian-influenced island, and on his return to Greece in 1888, the Cretan landowner reduced his demand to 40,000 francs and assured Schliemann that his presence in Crete was quite unnecessary to clinch the bargain; a deposit was all that was needed. Schliemann was tempted, but still wary, and probably more jealous of his hard-won earnings than was Sir Arthur Evans later to be, of his inherited wealth. When Schliemann discovered this time that there were 1,612 fewer olive trees than had been written in the deed, he declined the offer and never renewed negotiations.

It is interesting to speculate what Knossos would look like today had his pioneer technique in Troy been applied to the three palaces of Knossos, and had Sir Arthur Evans' representational restorations never taken shape. Personally, I like the Viollet–le–Duc-like restoration that Sir Arthur has given us, because it is the only such sample of its kind and a satisfying feast compared with the tantalizing fillip of a Phaistos or a Hagia Triada. Now, fifty years later, it may be the fashion to criticize the dedicated work of Sir Arthur Evans at Knossos, but it should be recalled that continuous research is not always corroborative. It may not always move forward, and succeeding generations have a funny way of changing their minds, as do individuals.

Our sixty-five-mile run north to Santorin, the southernmost island of the Sporades, occurred on another lovely sailing day. We had a fair wind and we carried all our light-air sails as we had from Nauplia to Crete and made eight knots an hour during the better part of our dawn-to-noon sailing day.

Though there had been severe earthquakes on these islands in the early fifties, they did not seriously affect the tourist side of Santorin, and there has been little change, tourist-wise, since we were there twenty-five years ago. Richard Delano has quite vividly described our visit to Santorin in his diary called "That Greek Trip," so I have little to say that would not be repetitious. We did, however, encounter one change in the form of a somewhat sinister warning after we had tied up to the one massive iron buoy, a hundred yards or so from shore. The water there is so deep that it is impossible to anchor, and the vast depth, even inshore, gives harborage to sharks more successfully than to ships. It was soon pointed out to us by a native that should we want to have a swim the only safe place would be not from our own craft, but from a tiny shelving beach close at hand. In general, we found sharks more feared and more talked about this year than we had on previous cruises. Santorin is well known for a variety of good, light, Madeira-like wines and the Cabots laid in a few samples that added to the gaiety of our evening meal.

The next morning, May 26, we made our accustomed early start, casting off from the giant buoy. As we approached Delos a few hours later, we soon realized that this island was to be one of our few changelings. When we had arrived in Delos on the morning of June 9, 1934, no ship was to be seen, except for the tiny motor boat that putt-putted out to guide us ashore. And when we had landed we were greeted by a nice-looking, dark-complexioned, middle-aged Greek accompanied by a little flock of children of assorted ages. He was obviously the harbor master so Paul offered him our ship's papers, which he promptly waved aside. "Don't you want to see our papers?" Paul had asked. "Oh no," was his indifferent answer. Paul then asked, "Oh, are you King?" "Yes, I King," said he. He had then waved for us to follow him so that he could show us the solitary and sacred island— so sacred indeed, in ancient days, that anyone about to be born or about to die had first to be removed to the neighboring island of Rhenea.

This time, however, we found that the confident "king" of 1934, with his court of assorted Delian children and his native pride in the importance of his job, had left no heir. In place of his small royal procession stood stall after well-stocked stall of native industries, being offered flamboyantly to a large crowd of customers of every nationality. Goatskin rugs, bags, and cushion covers woven of goat hair; and beads, carvings, and souvenir trinkets were temptingly displayed. Commercial steamers of all sizes and shapes, with an occasional yacht, were anchored within dinghy distance of the shore. In terms of Ancient Greece, the once-sacred and solitary little island was overrun with barbarians. Archaeologically speaking, the long line of magnificent seventh-century-B.C. lions stood their ground in the same excellence of condition in which we had first found them, though Delos generally typifies the sprawling disorder of some Greek ruins.

Leaving little Delos to her new-found crowded life of profane activity, we steamed towards Siros in the center of the Cyclades. As a matter of fact, at the beginning of the nineteenth century, Siros usurped part of the role once played by Delos in ancient times. Due to her excellent harbor with abundant ship-building facilities, Siros became the third port of importance in Greece, Athens being the first and Patras the second.

This deep harbor is sheltered on one side by a long breakwater, and on the other, by the Isle of Asses, and we moored, stern to, in the Mediterranean manner. As daylight faded, we watched the twinkling lights appear in tier above tier of houses that dot the slopes of two conical hills. The picturesque scene was completed as throngs of gay islanders appeared along the broad quay to take advantage of the evening breezes, and enjoy dinner or sip numberless tiny cups of coffee at the inviting restaurants along the water front. Another arena for the crowds of evening strollers, seeking the cool night air, is the broad handsome plaza in the center of the town, just beyond the quay. Strolling along quays or plazas in the cool of the evening and chatting with friends and acquaintances is a happy relaxation at the end of a long, hot sunny day, for those who live in a semi-tropical climate.

The following day we all had a breathing spell while Paul and Jay followed leads that suggested a possible winter berth for *Rara Avis*. I went off by myself in search of a till-then-postponed shampoo. At home there would have been dozens of women in the streets to put my questions to, but in Siros it was a choice of which man would give me the best advice. I settled on a nice, white-haired native, who turned out to be a small shopkeeper. Soon it was evident that I was to follow him to his own home, where his wife would then conduct me to the number-one beauty parlour in town, run by a cousin of hers; I was not to be neglected and left alone to lose my way in a foreign country.

As we talked and walked along side by side, I told my new-found friend that we had our boat in his harbor. He replied, with a shade of sadness, "the Greeks are a very poor people." You might suppose that this was a prelude to a request of some kind, but not at all, far from it—it was merely a wish to prepare me for the simplicity that I would find in his modest home. Throughout my encounter with this friendly Greek and his family, I was offered every hospitality that was available, without the slightest thought of any return. On my part, naturally, I was racking my brains to think how I could, without offense, reward their kindness.

Presently I found myself seated in a small Victorian living room, at a large dining room table, with the wife, the mother, the mother-in-law, the aunt, and a little daughter. I was being plied with tasty cakes and a sweet drink, and being offered homemade wine. My host soon disappeared about his business, and we women were left to carry on a deaf-and-dumb sign language. After having fed me, the young wife guided me through a few narrow streets to the fine open square, with century-old arcades that bespeak the halcyon days of Siros.

We then entered the door of the Elizabeth Arden of Siros, and I was introduced as an American to the pretty proprietress. They sat me in a comfortable armchair facing a mirror. An empty pail was placed on the floor behind my chair, my head was gently pushed backwards over the pail, and pitchers of hot soapy rain water were poured over my waiting forehead and locks. It was a painless and adequate proceeding that was attended by a lively conversation between my guide and her cousin.

When the shampoo was completed, my good Samaritan pointed the way towards the quay with a sweet smile and vanished. A little later, by dint of a good many enquiries, I managed to identify the shop and was able to send a bundle of silk stockings and canned food, which I hope turned out to be useful.

On May 28 we arrived at the southern side of the island of Keos. It was an unexpected landfall, for till that day, none of us had ever heard of it. Our hopes soared high when we read in Hachette's *Greece,* "Possesses a colossal antique lion, 29 feet 6 inches high."

Since then, interesting articles have been frequently in the news concerning excavations that were begun six weeks later on a northern promontory of Keos, St. Irene. Since Dr. Blegen's retirement, these investigations are being made by Professor John L. Caskey, the head of the Department of Classics in the University of Cincinnati, and his wife. They are proceeding under the direction of the American School of Classical Studies at Athens, and with the cooperation of the Ephor of the Cyclades, Mr. Zapheiropoulos. It was our misfortune to arrive at Keos too early to learn about this interesting find of one of the earliest of middle Bronze Age cities. It seems that the dead city of St. Irene was destroyed by earthquakes instead of by the fire and invasion that wrought havoc in Mycenae, Pylos, and Crete. The resulting comparisons between the damage done by fire and sword, and the damage done by earthquakes, may be of great interest in pointing up the history of the Achaeans.

We had no sooner landed than we found ourselves in the midst of an important cattle sale of nice healthy, brown animals with white noses and small black and white horns. Each cow carried a number on her flank, and there was an active veterinarian, dressed in a clean, crisp white gown, looking much like the doctors in the movie

"Men in White." He carried a stethoscope around his neck, and applied it attentively to the chest of each cow in turn. This was a tempting signal for Paul to play the farmer that he maintains he once was. Cigarettes, hats, and badinage in pigeon-Greek were bandied back and forth among the good-natured crowd, and pictures were snapped, while we waited for the one jalopy of the island to conduct us to the statue of the lion.

After much good-humored exchange between natives and tourists as to who should milk the cows, the car arrived. Like the lion, it also was colossal and antique, and we held our breath while we cavorted up the three-hundred-foot-high hill to the edge of the ancient town of Yulis.

At Yulis the road was no longer navigable by car, so we descended from the station wagon and were met by a guide. Yulis is a typical ancient hillside town with narrow wayward streets, often paved with marble slabs; where the going was steep the slabs turned into long marble steps—an aid to donkey or pedestrian. As usual, the little white stucco houses huddled close together, and sometimes it seemed as if we were walking through the retaining walls of an overpass that kept one house from sliding down on a lower one. Several times during that walk, we blessed Yulis for the guide it had provided us. Though you might think it impossible to lose your way in a tiny town built on the side of a hill, nevertheless the road had a way of shooting little bypaths off into back yards that would have delayed and puzzled us without him.

After quite a long climb, we came to an enclosure fenced in by an iron rail with a large padlock that could only be opened by the key possessed by our guide. There before us was indeed a colossal antique lion. Not only antique, but archaic. Twenty-nine-feet high and between fifty and sixty feet long, the recumbent figure lies on a huge slab of gray rock. The whole sculpture seems to be carved out of the matrix of the mountain, though a brick-work foundation is just visible beneath the slab of rock. The lion has the wide-apart, slightly bulging eyes of a magnificent archaic Kouros of the sixth century B.C., and he still wears a smile on his lips in spite of the violence that the Greek climate visits upon its outdoor treasures. He carries a brushed-back, upstanding mane and lies there with all the serenity and composure of a Greek philosopher. To us, he was an entrancing and unbeliev-able apparition, particularly fascinating because until that morning totally unexpected.

After lunching on board *Rara Avis*, we weighed anchor for Cape Colonna, and three hours later arrived in the protected harbor, south of the promontory crowned by the temple dedicated to Poseidon.

> Place me on Sunium's marbled steep,
> Where nothing save the waves and I
> May hear our mutual murmurs sweep;
> There, swan-like, let me sing and die.*

When Byron wrote those words, a hundred and fifty years ago, the mutual murmurs between poet and sea could well have gone unheard; even twenty-five years ago, the ghostly, white marble temple stood alone in its maj-esty. Now, the busy world has discovered it, and all our

---

* Lord Byron, "Don Juan," Canto III, Stanza 86.

powers of selectivity were challenged to blot out the surrounding havoc brought about by tourist demand.

When we arrived for the first time in 1934, the letters B-Y-R-O-N, carved on the north side of the Temple, were hard to find because they were cut in clean white marble and lost in the glisten of the sun's rays. Now they are hard to find because they are surrounded by myriads of other names—Arabic, English, French, German, Russian —all lost in a Tower-of-Babel-like confusion and clutter. Whether or not these letters were really carved by the poet, or even by one of his contemporaries, is a moot question that will never be answered. But let us not despair; while Sunium is within such easy reach of the great Mecca Athens, that it is inevitably overrun, there are still unfrequented regions to be read about such as the Mani, where goat-footed nymphs invite a traveler to the dance and trip him as he nears a precipice. Or there are faraway places in Thrace where wandering, picturesque and untamed Sarakatsans mind their flocks and live their lives in the worship of Artemis, as well as a Christian deity, and in fear, chiefly of the dark demon Daouti. Lonely and haunted regions still exist, but only a Patrick Leigh Fermor is clever enough and adventurous enough to offer them to us vicariously.*

At twilight, in the cool of a threatening sky, we swung at our anchor, getting constantly changing glimpses of the stark white temple high against black lowering clouds. We were thankful to have the enclosed feeling of a floating home, secure on the beloved element of Greek life, and not tempted to join the milling crowds on the acropolis. After dinner Tom Cabot read aloud to us

* *See* Patrick Leigh Fermor, *Mani* (New York: Harper & Brothers, 1958).

and we had much to discuss—of Byron—of Shelley—of
Aeschylus—of Sophocles—and of other great men, dead
and living.

As we parted for the night, we promised each other to
be up and off early in the morning, convinced that in
that case we couldn't fail to have the Temple to ourselves.
But no, with the first signs of the rose-fingered dawn the
crowds were already on high, and, metaphorically,
thumbing their noses at us.

As time advanced and the clock seemed to taunt us with
"now or never," we took the starboard launch ashore and
climbed the hill. On reaching the Temple it seemed that
each group of tourists, after doing their sight-seeing,
would file along the graduated steps on the north side,
and seat themselves for a well-timed photograph with the
Temple of Sunium for a background; after which, having
immortalized themselves with a proof of having been *in
situ*, they would board the buses and disappear to the
next Acropolis. So, as we watched the last group board
the last bus, the moment did at last arrive when we
were alone with the waves for a few minutes, and could
commune with them undisturbed.

By one o'clock that day, we were moored in Passalimani, and the hour was striking when we must let the
Cabots and Perkinses take wing. It had been an unforgettable month of sunshine, beauty, and interest, and
we hated to see them go. The end of a cruise such as this
is the signal for a general disbanding. The hard-working
crew deserves a liberty; there is some housekeeping to
be done, laundry to be sent ashore, stores to be bought
and stowed, and, unhappily, minor or major repairs sure

to be needed. These few days give the afterguard a chance
to live ashore, learn more about the country, see the
sights, revel in deep, hot baths, and generally go in dry
dock themselves. We stayed at the Grande Bretagne (or
at least I did) and had a room on the sixth floor, with an
unobstructed view of the Acropolis. Every early morning
hour that I spent at that open window, sipping my *café
complet* and feasting my eyes on the beauty before me,
was the height of my delight. No hour of sight-seeing later
in the day could ever match it.

When a window of your own gives on the Parthenon,
every sunrise brings the Age of Pericles before you, and
it is the man himself who speaks to you—speaks in those
eloquent phrases from one of his immortal funeral ora-
tions delivered over the bodies of the Athenian dead.

Our constitution is named a democracy, because it is in
the hands not of the few but of the many. . . . Our public
opinion welcomes and honors talent in every branch of
achievement. . . . We have no black looks or angry words
for our neighbor if he enjoys himself in his own way. . . .
We acknowledge the restraint of reverence. We are lovers
of beauty without extravagance, and lovers of wisdom without unmanliness. Wealth to us is not mere material for
vainglory but an opportunity for achievement. . . .
Such then is the city for whom, lest they should lose her,
the men whom we celebrate died a soldier's death. . . .
Such were the men who lie here and such the city that inspired them. . . . Let us draw strength . . . from the busy
spectacle of our great city's life as we have it before us day
by day, falling in love with her as we see her, and remembering that all this greatness she owes to men with the
fighter's daring, the wise man's understanding of his duty,
and the good man's self-discipline in its performance. . . .
So they gave their bodies to the commonwealth and received . . . the grandest of all sepulchres . . . a home in

the minds of men. . . . Their story is not graven only on stone over their native earth, but lives on far away, without visible symbol, woven into the stuff of other men's lives.*

The next lap of our cruise was to be all too short, as we had invited four young members of our families who had only a few days to spare to us before they returned to their jobs. Our time being limited, we remained within the familiar environs of Athens.

We made our departure from Passalimani with our great-niece and nephew, Pauline and Vieri Traxler on board, and headed for Itea at five P.M., on June 1. We had to wait at Isthmia for Canal clearance, after which we anchored for the night at Kalamaki. At five the following morning, we steamed through the Corinth Canal, the first ship of the day to go through. It is always exciting to sail through that feat of engineering, initiated by the emperor Nero in 67 A.D. It is so narrow that it can only serve one ship at a time, and there are moments when you can almost lean over and touch a vertical sandstony wall. A broad ribbon of blue sky forms a canopy overhead, and you sail under the bridge that connects Attica with the Peloponnesus. As you pass along you see a few naked brown-skinned youngsters tucked in cubbyholes at either end waiting for a chance to swim.

Our cousins Roxane and Shan Sedgwick met us in Loutraki, having driven there from Athens, and I must now make a slight detour to the other side of the Atlantic Ocean in order to introduce them properly.

* Alfred Zimmern, *The Greek Commonwealth* (New York: The Modern Library, 1956), pp. 204–209.

During Revolutionary times, and even before, the Sedg-
wick family of New England fell in love with the picturesque countryside round about the Housatonic Valley
and the Berkshire Hills. The first Theodore Sedgwick
was buried in Stockbridge, Massachusetts, in January
1813. He had served the mother country loyally until the
break came, and after that, his own country in many judi-
cial and other capacities. After the Revolution, he became
a member of the old Continental Congress and a member of the House under George Washington. Subsequently, he served as Speaker of the House and United
States Senator. The home that he built in Stockbridge,
and the circular burial plot that he bought and designed
at the same time, are still in the hands of his descendants
and are mentioned with due respect in Baedeker's *United
States*, published at the turn of the century.

The judge placed himself and his wife, Pamela Dwight,
in the center of the plot and around them, the six, widen-
ing pie-shaped pieces form a greater space for the increasing descendants of their children whose graves encircle
those of their parents.

The family house was inherited by my father, but having only two daughters, he sold it to Henry Dwight Sedg-
wick II, who had four sons and one daughter. By this time
it was a common saying that the katydids, frogs, and tree
toads in Stockbridge had a new song: "Sedg-wick, Sedg-
wick, Sedg-wick." One of my favorite cousins, born in
this house, but Greek by adoption, is Alexander.

Admiration for the Graeco-Roman world has always
been so much a part of the American heritage that we
have often, in odd ways, expressed it in the flattery of imi-
tation. With Yankee presumption, the city of Boston has
sometimes arrogated to itself the title of the Athens of

America and it must have been with this in mind that Sir Horace Walpole wrote on April 3, 1775, to his cousin Horace Mann, "The next Augustan Age will dawn on the other side of the Atlantic. There will, perhaps, be a Thucydides at Boston, a Xenophon at New York."* Moreover, though few may remember it today, it is a fact that the only requirement for entering Harvard College or the Boston Latin School at their inception, in about 1638, was the ability to read and speak Latin and to show some knowledge of Greek forms; mathematics was not a required study till the close of that century.

Be that as it may, Shan came to Greece in 1933. It was his second visit to a country which captured his fancy. Employed for several weeks as private secretary to his cousin Lincoln MacVeagh, recently appointed United States Minister to the then Hellenic Republic, he later joined the Associated Press, with which organization he remained until he became Athens Correspondent for the *New York Times*, a position which he held for thirty years. Shan's first assignment was one which dragged over months—the famous case of Samuel Insull, a Chicago utilities magnate, who was living in Athens as a fugitive from justice, Greece having in those days no binding extradition laws. However, the aged financier, finally venturing into Turkish territorial waters, was seized and sent home for trial. The charges against him turned out to be so complex that the jury couldn't understand them, and he was acquitted. He died shortly afterward.

In March, 1935, an attempted revolution by the follow-

* Wilmarth S. Lewis, *Horace Walpole*. Bollingen Series XXXV, 9 (New York: Pantheon, 1961), p. 183.

ers of Eleftherios Venizelos brought Shan into contact
with a beautiful and gifted young Athenian, Roxane Sotiriadis, daughter of George Sotiriadis, formerly Professor
of History and Archaeology at Athens University and first
Rector of Salonika University. Roxane had been employed by a Paris newspaper to cover the abortive coup—
her only venture into journalism. Her profession, law,
she abandoned after a few years of practice in Athens,
and she then became a student of classical archaeology in
which subject she later received her doctorate. Shan and
Roxane were married on May 17, 1935. Together they
have made an international contribution by continuously
fostering and deepening the native sympathy and understanding between our two countries.

Shan is witty and Pan-like; Roxane is clever and
Athene-like. Under their guidance and tutelage we spent
a blissful weekend, meeting them in Loutraki and sailing
around the Methana Peninsula, through the Poros Channel to Mandraki. When jellyfish chased us away from
there, we tied up, stern-to, in Hydra Harbor, and Roxane
led me up the steep hill to the little house she had recently purchased. Small, white, stucco box-like houses
climb the hillside from quay to sky line and stand so
close together that they overhang one another. Though
Roxane's house leans over the lower one in front of it
and elbows the ones on either side, it has great charm and
an enviable view of harbor and sapphire sea.

Two hundred years ago Hydra waxed rich and powerful through enterprising traders and privateers, a number of whom were of old Albanian stock. Some fortunes
were made by sponge-fishing off the North African shores.
A few of the wealthy built houses on a grand scale, which
today are show-pieces that may be likened to those hand-

some dwellings of an erstwhile splendor in New England's Portsmouth, Newburyport, and Salem. It is an island of fashion as well as of tourists, and daily transportation makes it easily accessible from Athens.

At this time, we had also on board our great-niece Pauline and her husband Vieri Traxler. Pauline and her brother John Rathbone had spent four refugee years with me in Syosset, from 1940 to 1944. With them came one of those peerless British nannies of whom paeans of praise are often sung in childhood reminiscences by the statesmen of England. Her name is Marjorie Morrell, and by relieving me of all responsibility and taking on her own capable shoulders all care of the children, she made the adoption a pure joy to me. During those years, as a little girl of five to nine, Pauline was unusually conscientious and self-denying; her favorite doll or toy was always being offered to another child. I used to think of her then as a very attractive, congenital public servant; unmarried, and devoting her maternal instincts to social welfare. I imagined her becoming a member of Parliament like her father before her, her mother, and her aunt Eleanor Rathbone, and other members of the Rathbone family of Liverpool. But no, she met the man of her choice at an early age at the beautiful and romantic Palladian Villa of Maser, near Venice, and in the face of some parental disapproval, on grounds of religion and nationality, they married young and she proceeded to devote her fires of self-sacrifice to an attractive husband, children, and the never ending duties of a diplomat's wife.

Coming to Syosset, Long Island, from war-torn England in July, 1940, Pauline and John had been warmly welcomed by the young Americans at the Greenvale School, and being, as their great-uncle affectionately called them, half-breeds, they soon adapted themselves to unaccustomed American ways and were often elected officers in their self-government classes.

Their father was tragically killed at Christmas-time, while flying in the R.A.F. over Germany, during our first year together. He was at that time not only an Air Force pilot, but a Member of Parliament from the Bodmin Division of Cornwall. After his death, his widow, Paul's niece Beatrice Clough, took his seat in the House of Commons. Beatrice thus became the first American-born member of the House of Commons since Lady Astor, and the second in history. In 1942 she married Paul Wright; with him, she carries on in a life of diplomacy, a life in which both of them shine.

After dinner, while the Sedgwicks and Traxlers were mingling with the heterogeneous crowds on the quay, and Paul and I were reading in the deckhouse, suddenly, through the darkness without, came a gay young voice addressing Jay, who was on deck.

"May I come on board? I recognized *Rara Avis* this afternoon by the tips of her three masts, and I know your *Landfall* too."

The voice soon was discovered to belong to a bronzed, featherweight Hermes, a young Swiss known as Claude Graf. His ketch was lying alongside, and he told us that she was largely designed by himself, was built in Ceylon, and that he had used Martinique as a home port before setting sail across the Atlantic.

"When do you go back to Martinique?" Paul asked.

"O, we never go back, we only go!" "We," it turned out later, stood for himself, his courageous young wife, and their angelic seven-month-old baby.

I asked him the name of his ship.

"*Taos Brett II*," was the answer.

Visions of D. H. Lawrence being lured by Mabel Dodge to join her coterie in Taos, Arizona, rose before me. I saw Toni throwing his Navajo blanket over his shoulder, and a picture of uninhibited, exuberant Frieda swam before my eyes. I saw Dorothy Brett cutting Mabel's hair and snipping off a piece of her ear at the same time. My expression must have betrayed what was passing through my mind for he added eagerly, "You know Dorothy Brett?—She was kind to me when I was in the United States, and I named my boat after her."

A few days later, we found the *Taos Brett II* in Tourkolimani Harbor, when we had a good opportunity to admire the fiberglas-covered ship with its many ingeniously thought out devices. After a thorough and admiring study of the unique craft, we took the little Claude Graf family to an attractive restaurant, overlooking the harbor, that seemed to welcome seven-month-old babies, and we all had a merry lunch.

From Hydra we sailed to Aegina and walked up the short path to the beautiful temple. Like the Parthenon and like Sunium, the Temple of Aphaia stands on high ground. The three temples form a roughly equilateral triangle about fifteen miles apart. When the temples were built in the fifth century B.C., they presented three lofty beacons useful as navigational aids for the little fleets that put out to sea to fight, to fish, or to trade.

The Parthenon still stands its ground in bold magnificence, and so does Sunium, but protecting evergreens have sprung up to shelter the feminine Temple of Aphaia. She has surrendered her might. No milling crowds surround her; there is a loneliness and sadness here that remind you of Olympia, where the wind sighs through the branches, whispering that the days of glory are gone. It was here that we found a name for the happy little group of black-uniformed high school boys and girls, omnipresent on every acropolis, like swarms of industrious little black ants. According to one Homeric legend, the original home of Myrmidons (Greek for ants) was Aegina. Here, after a plague that destroyed every inhabitant, the King of the Island, Aeacus, prayed to Zeus to renew his population. Zeus granted the prayer by transforming all the ants on the island into human beings, and they in turn have ever since offered especial thanks to Zeus for the precious gift of human life. These gay little swarms, being transported in busloads from one glorious temple to another, are quite obviously offering daily prayers of thankfulness for the blessings of their rich heritage, and so we christened them Myrmidons.

It is a short sail from Aegina to the harbor of New Epidaurus, where we left *Rara Avis* for a few hours while we drove to Mycenae, Tiryns, and the sanctuary of Aesculapius. The theater there is described by Pausanias as the wonder of Epidaurus, and even today it is the best preserved of all the ancient theaters. Hewn out of the steep northwest slope of the mountain, the fifty-five tiers of stone seats could accommodate 14,000 spectators when it was in its heyday in the fourth century B.C.

The Greeks worshiped health of mind and body and this was the greatest "spa" of the Peloponnesus, dedicated to the God of healing, Aesculapius. It may be that it was here that the ancient and revered caduceus, or doctor's emblem, renewed its magic, when during the Plague of 293 B.C., Rome sent an S.O.S. for the Serpent of Epidaurus.

The drama has always been to the Greeks a panacea and therapeutic measure, and every spa had its theater, large or small. The pilgrims seeking health and recreation journeyed there in great droves from far and wide, and it was a favored multitude that watched from this vantage point the plays of Sophocles, Aeschylus, and Euripides.

As it was early in June, the twentieth-century summer theatrical season had not yet begun and the theater was being made ready for the opening in July. A few masons and joiners were at work repairing the damages of the rainy, wintry season, and floodlights were being tested by electricians as the setting sun was bringing twilight upon us. Among random knots of tourists, seated here and there, high and low, was a group of Greek high school boys and girls, dressed in their simple black student uniforms—Myrmidons, of course. They were sitting together on the handsome, pink limestone armchairs in the front row, around the orchestra, occupying the *fauteuils* that used to be reserved for civic officers and distinguished guests. These boys and girls talked together with animation for a little while, and presently one of the girls walked onto the stage and stopped at the point from which a whisper may be heard in the far reaches of the topmost tiers. There, this tiny black figure of a sixteen-year-old girl took the center of the stage and faced the whole enormous amphitheater with utter composure and unselfconsciousness. She then recited for about fifteen minutes, in a clear, well-modulated voice, with unaffected charm and simple dramatic gestures, some Greek lyrics of her own choosing. The widely scattered audience, though small in number, were spellbound with delight, and clapped and cheered with great enthusiasm as this little fan of Sappho modestly resumed her seat.

In reluctantly turning our steps homeward, we felt that we had witnessed an unrehearsed Greek drama of touching, though miniature, dimensions, and we were thankful that the waning light of day had permitted that show to go on. As we drove back towards Old Epidaurus, we enjoyed recalling how directly our vocabulary of the theater derives from our Greek ancestors. *Tragedy, comedy, dialogue, characters, chorus, orchestra, musical,* and *scenery* are all legitimate and direct descendants of Greek dramatic vocabulary. Were Sophocles suddenly to make an appearance on Broadway at a summer opening of a musical comedy, he might well be startled, and probably shocked, but he could read many words in the program with comprehension, and he would be looking at one of his own offspring.

At the end of our short tour of some of the great sites in the environs of Athens—this time with the added benefit of the Sedgwickian knowledge of all things Greek—a transition period came upon us. The previous winter, when we were making our plans many months ahead, we had chartered *Rara Avis* to our friends the Lamotte du P. Copelands, who met us in Athens and took our ship over on June 10 for two weeks.

Paul and I were then able to enjoy a few more wonderful days at the Grande Bretagne. Athens was gay with myriads of Egyptian flags. Protocol was omnipresent, and *Rara Avis* had to move her mooring in Passalimani in deference to the visiting foreigners. President Gamal Abdel Nasser was paying a visit to King Paul and Queen Frederica (in order to effect a fair deal for the Greeks still in Egypt, I suppose) and the city groaned under the pressure of crowds of aliens.

Though I do as little shopping as possible when we are traveling, because of limited time and luggage, it was a pleasure to find three particular items for which money could be spent advantageously in Athens.

First come books: At every newspaper and magazine stand (and they are to be found at innumerable street corners) the reading matter offered is not so much newspapers and magazines as paperbacked Greek classics in English—in the Penguin, Pelican, Mentor, and other editions. The greatest choice and profusion of inexpensive, excellent little editions of Homer, Herodotus, Thucydides, Plato, and all of the Greek tragedies and comedies, are hourly being sought. In fact they are more frequently picked up on Venizelos Avenue than on Fifth Avenue.

Next come arts and crafts: They are to be found in a little craft shop near the Grande Bretagne that builds up their Majesties' Fund. This shop offers many beautiful examples of copies and originals, with an accent on the crafts that are made on the Island of Skyros. Attractive low oak chairs with rope seats and backs have been made on Skyros for hundreds of years, and an original is occasionally to be had. Beautiful copper kitchen utensils and charming ceramics also come from Skyros as well as from other islands. Skyros is particularly proud of its interior decoration; many of the houses are hospitably thrown open to the visitors who travel there, and quantities of their fine wares are sent to Athens for sale.

Finally, on Pandrosou Street, in the heart of the city, is an inexhaustible assortment of contemporary household goods, from chairs to ceramics, and from kitchen utensils to evzone costumes for children. These little shops with their small, square interiors open to the street remind you of the box-like Middle Eastern bazaars, and they are, indeed, visible traces of the Turkish occupation that lasted for three hundred years. The white interior walls are hung from floor to ceiling with tempting bargains, and the shopkeepers are busy with their tools, replenishing the diminishing stock, while attending to their customers. It is an area of frenzied finance called Monasteraki—a do-it-yourself, unsophisticated Madison Avenue.

As you shop or walk about the city, trying to decipher the signs, you are constantly discovering English words shining through the unfamiliar shape of the Greek alphabet. It doesn't require a talent for languages to realize that TAVERNA stands for the many taverns or restaurants in which the natives of all income brackets are apt to spend their convivial evenings, and it is only a mild surprise when you recognize the fact that the ladies' room is indicated by a word that looks like "Gynecology."

We had been able to secure our favorite archaeologist-chauffeur, George Pavlakis, for a week, and we drove about visiting the nearby sites such as the beautiful monastery of Kaisariani, the Agora, the gem-like Byzantine Daphne, Eleusis, and the recent fifth-century finds, unearthed by chance in a sewer during excavations preparatory to the construction of new buildings. On occasional afternoons we drove for a swim to suburban shores that offered neat bathhouses and snack restaurants.

Our niece and nephew, Kay and Alex Hammond, had given us a letter to the Swiss envoy to Greece, Ambassador Werner Fuchss, and one evening he and his wife and Horace Fuller's Greek wife, Dosia, dined with us and gave us an interesting evening of gossip about events social and political now going on in the Near East.

The Ambassador and his wife had thus far seen little of the Greek Islands and I hope that that evening led to their joining one of Hod Fuller's famous cruises later on. Hod Fuller, with his fine sailing craft, past and present, his experienced knowledge of the eastern Mediterranean, his well-known seamanship, and his delicious cuisine, has become a fabled Argonaut of the twentieth century. He now commands an able white-hulled ketch *Veilila* with copper-colored sails, 80 feet over all. She was designed and built by J. S. White of Cowes, England, and sleeps six with comfort. They are fortunate voyagers who see the Greek Islands with Hod Fuller.

Unluckily, his ship and ours have only here and there passed in the night, but Paul and he have occasionally found time in port in which to exchange weather predictions, general information, and the latest innovations in gadgetry.

Before many days had passed we boarded the comfortable little Greek steamer *Colocotronis*, outward bound for Rhodes, where we would soon be met by Lawrence Pool, his son (named after his father but known as Mike), Halsey Herreshoff, and my grandson Arthur W. Schwartz.

The journey from Athens to Rhodes, at first threading the islands of the Cyclades and later the Dodecanese, is full of interest, and we were, as always, accompanied by bright, hot sunny skies. The islands on the north side follow one another so quickly that they form an almost continuous line to the eye all the way, and as you near Rhodes, the capes and points of the Anatolian coast, with islands like Simi and Kos distinct from the mainland, form another unending line.

The sea was smooth, the crew (from the captain to the bilge-boy) attentive, the ship well managed, and the food very good. The only fault we could find was with an unfortunate broadcasting system that pervaded saloons and decks indiscriminately and invaded, with popular tunes of doubtful quality, the most private recesses during all of our waking hours.

Upon our arrival in Rhodes, we took our many bags to the same hotel at which we had stayed in 1934. The Hotel des Roses, an old-timer of real distinction, has the perfect setup that permits you to put on your bathing suit in your bedroom, descend in the elevator, and step from the deepest recesses of the hotel out onto the sunny beach and glorious sea. It is a counterpart to some of the hotels on the Lido in Venice and the Grande Bretagne (without beach) in Athens.

Rhodes is like Janus, double-faced and looking both backwards and forwards—back to the dimmest reaches of the past, and forward to a bright future. The Italians began the occupation of the Island in 1912, when they made many beautiful restorations of the historical buildings, and Mussolini carried on the good work by directing a general redecorating and clearing up under the supervision of one of his ablest lieutenants. Outside the walled city are modern suburbs and public buildings, shops and hotels, and villas belonging to wealthy officials and businessmen. There are Greek, Italian, Jewish, and Turkish quarters, and neither race nor religion seems to prevent the inhabitants from living amicably, side by side. The average modern Turk on a Greek island usually outdoes himself in gentle manners.

A short walk from the Hotel des Roses takes you past the ancient "Harbor of the Galleys," through the Liberty Gate to the old walled city. Unbelievably and ridiculously picturesque, you think that you are dreaming and that you have suddenly come upon the home town of Aucassin and Nicolette. The two finest architectural ornaments are the "hospital" itself and the "Street of the Knights." The latter, only a few hundred yards long, mounts steeply up to the Grand Master's palace which dominates everything, as would a keep. The Street of the Knights is made up of the *auberges* of the different *langues*—the Tongue of France, the Tongue of Spain, of Provence, of Auvergne, of Germany, of Italy, and of the Englishman, who stands characteristically apart. Each of the seven nations represented was given a separate section of the walls to defend. The *auberges* are gems of medieval architecture, like little college halls; and indeed once served that purpose. I am told that to this day each nation still maintains a tiny foothold in her own *auberge*, bequeathed her by her intrepid and crusading forefather armed cap-a-pie.

Surrounding the medieval city, and inviting you to walk the upper rim of the circle, are huge, massive fortified walls, reminiscent of those on the island of Cyprus— Cyprus, of course, because when the Knights of St. John lost their foothold there, they repaired to Rhodes and once more built themselves in with their iron will and determination. The walls have kept their integrity and continuity, though time has taken its toll and they have had to be rebuilt somewhat.

The landscape gardening has been an important part in the renaissance of the medieval town. The profusion of flower borders are a delight to the eye, and the affectionate use of cannon balls as opposite numbers to delicate hibiscus, morning glories, and geraniums startles you at first. Stone cannon balls of all sizes are selected with care, matched like pearls, and piled in pyramidal shapes as ornaments. They are stood in rows against the walls and fill every vacant space, while small fragments are carefully preserved to edge the flower borders. The thousands of huge, sixteen-inch cannon balls must have hit the resistant buttresses and stone pavements with a thunderous roar, and the Turks certainly did batter great breaches in the walls. But the defenders themselves generally escaped, for there was a man who rang a bell whenever he saw that a Turkish piece was about to be discharged.

There are many small shops in the old city, and soon Paul had ordered three suits from a Rhodesian tailor— one for Larry, one for Jay, and one for himself—and had made three fitting appointments for the following day.

Retracing our steps, we returned through the Liberty Gate and left the old quarter for the new; as we did so, we saw that Carl Koch's 40-foot yawl *Jen* was tied up almost alongside *Rara Avis*.

Carl is one of those clever amphibian architects who is equally at home in creating a design-for-living afloat or ashore. Early in his architectural career he constructed a barn in which to build a boat in Belmont, Massachusetts. Before he had achieved his ambition, however, he was forced to move, and so with spider-like persistence and industry he built another barn for the same purpose, twenty miles away in Concord. He and his young wife were now in the midst of an adventurous cruise that had started in Marseilles on May 1. Sometimes they were joined by another couple, sometimes they were alone, but no matter what the crew, the cleverly designed *Jen* was proving all that they had hoped for. They lunched with us at the hotel one day and we compared notes as to our courses, which turned out to have differed in many respects.

A little farther along, in the commercial harbor—the only one that can accommodate big ships—lay Dr. Matthew Mellon's able craft *Vagabondia.* He had written us that he hoped we would see his ship, even though we would not find his wife and himself, because they had returned to America for a son's graduation. His sailing master invited us on board and we found an attentive captain and crew looking after not only his splendid yacht, but a charming miniature poodle that was languishing for her mistress and presently proceeded to rebel by going A.W.O.L. on the town. After two days of sight-seeing and fraternizing with Rhodesian dogdom she was carefully returned on board, none the worse for her adventures.

Dr. Mellon is an intrepid and serious yachtsman who has a navigator's license, sails his own ship with his wife for several months of the year, and explores the coastal regions that entice him into a life largely devoted to the observation, enjoyment, and study of the world. For the last seven or eight years Matt has sailed the Turkish coast, and his forthcoming book on his experiences will be a very interesting one. Paul had, in his pocket, a wonderfully detailed letter from him, which proved invaluable to us later on, with suggestions and admonitions relative to the coast of Asia Minor.

Somewhere, not far from the Liberty Gate and certainly guarding the Harbor of the Galleys, once stood the huge bronze statue of the sun-god Helios, Colossus of Rhodes, one of the Seven Wonders of the World. The legend is that he carried a beacon light in his raised hand, and that the ingoing and outgoing ships passed between his legs. It was designed by the sculptor Charos, a native of nearby Lindos, and it is said that its completion took twelve years and that when finished it stood 200 feet high, or about the same height as our Statue of Liberty. An absolutely magnificent sight it must have been, in shining bronze. It was thrown down by an earthquake in 224 B.C. and lay there in fragments for nearly one thousand years before being bought and carried away by Saracens to be converted into instruments of war.

Paul has much enjoyed telling his friends that he designed and topped off *Landfall*'s mainmast to the dimensions required to permit her to sail between the legs of the Colossus, but found to his chagrin, upon arrival at Rhodes in 1934, that not even the pedestals were standing.

Returning to the hotel for lunch, we were happy to be joined by Mary Peltz and Walter Phelps Warren. They had made a quick trip to Crete the day before; too quick it seemed to me to be the pleasure that it should be. But on occasions when you only have a little time to spare to an island of infinite variety, you can simply let it whet your appetite for a return engagement.

The following afternoon we made the exciting excursion to Lindos. Just as the Rhodes that we left behind us typifies the picturesqueness of a somewhat hidden medieval town, Lindos typifies the majesty and aspiration of a once pure Greek Acropolis. As you approach, the rocky prominence seems to soar toward Olympus, announcing that though it was originally built for defense, endowed with human purpose, and dedicated to the gods, it stands now, in its ruins, for beauty alone. In an orderly way, the evolving architectural styles of civilization—Doric, Ionic, Corinthian, Roman, Romanesque, Byzantine, Frankish, and Venetian—are conspicuously displayed. This acropolis is a giant guidepost in time, pointing to the two vistas of history, the past and the future.

From the great height of Lindos you look down on the exquisite miniature harbor of St. Paul, one of the landfalls of the Apostle's lengthy voyages, during the course of which his labors of love and of teaching were so often interrupted by disasters at sea. Like the Phoenix he rose, not from purification by fire, but from baptism in the depths of the sea, and proceeded on his pilgrimage. My Paul shakes his head as he looks at the telltale rocky headlands and emerald green water, the scene of one of St. Paul's shipwrecks. "A poor navigator," he says sadly.

On the afternoon of June 21, Monique and Philip Wiedel, with their two little girls, Janine and Suzanne, came on board, and that evening we all dined together. Dr. Wiedel is an amateur ornithologist and was observing through his field glasses with close attention the birds of the eastern Mediterranean. I begged him to send me some of the results of his observations, and the following quotation was contained in a letter I later received from a keen bird watcher.

I have never seen such a concentration of Shearwaters as we saw over the water from our balcony at the Hotel des Roses. Most of them were Cory's Shearwaters, but many more were also identified as Manx. This, at least, is what they have usually been called, but since then, in conversation with Dr. Robert Cushman Murphy, I have learned that he thinks that they should be called Levantine Shearwaters, and that while in plumage they resemble the Manx, their flight is quite different and far more similar to that of the Fluttering Shearwaters of the Southwest Pacific. In any case, these two Shearwaters are the common seabirds of the eastern Mediterranean.

Ashore on Rhodes, Little Owls (*Athene noctua*), Athene's symbolic bird, were a common sight sitting on the wings of windmills. House Martins and Barn Swallows swooped about the town. Along the roadside, Bee-eaters were seen sitting on telephone wires. These brilliantly colored birds are hated and hunted by beekeepers. White-throats and Blue Tits were also seen along the roads.

Among the ruins of Athene's temple at Kamiros the Black-eared Wheatear was common. I saw my first Long-legged Buzzard at Lindos, flying over the bay, pursued and harassed by Kestrels. Crag Martins soared around the sea cliffs there, where St. Paul landed a few years ago. Swifts and Alpine Swifts were seen there too. Crested Larks and Hooded Crows were numerous along the road. Woodchat Shrikes were a common "wire-bird." This is the bird which is most perfectly illustrated in the Egyptian wall paintings at Beni-Hasan dating from the twelfth dynasty.

The next day we weighed anchor early in the morning and set our sails for Kos, the island forever dedicated to the medical profession.

The god of the island, Aesculapius, was the son of Apollo, God of Healing, and "one who did only kind things." You will remember the famous Sanctuary of Aesculapius in Epidaurus; from thence came the first settlers of Kos.

Our human Father of Medicine, Hippocrates, who gave mankind the Hippocratic Oath, was born here about 460 B.C. He seems to have shed preconceived ideas, and observed and inferred for himself. He was so greatly revered in his lifetime, and for many centuries thereafter, that there developed a habit in classical times of attributing all the wise sayings and treatises on medicine to him; there arose a sort of Old Testament of healing, known as the Hippocratic Collection.

A significant fact is that though the Hippocratic Collection is frequently guilty of error, it contains practically nothing of superstition. One treatise, *Ancient Medicine*, foreshadows the Freudian creed in dealing with certain kinds of dreams. Another treatise, *In the Surgery*, reads: "Practice all the operations with each hand and with both together, your object being to attain ability, grace, speed, painlessness, elegance and readiness."

In the center of the town of Kos stands an ancient plane tree now overgrown to elephantine proportions. Its far-reaching and sagging branches are supported by marble columns, wooden spars, and any Atlas-like prop at hand. Legend has it that it was under these branches that the great physician taught his students and healed the sick and you can always let legend have its say.

It was because of his deep interest in Kos, the birth-place of medicine, that we now had with us on board our own beloved surgeon, Lawrence Pool. Larry knew, when he was still at St. Paul's School that he wanted to follow in the footsteps of his father, Dr. Eugene Pool, and one summer, father and son made a European tour under the aegis of the Travel Club of Surgeons. This must have been a great opportunity for the boy, not only to profit through travel abroad, but to associate with interesting and stimulating men of the profession.

Always an ardent athlete, Larry is a skier, was twice national champion of squash racquets, held a private pilot's license, and most outstanding of all, was and is a sailor. He crossed the Atlantic four times on sailing craft, sometimes racing, sometimes not and was one of Paul's crew on *Landfall* in his race from Newport, R. I., to Plymouth, England, in 1931.

While still a medical student Larry decided to specialize in neurosurgery and seized the opportunity to work under Dr. Allen O. Whipple, Dr. Byron Stookey, and one of the deans of neurology, and psychiatry, the late Foster Kennedy. During World War II, Larry served with the Ninth Evacuation Hospital for four years, three of them in North Africa, Sicily, Italy, France, and Germany. He is now Professor of Neurosurgery at the Neurological Institute in New York, and has been an Overseer of Harvard University. "My great passion is pioneering work in the surgery of aneurysms," he says, "those lethal time-bombs in the head, like blowouts in an automobile tire."

Larry's son Mike is a gentle, thoughtful youngster who is interested in the humanities. While he was at the Buxton School in Williamstown, Massachusetts, he had taken part in Oedipus Rex and other plays, and coasting along the shores of Ancient Ionia appealed to him particularly. As we sailed along, he took delight in the panorama of constantly changing theatrical sets; to him the cruise was a living, never-ending drama. He is at present intent, like all young men of his age, on developing his own tastes and talents into maturity.

When we invited our grandson Arthur Schwartz to join us in Rhodes and sail up the coast of Asia Minor and thence to Greece, it was partly because we knew that he wanted to become an architect. But having completed only his first year at Princeton, we had no idea of the excellent preparation he would bring with him for viewing the treasures of Priene and Miletus, Didyma and Ephesus. He had had the good fortune to take "Architecture 201, The History of Ancient Architecture," a course usually reserved for sophomores, and he had profited greatly under professor of Classical Architecture, Richard Stillwell. The only really successful way to see the great sites of history, archaeology, and architecture is to bring your information with you, not expect to find it ready at hand after you have arrived on the spot. Sight-seeing and study are a give and take, and need a constant interchange, as Bernard Berenson, "the passionate sight-seer," so well knew.

An interesting coincidence is that twenty-six years earlier, in 1934, we had taken along another young would-be architect, Richard Delano. Dicky eventually gave up the profession and turned to other pursuits, but he too benefited through the teachings of Richard Stillwell. The latter was then a young man in his early thirties directing the "Dig" at Corinth under the auspices of The American School of Classical Studies at Athens, and setting up once more some of the fragments of the ancient buildings —a project which was generously being subsidized by Mr. Malcolm Chace.

Professor Stillwell is now Howard Crosby Butler Memorial Professor of the History of Architecture at Princeton University, Editor-in-Chief of the American Journal of Archaeology, and also Field Director (alternating with Professor Erik Sjoqvist) of the excavations of Morgantina in Sicily, a project of the Princeton University Expedition in Sicily. Our experience in having found two young men who had benefited from Professor Stillwell's teaching is only a small sample of the wide influence that he has exerted over the lives of talented young men in their architectural studies at Princeton University.

Our other guest, several years older than Mike and Arthur, was Halsey Herreshoff, the son of Sidney de Wolfe, nephew of Francis and grandson of the great Nathaniel G., the most famous of United States yacht designers. Without fear of exaggerating, I can say that Halsey is one of the best all-round examples of excellence in a young man of his age that can be found. Intelligent, sensitive, observant, imaginative, and keen, he has taken honors in his preparatory schools and in Webb Institute, where he studied Naval Architecture. He was a most useful, reliable, and companionable shipmate, and was equally enjoyed by those of all ages.

The Eugenics International Congress once accorded the Nathaniel Herreshoff family a niche in their hall of fame. In one of their exhibitions that was displayed at the Natural History Museum in New York in 1921 was hung a large chart designed to show recurring hereditary traits in seven generations of several distinguished families. The Herreshoff family was one of these. The aptitudes featured, with boat-designing and mechanics, art, music, and writing, formed a rich crop for any hereditary tree to boast.

Only a few miles from Kos is Cnidus, where we looked in early the following morning. Cnidus flourished with Kos, during the same era, and is thickly strewn with the architectural ruins of a well laid-out city; among these an agora, a theater, and a temple of Aphrodite that was once adorned by a lost goddess wrought at the hand of Praxiteles, are outstanding. From the vanished treasury building, exquisite fragments of metopes have been salvaged and are now beautifully displayed in the museum at Delphi. There is also a colossal lion here, carved out of one block of Pentelic marble, smaller and later than our archaic lion of Keos. Another fact of interest is that, of the two schools of medicine on the coast of Asia Minor, the one of Cnidus antedates Kos; the latter, however, stole a march on Cnidus by giving to the world one of its immortals.

We steamed toward the town of Cnidus with high hopes that morning, only to find an open roadstead with nothing visible except rocks, two or three stony houses, two men in army uniforms, and a poor holding ground. Conscious of the fact that only two months earlier the reins of the Turkish government had changed from the hands of the former Premier Adnan Menderes to a military junta in what the Turks called a "well-mannered revolution," we studied, through our glasses, the expressions of the soldiers on guard. They, like the rocks, gave us an impression of stoniness, and when they began to gesticulate quite violently and we couldn't decide whether their gestures were welcoming or threatening, we chose the better part of valor and withdrew.

By noon we had reached one of the greatest of all sites of antiquity, Halicarnassus, now known as Bodrum. It is partially surrounded by a circle of hills, overlooks the sea, and faces the island of Kos. Here the indefatigable Knights of St. John stood their ground after being driven out of Rhodes, and dug themselves in by building a giant fortress-castle that dwarfs and dominates the modern town and all about it. The immense size, the faintly golden color, and the stark simplicity of line are impressive. Looking more closely, you find that great numbers of fragments and even large pieces of Greek sculpture have been ingeniously incorporated into the walls by artisans who recognized their potentiality and beauty.

The Knights of St. John dedicated their castle to St. Peter and used it as a base for raids on the mainland. The castle was also used as a sanctuary for Christian slaves and it is said that a breed of dogs with delicate scent could distinguish Christian from infidel and brought the slaves in from the surrounding country to the safety of the fortress.

But it is really ancient Halicarnassus, the greatest and richest city in the province of Caria, that seizes the imagination. There is, of course, nothing to be seen of the tomb of Mausolus, one of the Seven Wonders of the World, except in those fragments mentioned above, and you can only guess how and where it was placed. Because of its natural stronghold and excellent harbor, this site must have had importance even before the Ionian influx, about 1100 B.C. Perhaps the name comes from those earlier settlers, for the word is said to have no Greek roots. Later, it became a member of the Six Towns or Hexapolis which together formed the State of Halicarnassus. It was here, about 484 B.C., that Herodotus was born.

The reigning sovereign of the State was then a Queen Artemisia; the family of Herodotus belonged to the upper rank of citizenry. His uncle or cousin, Panyasis, was sufficiently important to be put to death for dangerous political opinions, and it is likely that Herodotus, sharing his relative's leftist leanings, was exiled to the Island of Samos. Or he may have chosen to live on that island because he could there practice his own brand of civil rights with greater freedom than on the mainland; at any rate, it is apparent that he devoted his early years to serious thought, to instruction, and probably to proselytizing.

Herodotus traveled extensively, not only through Asia Minor and the mainland of Greece, but also to all the important islands, such as Rhodes, Cyprus, Crete, and Delos. He undertook the arduous journey from Sardis to the ancient Persian capital, Susa, visited Babylon, and traveled along the west shore of the Black Sea as far as the estuary of the Dnieper. He explored Sidon, Tyre, and Gaza as he coasted along the shores of Palestine, and probably made a long stay in Egypt.

As he journeyed he inquired, he observed, he made measurements, he accumulated materials, and somewhere, later on, he settled down and formulated his mature thoughts and experiences in the shape of his great history. The haven where he finally decided to do his writing may have been the small town of Thurdium in the south of Italy, we do not know.

As *Rara Avis* lay off Halicarnassus, I was reading *The Persian Wars* with increased interest. Most of the classics on President Eliot's five-foot shelf I find very difficult reading, but Herodotus is different. He has a facile way of telling anecdote after anecdote in short, easy stages, referring again and again to his main theme so that your attention is not allowed to wander.

Being a Greek at heart, he was as familiar with the *Iliad* and the *Odyssey*, as any Anglo-Saxon scholar is with Shakespeare and the great authors of his own literature; having been born and brought up a Persian, he was naturally preoccupied by the Persian Wars. It follows, therefore, that when he came to write his great history, he was well qualified to write with literary skill.

Herodotus recognized the importance of a comprehensive "introduction" to his history, in which little-known parts of Asia are involved. He therefore gives full descriptions of the lesser-known nations with graphic sketches of the generals and leaders that figured, and this preamble adds to his volume a rich background of the geography, biography, and government of the nations of the known world. Small wonder that he has come to be called the Father of History. While I was engaged in discovering Herodotus, I came upon the following passage in Book VIII: "Nothing mortal travels so fast as these Persian messengers. The entire plan is a Persian invention, and this is the method of it. Along the whole line of road there are men (they say) stationed with horses, in number equal to the number of days which the journey takes, allowing a man and horse to each day; and these men will not be hindered from accomplishing at their best speed the distance which they have to go, either by snow or rain, or heat, or by the darkness of night." *

It rang a bell. Suddenly, I was back in New York on Eighth Avenue opposite Pennsylvania Station, looking at the inscription on the façade of the Post Office Building. "Neither snow nor rain nor heat nor gloom of night stays these couriers from the swift completion of their appointed rounds."

It seemed to me that these sentiments, though elaborated, must have been inspired by Herodotus and his Persian messengers, but whom to go to for the proof? After our return I began casting about for the right source of information, and at a suggestion from his sister, Mrs. Frederick Osborn, I telephoned Mr. Bayard Schieffelin,

---

* Herodotus, *The Persian Wars,* Trans. by Geo. Rawlinson (New York: The Modern Library, 1942), p. 633.

the executive officer of the New York Public Library. Within twenty-four hours I had received from him the following quotation from the magazine, *The New Yorker* (February 12, 1938), describing the inscription:

Your general reading has probably made you familiar with the fact that the sentiment carved on the façade of the main Post Office Building, over on Eighth Avenue, is from Herodotus. You may not know, however, that the translation, which is a rather free rendering of the original Greek, is by the architect, Mr. William Mitchell Kendall, who designed the building for his firm, McKim, Mead & White. Mr. Kendall, a courtly gentleman now in his eighties, has been a partner in the firm since 1906. He told us lately that when he designed the building he realized he was going to need an inscription to go above the 280-foot frieze, and just kept his eye open for a likely sentence. One night he was reading Herodotus (Mr. Kendall's father was an instructor in classical languages, and he reads Greek for fun), and stumbled on just the thing in Vol. VIII, Chapter 98.

After making a study of several translations and writing to his friend, Professor George Herbert Palmer of Harvard for further advice, Mr. Kendall finally adapted them all to a more poetic pattern of his own.

It may have been Herodotus of Halicarnassus who first observed and described the miracle of the swift Persian messengers during the Persian Wars, but it was our own Mr. Kendall of McKim, Mead and White who recognized in the postmen of New York the same qualities of courage and stamina to which Herodotus alluded.

We departed Bodrum in the early morning on June 24, and a few hours later let go our anchor in the harbor of a beautiful island—dominated by the most striking of fortress-like monasteries, or monastery-like forts— Patmos. The bare, volcanic terrain rises steeply for almost a thousand feet from a deeply indented coast. Magnificently placed on the summit, crowning the height and dominating the whole landscape with a great, dark-gray mass of tower and battlement against the bright blue sky, and surrounded by a flock of little white houses clinging close for protection, stands the monastery of St. John.

Though Ionians settled early on Patmos, and it is mentioned in the fifth century B.C. by Thucydides and later by Strabo and Pliny, its early history has little to offer. Its fame rests on the heavenly vision that appeared to St. John the Evangelist in the latter part of the first century A.D., while he was imprisoned in a grotto high on the hill. There he is said to have written the Apocalypse, and on that island The Revelation came to him.

Scholarly and welcoming monks, designated as guides, lead you through architecturally beautiful passages, arches, and terraces into roomfuls of Greek Orthodox treasures and large numbers of priceless books of many centuries, including important incunabula.

With our usual early start at 5:00 A.M. the following day, our next stop was the town of Tigani, reposing on the foundations of a city that belonged to the period of Polycrates. It is the port of Samos, one of the Greek islands nearest to the coast of Asia Minor, only about a mile distant.

Samos is a giant of antiquity, and we saw enormous archaeological remains along the route of a rickety station wagon, bounding on a worn and ancient highway. The cynosure of this prospect is the one immensely high column which gives the name to nearby Cape Colonna. With huge drums, crazily aligned, it is now the one and only surviving column of the great temple of Hera. The drums look quite tottery, though I daresay they will continue to stand, unless an earthquake does the deed, for many another century.

Under the tyrant Polycrates, the island reached a time of great prosperity, and from her deep-sea harbor "ruled the waves." He it was who commissioned the building of one of the Seven Wonders of the World, a tunnel, over 380 yards long, pierced through the mountain in order to supply the town with drinking water. There are still vestigial remains of that tunnel to be seen and explored at the present time.

Herodotus tells us a fabulous tale of a ring set with an enormous emerald, a symbol of prosperity so dear to the heart of Polycrates, that, in his fear of tempting fate, he one day cast it into the sea as a sop to the gods, only to have it scornfully returned in the belly of a dolphin.

The Samians were for centuries so loyal to Greece that they were accorded special privileges in the Delian League, but in 440 B.C., during a dispute with Miletus, they seceded from Athens. Their subversion ended in their defeat at the hands of the Athenian fleet, led by Pericles himself. The facts surrounding this battle provided the source of Byron's lines, "A land of slaves shall ne'er be mine—/Dash down yon cup of Samian wine!"

It is difficult, while you stand in the presence of the desolations of today, to imagine this once powerful area building the greatest of ships, launching them in a new deep-sea harbor, and victoriously blockading the Persian coast. The ruins of the overthrown columns; the rampant, unkempt covering of ragged growth and weeds; the general devastation of the ancient city and its environs; and, above all, the now shallow and muddy shores, clogged with the silt of ages, have changed the scene beyond recognition. But the fascination of history outlives every visual change.

A six-hour sail took us to Kusadasi, the important center from which, with two long days of driving, may be seen Priene, Miletus, Didyma, Ephesus, and Pergamum; the latter, however, we did not have time for. Nowhere else in the world, I suppose, within so small a compass, can be found the substantial ruins of five such prominent cities of antiquity, claiming so many famous sons. It is equally feasible to use Izmir (ancient Smyrna) as a steppingstone to these cities, but we chose Kusadasi because Matt Mellon had given us a letter to a young Turk who lives there and speaks English. His name is Sumer Erdem; to us he was Sam, and a very useful and helpful guide he became.

A guide is more necessary in Turkey than in Greece. The whole of Asia Minor is farther from the main arteries of travel, and the people are unprepared for an influx of hungry, weary, or demanding tourists. The language is even less familiar to Westerners than is Greek, and the differences in custom and culture are more divergent. There are fewer hotels and restaurants, fewer conveyances, fewer guidebooks in English and fewer guides speaking English.

By the time we reached Kusadasi, on Saturday, June 25, the Revolution had been in full swing for two months, and flags were already flying, proclaiming the first "Freedom Day," to be celebrated the following Wednesday.

People were explaining the situation by saying that Atatürk had brought about, overnight, the metamorphosis from an eastern civilization that had endured for thousands of years, to a modern democracy of the twentieth century. He had done away with the fezzes and turbans worn by all Turkish men to denote the rank, profession, and status in the Moslem hierarchy to which every educated Turk belonged, and made them suddenly appear incognito in western-style fedoras and caps. Regarding the Turkish woman, Atatürk decreed that she should have equal rights with her man, and he demonstrated her emancipation by depriving her of her veil, thus incurring the displeasure of many of both sexes.

For political purposes, the Menderes regime was quick to take advantage of a conservative Moslem resurgence among the large majority, the fires of which were burning unquenched. All that was necessary to win a popular support was a de-emphasizing of Atatürk's so-called reforms.

Halsey had little difficulty in locating Sam. There is a living, wandering grapevine in the Near and Middle East, that intuitively answers any traveler's request, and in a couple of hours there was Sam standing before us, dressed in a trim, khaki uniform and looking young, happy, and interested. He told us that his induction into the army was imminent, but that he would just have time to give us the better part of two days. He reminded us to bring our own lunches, for there would be none to be had along the way, and the following morning at eight o'clock he and a station wagon and chauffeur were waiting for us.

Our first stop was at Priene, the smallest of the twelve city-states that formed the Ionian League. It had protected itself by backing up against the foot of a rocky acropolis, and looks out on a pretty view of gently sloping ground toward the plain of the Maeander River. It is not surprising that this wandering river, over two hundred and fifty miles long, bequeathed us the gentle verb "to meander." The strange thing is that it was, during the rainy season, a fiercely destructive force that invaded private property and changed boundaries to such an extent that it was frequently named the defendant in suits brought by angry landowners.

Perhaps because of its small size Priene early embraced a policy of nonaggression, of live and let live, and developed its natural, humanistic talents to a high cultural level. The people chose to submit to their ambitious neighbor, Miletus, and other envious city-states, and accepted their domination with dignity. There is no better example of their way of life than their exquisite theater of intimate proportions and simple design looking toward the valley of the Maeander. The semicircular floor of the orchestra has a row of seats with backs, and at intervals there are five thrones, placed equidistantly, that were reserved for honored guests or distinguished civil servants. The thrones were probably spaced so that between the great figures lesser men could sit, enjoying the privilege of nearness to the illustrious. The theater is carved out of softly tinted gray marble, and two or three of the thrones look almost polished and in pristine perfection. They had comfortably curved backs and the graceful arms end in hand rests skillfully turned in the form of a scroll. Their excellent condition testifies to the enduring powers of survival in peaceful coexistence.

In the residential quarter, a few hundred yards back from this model theater, is further testimony of attention to the arts and a high standard of living. The streets and avenues are wide, with marble pavements and steps along the sides. Though the houses are small, they are spacious and well lighted through interior patios, and give on little gardens and fountains and open squares. The walls were stuccoed and frescoed with decorative designs, and an ample supply of wells throughout the city once afforded running water in every important room.

Turning our backs slowly and reluctantly on peace-loving Priene, we faced quite another type of city-state, Miletus, just across the river Maeander.

Thales was only one of the many distinguished men who came from Miletus. According to Greek history, it was a breeding-ground of scholars; their birthrate was certainly high. Among them were the philosophers Anaximander and Anaximenes; the historians Cadmus and Hecataeus; and Hippodamus, the architect who invented city planning. The latter was of the fifth century B.C. and planned the harbor town of Piraeus for Athens. Perhaps pride in these compatriots was what initiated the general ambition for expansion, the will to win, the aggressiveness and the bigness.

Miletus developed great naval wealth and power through her four convenient harbors on the Ionian Sea of classical times, and enjoyed a long supremacy before the silting up of the Maeander River and the retreat of the shoreline caused her downfall. In her heyday, she is said to have developed, through her bold seafaring people, as many as eighty colonies (more than any other classical city), an empire that reached to the Black Sea and the Atlantic.

The theater of Miletus, though almost as large as the theater in Epidaurus, having fifty-four tiers, is not fifth century but Graeco-Roman, with a heavy Roman look,

more weathered and less impressive. It is very handsome
and striking, however, with its two Roman arched stairways, one on each side of the proscenium. We were soon
thankful to be able to take cover from the burning sun
and break out our picnic lunch on the steps, in the cool
shade of one of the imposing covered stone stairways.

Of all the Miletan scholars, Thales, who was born in
the seventh century B.C., died in the sixth, and is reputed
to have lived for ninety years, was the most distinguished.
He was one of the Seven Wise Men of ancient Greek
philosophy, and his aptitudes and attainments were so
varied that he seems to have been a spiritual forefather of
my own favorite philosopher, Benjamin Franklin. As with
Poor Richard, many acts and sayings popularly associated
with wisdom are attributed to his name. It is understood
that he introduced geometry into Greece. One of his
studies in that field was the measurement of the pyramids
in Egypt; another was the calculation of the distances
from shore of ships at sea. As an astronomer, he advised
navigators to steer by the Little Bear, rather than the
Great Bear, and it seems to be generally agreed that he
foretold the eclipse of May 28, 585 B.C. Philosopher,
mathematician and astronomer, he was also a practical
statesman who, according to Herodotus, advised the
Ionian cities to federate. Aristotle leads us to believe that
Thales may have been the first man to corner the olive
market. Being weather-wise, he once foresaw an olive fam-
ine. Possibly for his own benefit, or more likely for the
good of the community, he cleverly procured all the olive
presses, and in the hour of need there was plenty; which
shows that a philosopher and scientist can also be an economist and philanthropist. To top the stories about him,

it was he who provided the subject for the nursery rhyme "Johnny Look-in-Air"; once, while gazing at the stars in the dark of night, he tripped and fell into a well.

After a refreshing siesta under the cover of one of the stone stairways that once led to the upper tiers of the theater, we continued our drive through the lovely countryside of ancient Didyma. Whereas Priene is remembered for its exquisite theater, and its cultivation of the peaceful arts; Miletus for its immense theater, aggressive naval power, and far-flung colonies; Didyma's vast proportions are recalled as the Asiatic opposite number to the oracle of Delphi. Wars were not often declared, nor peace concluded, without well-rewarded advice from one of these oracles. So large was this temple conceived that it never came to completion.

The founder of the temple of Apollo was Branchus, endowed with the gift of prophecy; he may have christened it Didymaeon for the twins beloved by Apollo, Castor and Pollux. It is remarkable not only for its size, but for the rich ornament of its massive column bases and the variations in its Ionic capitals. Unlike other temples, its plan is laid on several levels and it surprises the unsuspecting observer with its baroque style. Two huge outer columns still standing in their entirety on the northeast flank, and a third, a great distance away, help to complete a visual impression of the temple's gargantuan size. Strabo ranked it the greatest of Greek temples, and Pliny placed it second only to the temple of Artemis at Ephesus.

We returned to *Rara Avis* late that afternoon after a happy day replete with our first impressions of what Lord Kinross calls "Europa Minor," an apt title, for that coast turns its face towards Europe and its back on the ancient foes of Greece, Darius and Xerxes of Persia.

The next morning, Jay departed Kusadasi and took *Rara Avis* around to the port of Cesme, while we resumed our inland trek, with our guide, chauffeur, and station wagon, to one of the greatest of all Christian, as well as pagan, sites.

Diana of the Ephesians must not be confused with her Greek counterpart, Artemis. She was of pure Asiatic extraction and a divinity that the Greeks found already established in Ionia when they first planted their colonies there in the twelfth or eleventh centuries B.C. Perhaps she belonged to one of those early peoples who gave its name to Halicarnassus, a name, as I understand it, without Greek roots.

The Greek Artemis was represented as a huntress or Goddess of the Moon, twin sister of Apollo and daughter of Leto and Zeus. She was armed with bow, quiver, and arrows, and was sometimes a killer of men or animals, but always a protectress of the young. She was unmarried and guarded her maidenhood fiercely. By commonly accepted standards, she was beautiful.

Diana of the Ephesians was reborn seven times. Her first temple was probably a tree trunk and her first image had fallen, a gift, from the skies. With this embryonic beginning she rose seven times with greater and greater stature, always true to the Asiatic conception, till she became the Roman Diana of the Ephesians. Though Pausanias said that the temple in which her statue stood "surpassed every structure raised by human hands," I cannot believe that the woman within reached the noble proportions of the temple. The lower half of her body was swaddled and swathed in mummified fashion. As she was the goddess of fertility, she had many breasts and the upper part of her body was adorned with what archaeologists and insectologists have diagnosed as the ova of the fertile bee. She must have been a sorry sight.

It was a fair wind, not a shipwreck, that brought St. Paul into Ephesus from Corinth, propelled with the aid of the square sail and long oars gripped by the muscular hands of men. His landing place and the baths nearby, where travelers were then expected to wash away the grime and sweat of the journey, can only be imagined by the wayfarer today. The long, broad, white marbled street up which he walked to the city, as well as the many buildings of importance, have been handsomely exposed to view by archaeologists. Both sides of the street are adorned with statuary, sometimes well preserved, sometimes in ruins, and this great white way leads to the famous amphitheater, that, in the first century after Christ, rang to the words of one of the greatest preachers ever known.

As St. Paul's teachings became more and more eloquent, and more and more popular, the eyes of the idolaters were gradually beginning to be opened to the value of the Word and the Truth. Soon some of the pagans were averting their gaze, not only from the original misshapen effigy, but from the small graven replicas in which the silversmiths had hitherto carried on a thriving trade.

After a stay of almost three years, the influence of the Saint's persuasive words were taking strong hold, and during a month of the Artemesian Festival, when the city was overcrowded with visitors, Demetrius, the master craftsman, called a meeting. No words of mine can be as vivid as these in the Acts of the Apostles:*

---

* Acts 19:24–30, 32, 34, 35, 36, 38, 40–41.

A certain man named Demetrius, a silversmith, which made silver shrines for Diana, brought no small gain unto the craftsmen; whom he called together with the workmen of like occupation, and said, Sirs, ye know that by this craft we have our wealth. Moreover ye see and hear, that not alone at Ephesus, but almost throughout all Asia, this Paul hath persuaded and turned away much people, saying that they be no gods, which are made with hands: So that not only this our craft is in danger to be set at nought; but also that the temple of the great goddess Diana should be despised, and her magnificence should be destroyed, whom all Asia and the world worshippeth.

And when they heard these sayings, they were full of wrath, and cried out, saying, Great is Diana of the Ephesians.

And the whole city was filled with confusion: and having caught Gaius and Aristarchus, men of Macedonia, Paul's companions in travel, they rushed with one accord into the theatre. And when Paul would have entered in unto the people, the disciples suffered him not . . . The assembly was confused; and . . . all with one voice about the space of two hours cried out, Great is Diana of the Ephesians.

And when the townclerk had appeased the people, he said, Ye men of Ephesus, what man is there that knoweth not how that the city of the Ephesians is a worshipper of the great goddess Diana, and of the image which fell down from Jupiter? . . . Ye ought to be quiet, and to do nothing rashly. . . . Wherefore if Demetrius, and the craftsmen which are with him, have a matter against any man, the law is open, and there are deputies: let them implead one another. . . . For we are in danger to be called in question for this day's uproar, there being no cause whereby we may give an account of this concourse. And when he had thus spoken, he dismissed the assembly.

And after the uproar was ceased, Paul called unto him the disciples, and embraced them, and departed for to go to Macedonia.

We cannot watch St. Paul continue on his travels without recalling a few of his oft-repeated, favorite verses. Though they are quoted in the Book of the Acts as belonging to the Epistle to the Corinthians, it was at Ephesus, during these days of tension and trial, that they were written.*

Though I have the gift of prophecy, and understand all mysteries, and all knowledge; and though I have all faith, so that I could remove mountains, and have not charity, I am nothing. . . . Charity suffereth long, and is kind; charity envieth not; charity vaunteth not itself, is not puffed up. . . .
    When I was a child, I spake as a child, I understood as a child, I thought as a child: but when I became a man, I put away childish things. For now we see through a glass, darkly; but then face to face: . . . And now abideth faith, hope, charity, these three; but the greatest of these is charity." †

Chios is an Aegean island, not much more than a stone's throw from the Turkish coast, and we had almost forgotten that on our arrival, we would be crossing the tracks of Christopher Columbus. It is probable that in his early youth, Columbus made several short voyages in the Mediterranean and at least one long voyage to Chios, let us say in 1472. This latter must have been a merchant voyage from Genoa, which had a trading station on the island to exchange consumer goods for the local product of gum mastic. This is a resinous shrub that grows about six feet high and is to be found in Chios in great abundance.

* H. V. Morton, *In the Steps of St. Paul* (London: Methuen, 1959), p. 308.
† I Cor. 13:2, 4, 11, 12, 13.

While Columbus was coasting along the shores of Cuba on his first major voyage of discovery, he was making every effort to recognize in the yams, corn, cotton, and other shrubs the vegetable growth that he passionately hoped and expected to find in the Indies. He collected specimens that would enable him to prove that he had at least touched the fringe of Asia. One of these shrubs "smelled something like cinnamon, and so it must be cinnamon"; * what was really gumbo limbo he hailed as the gum mastic that he had procured for Genoese traders in his early youth on the island of Chios, off the shores of Asia Minor. That was the only place, Columbus was convinced, where it could be found outside the continent of Asia.

Chios is green and luxuriant, grows fruit and vegetables in great quantities, and is dotted over with hills. We drove along a pretty shore road for about half an hour and up to the ancient Homer's Stone. About two hundred feet above sea level, skillful stone masons, aeons ago, had carved a huge round terrace out of the natural rock; the terrace was rimmed by a circular podium that afforded seats for Homer's listeners. The blind poet must have sat in the center, surrounded by his rapt audience, while he recited chapter after chapter of the *Iliad* or the *Odyssey*. The story of Homer's Stone is a thrice-told tale, for after his death it was used for the same purpose by a cult of young poets, the Homeridae. They persuaded their followers that they were Homer's direct descendants, and they undoubtedly went far to popularize his two great epics and make them the best sellers that they are today.

After the life of Homer, which probably occupied the better part of the ninth century B.C. and after the many lives of the Homeridae, the "singers of woven lays," had

* S. E. Morison, *Christopher Columbus* (London: Faber, 1956), p. 82.

passed into oblivion, there came to be another use for the great stone carving. The nearby city of Ephesus sent an offshoot of a religious nature to the neighboring island, and the central dais must then have become an altar, surrounded by worshipers belonging to one of the Ephesian cults.

We departed Chios at 5:30 A.M. the following morning and saw only the islands of Psara and Antipsara all day. We were headed westward toward the easternmost island of the North Sporades, Skyros, and arrived just in time for supper.

There are two villages on the island of Skyros. The one on the west, where we anchored and made fast behind a miniature breakwater, is occupied by fisherfolk of the island. We were just beginning to feel hungry when a fine, strong middle-aged lobsterman and his son sculled out to us with a mess of lobsters lying in the bottom of his boat. We paid for them gladly and he promised to make arrangements for a car to meet us the following morning.

Up to the other village we went the next day. Its glistening white houses and pavements wind their way up the sizable acropolis, along tortuous narrow alleys to the point where Rupert Brooke's memorial statue overlooks a magnificent panorama of sea, sky, and distant islands. On the way we passed a tiny terrace, shaded by a grapevined canopy, where four men sat playing cards and occasionally breaking into song. The sight awoke memories of twenty-five years before, when the preceding generation had formed almost exactly the same picture for us, and perhaps sang the same song. No doubt the scene had not changed much since the Peloponnesian Wars. This morning it was World War II that was in the memory of these four men. There has always been a war to remember and a song to be sung.

Beautiful as are the near and distant views at every turn, the interiors of the houses match them, for these homes are the minute museums of Skyros. Traditionally, a living room contains a large bronze coffer, low tables that hook along the white walls, and low rope-seated chairs with clever carvings of double-headed eagles, or geometric designs. There are old ceramics and modern pottery standing on shelves; textiles old and new; and highly-polished copper kitchen utensils decorating the walls. Some of these works of art are native and some are the spoils that the hardy seamen have brought back from long voyages to distant shores.

Skyros will always be remembered by Anglo-Saxons as personifying the supreme sacrifice of World War I made by the youths of Great Britain on the shores of the Dardanelles. Early in May, 1915, Rupert Brooke, at the age of twenty-eight, died on board the French Hospital ship *Duquay-Trouin*, then lying off the island of Skyros—the same island, legend tells us, where Theseus was buried.

The coffin was carried by his "A" Company petty officers, by lamplight, that same evening, up the rough, narrow pathway to one of the loveliest spots on earth. Gray-green olive trees surrounded the little group of mourners, and they stood on a carpet of flowering sage that filled the air with its exquisite fragrance. His friends had lined the grave with flowers and laid a wreath of olive on the coffin. There they left him, where they knew he wished to lie. The soldier-poet had had a premonition of the manner of his death, and had expressed it in his sonnet, "The Soldier."

If I should die, think only this of me:
That there's some corner of a foreign field
that is for ever England.*

By the time it came to say goodbye to our helpful fisherman we were fast friends and he invited us to pay him a
visit in his own little museum. It was the typical Skyros
interior with the addition of two framed photographs
hanging on the wall—one of his Queen, holding in her
arms a six-month-old baby, and beside it the portrait of a
happy young Greek sailor. Those two pictures told the
story of the days in World War II when Queen Frederica
traveled from island to island, prophesying to her people
better days to come, cheering them on the road to victory,
and expressing to them with her contagious gaiety the
sympathy and understanding that she felt for every member of the Greek Commonwealth.

Continuing from Skyros, in a westerly direction, and
once in the Atalanta Channel which divides Euboea from
the mainland of Boeotia and Attica, we were entering the
battle-lines of the land- and sea-forces of the Graeco-Persian Wars. The steep coasts of Euboea are treacherous for
yachts as well as fighting ships, and caution is required,
for the few anchorages are only on the Boeotian shore.
Moreover, sudden blasts of wind coming down from the
mountains are dangerous for sailing craft.

We passed through the Oreos Channel, which separates
the northern end of Euboea from the coast of Thessaly,

* Rupert Brooke, *The Collected Poems of Rupert Brooke* (New York:
Dodd, Mead, 1946), p. 105.

and anchored for the night in the Atalanta Road, near a smart white cutter, *Korby*. The owners, Captain and Mrs. H. M. Denham, have enjoyed her as their summer home for many years, and they and their guests gave us a lively evening by joining us on our ship and telling us of their many experiences in Mediterranean waters.

As we approached the scenes of the great battles between the Greeks and Persians, we became more and more interested in what Herodotus has to say of the Kings of Persia.

It seems that Cyrus, the father of Darius, welded the tribes into a single nation in the latter half of the sixth century B.C. The weapon on which the Persians chiefly relied was the bow and arrow. While his infantry knelt to shoot a hail of arrows, his cavalry threw the enemy lines into confusion. In fighting with the Medes and Babylonians, these tactics were highly successful, and though the foot soldiers carried short lances and daggers, they were not often engaged because the Persians were able to keep their enemies at the desired distance. It was not until Marathon that they met their defeat in hand-to-hand fighting dictated by Greek courage and Greek understanding of strategy, phalanx, and terrain.

Darius the Great was an unsurpassed leader of the ancient world, in peace as well as in war—the greatest commander and organizer that the world had yet known. His policy was that of an empire-builder, and before invading Greece proper, he had already annexed Egypt and Thrace, forced Macedonia to her knees, and conquered Greek cities in Asia Minor as well as some of the off-shore islands.

His first act of aggression against the Greek mainland was to equip and launch a fleet under Mardonius, which was destroyed by storms off the promontory of Mt. Athos. A second expedition was sent by direct sea-route, through the islands to Eretria, and to the Bay of Marathon, where the Persians received their first overwhelming defeat, in 490 B.C. Five years later, when Xerxes inherited the power and the spirit of revenge bequeathed him by his father, he created a fabulous war machine.

For several years, men, ships, horses and provisions were being requisitioned in every part of Asia, with the understanding of a general attack on Greece. Xerxes cut a canal through the isthmus of Mt. Athos in order to avoid a repetition of the disaster that befell Mardonius and also with the intention of keeping the fleet close to the army. With the rocky promontory of Athos behind them, army and navy could then proceed to Therma, to Artemisium, to Thermopylae, through the straits of Khalkis, and eventually to Athens.

It was near Thermopylae that the land- and sea-forces of Xerxes conjoined most closely in 480 B.C., and it was to the famous Pass of Thermopylae that our course was directed. Here Leonidas, King of the Spartans, made his heroic stand against fabulous armies of Persians. Permitting the Greek army of about 7,000 men to be deployed to the rear of the pass to defend their flank, Leonidas kept 299 of his bravest hoplites ready to sacrifice their lives if need be. Overwhelmed by numbers, there they fought, and, fighting, died to a man. On a white, marble slab that commemorates the site of the battle, an inscription is carved. That particular translation sounds to my ears like a cry of distress. To me, that voice should have the ring of victory and command, as it has in the translation by William Lisle Bowles.

Go tell the Spartans, thou that passeth by,
That here, obedient to their laws, we lie.

Near the inscription stands a lion for Leonidas, and
three hundred cypress trees raise their dark green, spearlike points up toward the blue sky, in memory of the
honored dead.

While the armies were engaged at Thermopylae, the
Greek fleet was standing by at Artemisium, the northern
tip of Euboea. What precipitated the move that led to the
Persian downfall was the cunning message, simulating
treachery, sent by the leader of the Greeks, Themistocles,
to the King of the Persians, assuring the latter that the
Greek galleys waited at Salamis only to betray the Greek
cause.

The picture of Xerxes, enthroned on a hilltop above
the Bay of Salamis, watching the defeat of his long-
vaunted navy, is every school child's memory of one of the
decisive battles of the world.

Soon after the victory of the Greek fleet in the Bay of
Salamis, the Persian general, Mardonius, persuaded
Xerxes to return to Sardis, leaving him to deal with the
ground forces.

For some months his army harried and engaged the
various Greek contingents. With a final clash of great
numbers of infantry, in which the heavily armed Persians
were at a disadvantage against the lightly equipped hoplites in the hand-to-hand fighting, Mardonius himself
fell at Plataea and the Graeco-Persian Wars came to an
end. This victory of 479 B.C. belonged to the Plataeans
who had raised volunteer armies from thirty-one city-
states. Their next step was to dedicate a tenth of the spoils

of war to the Delphic Oracle, and to set up the famous bronze serpentine column to their illustrious dead near the Temple of Apollo. It was created in the form of three gigantic snakes twisted together, about thirty feet high. The three serpent heads at the top supported a sacred tripod of gold, and this in turn supported a golden urn. For eight hundred years it stood there, the cherished symbol of victory to the Hellenes, until the Emperor Constantine ordered the column to be removed from its pedestal and transported to Constantinople to adorn his hippodrome.

It is said that the column, on which are engraved the names of the thirty-one city-states, represented in bold Greek script resembling the graven letters on the helmet of Miltiades, was wrought from a single block of metal. The golden tripod and urn have long since vanished, and nothing remains in Delphi but the bare stone base near the Temple of Apollo. To see what does remain you must go to Istanbul as well as to Delphi; this is one of the visual crosscurrents of history that flows between Greece and Asia Minor, a lesson taught to us by Sir John Forsdyke when we found him in Istanbul with Tom Whittemore in 1935, and sailed him back with us to Delphi. Sir John is a distinguished classical scholar who was for many years the head of the British Museum in London, the home of the Elgin Marbles, and is the author of, among other publications, *Greece Before Homer*.

On our way back to the ship after an absorbing interlude of sites and memories of Graeco-Persian battles, we stopped at a nice little restaurant at Kamena Vourla Spa. These thermal springs are radio-active and were rediscovered in 1935. The radio-active properties of these waters must have been well known to the ancients, for a neighboring rock was early dedicated to Aesculapius. After a refreshing, and medicinal swim, preceding a very belated lunch, we resumed our homeward drive to *Rara Avis*.

The following morning we steamed through the Atalanta Channel between Euboea and the mainland. At the narrowest part, for about six miles, the Euripos (meaning "swift current") has been deepened and widened to form a navigational passage. This portion of the Euripos is celebrated for a phenomenal alternating of currents, and we were lucky to have a wait of only half an hour before the tide allowed us through.

For millenniums the two ports at the upper end of this gateway, the "Thermopylaes of the Sea," have kept a control over the flow of commerce and colonization between the rich island of Euboea and the mainland, and when necessary, have blocked the entrance. Once through the swing-bridge, we landed and went ashore to see a small museum. That night was spent anchored in the stream, and the next morning we departed for Marathon at 8:00 A.M. Due to a restricted military area we anchored in Rafina Harbor and drove eight miles to the scene of the famous battle.

The rough green scrubby crescent-shaped plain of Marathon lies between the bay and the great mass of steep semicircular rocky mountains that are the bulwark of Attica. Somewhere, felt but unseen, is the ancient carriage road along which Phidippides ran, which penetrates the range of mountains and arrives at Athens. Here, in 490 B.C., was the first overwhelming Greek triumph in the Graeco-Persian Wars, and it is impossible to overestimate what this victory did for the morale of the city-state forces. It raised the Athenians from a second-rate to a first-rate power, it accentuated to them the need for co-operation with their rivals, and it taught them the value of a sacrificial stand.

The hero of Marathon, Miltiades, came from a family that claimed descent from Aeacus, the son of Zeus and Aegina, and who was once king of the island of Aegina. This Olympian ancestry therefore surely gave him the divine right of kings, and in addition, he combined an insatiable ambition with a conspicuous courage. More than once, in his youth, he was impeached for making laws unto himself, but when the Persians were known to be approaching, he was needed, and was made one of the ten generals to defend Attica. Eventually posterity acclaimed him the victor of Marathon.

Here, with the Greeks greatly outnumbered by the Persians, the superiority of the Greek phalanx was demonstrated. The Persians lost several thousand men while the Greeks lost only 192. These heroes were cremated at the end of the battle and the sepulchral mound under which they lie is in the center of the battle field. Steps lead to the top of the tumulus, and except for archaeological searchings, the scene has remained as of old, with little change for twenty-five hundred years.

There are touching reminders here, as in Olympia, of patriotic dedication, other than being slain in battle. The Marathon race (staged for the first time in the Olympic Games that were revived at Athens in 1896) was won by a Greek, Spiridon Loues. The race commemorates the sacrifice of Phidippides, who covered the distance from the plains of Marathon to Athens, twenty-six miles, to bring the news of the Greek victory, and fell dead, his mission accomplished, with the words "We won," on his lips.

Again Boston claims its Athenian descent. Second only to the Marathon race, run in the modern Olympic Games, the most notable long-distance race nowadays is the annual Marathon run by the Athletic Association of Boston. Sir Horace Walpole might have added, in his letter to his cousin Horace Mann, that besides a Thucydides at Boston and a Xenophon at New York, there will perhaps be a Phidippides in Boston. This race has been featured since 1897, and from 1945, for eleven years, the winners were from nations other than the United States.

We had now only the familiar waters to navigate that we had already so often sailed through on our way between the Aegean and the Ionian islands. We rounded the Attic Peninsula, spent a moonlit night in the harbor beneath the Temple of Sunium, and started the last lap of our 1960 Cruise by anchoring in Kalamaki Harbour, in the Saronic Gulf, on our way to the Ionian Sea.

For the fifth time in two summers, *Rara Avis* entered that product of necessity, the Corinth Canal. As we passed through its massive walls of sandstone, we thought of the days of antiquity, when shallow-bottomed galleys were dragged across the isthmus by manpower, and we blessed the emperor Nero and the profession of engineering for making it possible for mariners of today to sail, with so much ease, from the Aegean to the Ionian Sea. Continuing on our way through the Gulf of Corinth, we took a northerly course for a somewhat hidden island between Levkas and the mainland.

"This is the island," said Jay, as we approached a particularly pretty, lengthening, narrowing harbor, "where they don't want any money, they only want things." The gray-green foliage of old gnarled olive trees soften the out-lines of the hills, and ancient individual trees shade the banks close to the water. The high ground rises obliquely and irregularly back from the shore road, making a mys-tery of what lies beyond. It is the westerly harbor on the north coast of Meganisi, one of Bobby Somerset's favorites, that he had begged us not to miss.

In cruising among the Greek Islands, at one end of the pole is the majesty of the Parthenon or the sight of the Temple of Sunium standing proudly high against the sky on Cape Colonna; at the other end are numberless small islands of enchantment that are unheralded and un-sung, but that quietly etch themselves indelibly on your memory. They do not present archaeological paths of stone that wind through twenty-five hundred years into the past, but what they have to offer is ancient history that is alive today. The inhabitants are often dressed in the same garments, living the selfsame kind of life, and oc-cupied in much the same manner as were the peasants of the faraway centuries before Christ was born. They are concerned with bringing up their sons in the old tradition of farming, fishing, shipbuilding, and protecting their way of life; and their daughters in the lore of homemaking, motherhood, and human relationships. These parents have no cars, no television, no kitchen aids, no school-busses, and I can only suppose, no bank accounts.

Within a few minutes we were secured, stern-to, to an ancient olive tree, our broad, flat bottom swinging free in the transparent shallow water. A dark chestnut-colored awning slung between deckhouse and cockpit shaded our lunch table from the cloudless sky and the burning mid-day sun. No human being was in sight. It was siesta time for man and beast.

It wasn't long, however, before a dozen little boys of varying ages and sizes, some with swimming trunks and others without, appeared from nowhere and were soon swimming around the ship with shouts of glee and wonder. A great deal of sign language was added to Greek and English, and after many questions such as "Inglesi?" "Amerikani?" "Where from?" we thought it was at last siesta time for us, and we waved them off with a "shoo—shoo." They gradually took the cue, and disappeared amiably, but temporarily, to the oblivion from which they first appeared.

Then came our turn for a delicious swim off the boat after which the heat robbed us of all ambition and not one of us showed the slightest curiosity about going ashore to investigate and explore. This proved fortunate, for while we sat on deck, absorbing the beauty and sunshine, we presently became aware of a scene and a stage-set such as dreams are made of.

On one side of our narrow harbor sprawled a great olive tree, with gnarled gray trunk and bearing leafy branches that shaded a few large flat-topped field stones. Presently out of the blue, much as our little swimmers had previously appeared from nowhere, there approached three tall, slight, graceful female figures. They were dressed in soft black drapery that fell in folds from neck to toe, and were easily belted at trim, neat waistlines. In the crook of one elbow, each carried an armful of yellow wheat, and between them they brought along one gavel-like wooden hammer. With great dignity and equal grace, they sat down on three of the flat field stones, under the shady olive tree, and there they proceeded to spread their bundles of wheat in front of them and to thresh by hand the grain from the stalks. They seemed to talk quietly together as they worked and they showed no interest whatever in our admiring and absorbed attention. We, on our part, felt that we were watching the Three Graces, Aglaia, Euphrosyne, and Thalia, not standing in statuesque marble perfection, but seated at ease, very much alive, and enjoying one of their familiar and daily tasks. Had I taken a step forward, with my Leica, they would probably have vanished in thin air.

A sight such as this was what we had come four thousand miles to see. There before us was the living counterpart of a black-figured terra-cotta vase of the seventh century before Christ, representing the Three Graces. We were touched with gratitude and Jay's words sprang to our minds. "This is the Island," he had said, "where they only want things."

The things that we were able to gather together fell very short of what we would have liked to give them. You are inclined to horde your travel-limited clothing because it may prove irreplaceable en route. We gathered together a pair of shoes that might be worn in the coming winter, some underclothes, and some S. S. Pierce cans of food—a pitiful little offering in exchange for so much beauty and inspiration. We put them in a bag and sent it ashore via one of the boys.

As soon as the graces perceived our efforts in their direction, one of them rose nervously, as if we might have had an evil eye among us, and started to make off. This attitude alarmed us and we waved friendly gestures that were intended to reassure them as to the contents of the bag, and to suggest that it contained something worth looking at. Apparently our signs were propitiatory because the timid one seemed to relent and relax, and pretty soon the suspicious-looking Pandora's bag was being gingerly unzipped and no horrors were flying out. Instead, the shoes were examined with approval, the undies were held up with recognition, and the preliminary reluctance was being replaced by acceptance. By this time the sun was low in the heavens and our Three Graces quietly repacked the little bag, picked it up with the wooden gavel, left the chaff on the stones to dry, and wended their way homeward in single file.

We spent one more night in this peaceful haven of a primitive existence, and the next morning, at 7:00 A.M. took our departure for Corfu. We were soon steaming north, through a passage about four miles long, between Levkas and the mainland—a passage so narrow that it has the character of a green, steep-sided canal. Once through, we soon left the harbor of Preveza on our right, and in another few miles, the island of Paxoi on our left, and made our landfall. At about five o'clock that afternoon, we let go our anchor in the commercial roadstead north of the city.

That evening we dined at a handsome new hotel facing the east harbor, Kinopiastais. The hotel was one of those built after the war, on Marshall Plan funds.

The Island of Corfu is often a foreigner's first impression of Greece, as it occupies an important location at the end of a well-traveled highway between Italian and Greek waters. The lush, soft, verdant quality of Italy (to which Corfu belonged for centuries) still lingers there. The Venetian occupation even went so far as building a walled city, with narrow streets and thoroughfares. Placed within those walls were several sixteenth- and seventeenth-century Palladian villas, with their conventional symmetry, style, and taste.

In Graeco-Roman times, it was the fate of Corfu to lie on a fringe between powerful nations, and in the neighborhood of envious city-states, and twenty-five hundred years ago, it developed an independence that sometimes challenged even the mother city, Athens.

Just as the island of Gozo is identified with the Homeric Ogygia, where Odysseus spent seven long years under the spell of the divine Calypso, Corfu is identified with Scherie, the home of the Phaeacians, ruled over by the good King Alcinous, father of the beautiful Nausicaa. This historic legend is preserved in the names of such landmarks as the ancient Port of Alcinous, the Phaeacian Highway, and the tiny islet, recognized as the Ship of Odysseus, turned to stone by Zeus for disobedience to his command, and popularized by the Swiss painter Arnold Boecklin.

There are many first-rate hotels and numerous restaurants and cafés, not only in the city, but dotted along the main highroads of the island. We lunched at one of these restaurants, called Avra. It is perched on a high cliff, overlooking enchanting views of sunlit seas, and as you glance down a steep embankment, about a hundred feet beneath you, a small, shallow bay of dazzling white sand is lapped by aquamarine wavelets and shaded by gray-green olive trees. Who can say that this crescent-shaped beach was not the one where Odysseus was cast ashore, and where, after a deep sleep of exhaustion, he was awakened by the feminine voices of Nausicaa and her gentlewomen?

A Royal Palace, dating from the British occupation in 1815, and built of blocks of Maltese stone, is situated on the handsome Garizza Esplanade, which, toward the west, leads into the Garizza Boulevard. With a view over the Bay of Castrades, the Esplanade is the favorite site along which the evening strollers spend their hours of rest and conviviality, at the end of the long languorous days of summer.

The Garizza Boulevard takes you out to the picturesque and beautiful countryside. Groves of olive trees, oranges, and lemons are pointed up with dark green spearlike cypresses, and the ground cover is a mass of flowering shrubs with incidental gray rocks to set off their delicacy. All over the island, singly, and in groves, venerable olive trees flourish, encouraged by government subsidies, and they add charm to the landscape as well as value to the land.

In the midst of all this natural beauty, about three miles outside of the city, stands a tasteless palace that is a jumble of many periods of architecture. It was built about 1890, for the Empress Elizabeth of Austria and was subsequently owned and occupied by Kaiser Wilhelm II. It is called The Achillaeum. On a terrace in the park, where deciduous trees frame colorful views of sapphire sea, lies a recumbent statue of the emperor's hero Achilles, formerly inscribed "To the greatest of Greeks, from the greatest of Germans."

Not far from the Garizza Boulevard is a strange circular cenotaph to the memory of Menecrates, a proxenos of the Corcyreans who perished at sea in 664 B.C. The earliest naval battle recorded in history was one of that date, between the Corinthians and Corcyreans, but there are no known facts to establish a connection between his death and the battle.

The museum contains small and large fragments of the

ancient necropolis and of a gigantic sixth-century Temple of Artemis. Quite unlike the beautiful sixth-century archaic pediment of the temple of Zeus in Olympia, the main feature of this one is a colossal snake-engirdled gorgon, to which is added a sleeping panther, and a combat between Zeus and Titan. In addition to the richness of this legendary and historic past, Corfu now enjoys a renewed vitality brought to it by the presence of the Royal Family, whose summer palace, "Mon Repos," is situated on the sea front.

In the early morning, on the day after we arrived, the authorities brought us the welcome news that King Paul and Queen Frederica would honor us with a visit. At the same time, the harbor master advised us that strong northwest winds were predicted, and that it might be advisable for us to shift to a more protected anchorage. Of course we followed his directions, but as no strong winds developed, it seemed to us more likely that *Rara Avis* was being moved to Garizza Bay, south of the city, because it was a less public berth and a more convenient distance from the royal residence.

It was not to be our first meeting, because, in the late twenties, when Prince Paul was a young bachelor and Greece was temporarily a republic, he had left his own country in quest of a livelihood and in order to learn his way about among other peoples. He visited both England and the United States, and worked in factories in both countries as a mechanical engineer. Everywhere that he went, he made friends and was warmly welcomed.

When Prince Paul arrived on Long Island, it was to stay with his cousin, Princess Xenia, who had married an American and was living in Oyster Bay. My Paul was then also a bachelor and living in his Cape Cod cottage in Syosset, and it came about, probably because they were both sailors, that Prince Paul's next visit was to him at Muttontown Lodge. It was just before the colleges reopened, so the season for debutante parties was in full swing. Though a hard-working schedule limited Paul Hammond to Saturday-night conviviality, a full social agenda was a must for his royal guest. Many a morning, when the sun was well up, Prince Paul would be gaily entering the garden gate, headed for a well-earned sleep, while his host would be emerging from the front door, on his way to an early train, to put in a long day earning his bread and butter.

Those weeks were again recalled when King Paul and Queen Frederica came to the United States in 1953, on the occasion when the King was invited to address the Assembly of the United Nations in New York. We went to the meeting and heard a very interesting and modest speech, beautifully delivered, that has ever since connected him in my mind with the Greek aphorism "Moderation in all things."

Saturday, July 16, 6:30 P.M., was the appointed hour, and on the dot, a smart blue-and-white launch, steered by the King, made a good landing at our starboard gangway. Soon after the King and Queen came on board, we were joined by the Crown Prince Constantine. He came alone by way of an albatross outboard. During our cruises of 1959 and 1960, whenever the Prince's name was mentioned, in whatever company, there was always a chorus who would say, "He's a good boy." We were therefore all the more interested when he stood before us, manly, grave, and self-confident, bearing the title of Duke of Sparta. Later that summer, he won with his *Nereus* the

Dragon Class series in the Olympic sailing races, which took place in the Bay of Naples, thus securing for Greece her first Gold Medal in an Olympic yacht race.

After they had all "inspected the ship" from stem to stern, the Prince left us while the King and Queen stayed on board for another hour, discussing Near-Eastern and world politics.

Queen Frederica is well known for her youthful charm and vivacity and she gave us a vivid account of a journey she and her children had made to the United States in 1958 in connection with the Atomic Energy Commission. She is a great admirer of Admiral Rickover—"My Dictator," as she calls him, and she made us laugh over her lively description of running arguments between the Admiral and some of the security officers, all ardently and equally concerned over her welfare and safety. "I will take Her Majesty in my helicopter, to such and such a place." "No you won't." "Yes I will." The arguments usually seem to have ended with the Yes, I will's. The royal visit was a sentimental farewell, closing our long chapter of happy cruises in Greek waters.

Starting at 4:00 A.M., July 17, it took thirty-three hours to cross the Ionian Sea to Messina, where we spent the night. On July 19 we departed Messina for the island of Ischia. On the way, however, we were forced to change our plans when the starboard engine broke down. We put in at Naples, where we had one of the delicious dinners for which the de luxe Hotel Excelsior is famous, and remained till the following morning.

The next day we left *Rara Avis*, with our blessings, to the tender mercies of mechanics and electricians, and took a ferry to Ischia. Though I would not see her again

1. Rara Avis. Sailing trials in the Solent after completion of the rig by Groves and Guttridge Ltd., East Cowes, Isle of Wight. Constructed at Terneuzen Shipbuilding Co. Ltd., Holland.

Courtesy of Beken & Son, Cowes

2. *The author on board* Rara Avis, *holding the Sperry hydraulic tiller.*

3. *Paul Hammond, a sailor in peace or war.*

4. *Paul and Susan Hammond in Cartagena with their guests Mary Sears, Amanda Kane, and Henry Sears.*

Courtesy of R. Keith Kane

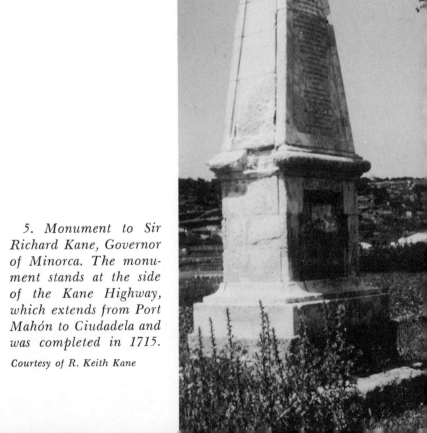

5. *Monument to Sir Richard Kane, Governor of Minorca. The monument stands at the side of the Kane Highway, which extends from Port Mahón to Ciudadela and was completed in 1715.*

Courtesy of R. Keith Kane

6. *Fishermen going to sea after a storm.*

7. *Harbor of Qala Tad-Dueira, Gozo.*
Courtesy of T. D. Cabot

8. *Temple of Apollo at Bassae.*

10. *Unusual base of an interior column.*

9. *Susie Saarinen sketching.*

11. *A jolly monk of Corfu.*

12. *Ship of Odysseus, turned to stone by Zeus.*

13. Monoliths of the Temple of Apollo, Corinth, 1934.

14. Corinth Canal, 1960.

Courtesy of T. D. Cabot

15. *Temple of Aphaia, Aegina.*

16. *Little beasts of burden.*

17. *Sunset from the Palace of Mycenae.*

18. *On the road to Mycenae.*

19. *The Temple of Poseidon, Sunium.*

20. *Temple of Apollo, Delos. Richard Delano (left) and guide.*

21. *Archaic lions of Delos,* ca. 700 B.C.

Courtesy of T. D. Cabot

22. *Santorin.* Rara Avis *as seen from lofty parapet.*

Courtesy of T. D. Cabot

23. *Climbing the 900 feet to the summit.*

24. *Lion of Keos*, ca. *600 B.C.*   *Courtesy of T. D. Cabot*

25. *Another view of the archaic smile.*   *Courtesy of T. D. Cabot*

26. Landfall. Designed by L. Francis Herreshoff.

27. *Paul Hammond (left) and Professor Blegen, Troy, 1934.*

28. *Heinrich Scliemann's pioneer cut, made about ninety years ago.*

29. *Troy VI and VIIa, the walls of Homer's* Iliad.

30. *Marble ramp of Troy II.*

31. *Lillian Gish plays a new role. Egypt, 1934.*

32. *Our camp on the desert.*

33. *The goddess Sakhmet, Temple of Mut, Luxor.*

34. *Horns of Consecration, with colossal oil jars. Crete, 1934.*

35. *The storehouse.*

36. *Fresco of the Minoan Games. Palace of Knossus, 1934.*

37. *Entrance to the harbor of Rhodes, 1934.*

38. *At the first alarm, a man rang a bell.*

39. *Lindos seen through the rigging of Landfall.*

40. *The Sea of Galilee.*

41. *Jane Nichols and Kim Norton, 1937.*

42. Capitana.

43. *Samuel E. Morison, in command of the Harvard Columbus Expedition, at the helm. Beside him, Jariilo Walter, sailing master.*

44. Mary Otis, *with jury rudder, returning from Santa Maria.*

45. *Dwight Morrow and Jim Byrne help the crew furl the forecourse.*

46. *Paul Hammond, in command of* Capitana.

47. *Young Azorian
wields a heavy oar.*

48. *Corvo's only landing.*

49. *Church of the Carmo in Lisbon, where Columbus'
wife, Dona Felipe Perestrello, is buried.*

50. *La Rábida, little changed since the time of Columbus.*

51. *Fray Juan Perez de la Marchena, who harbored Columbus and his little son Diego for five years, and relayed their story to Queen Isabella.*

52. *Gertrude Whitney's statue of Columbus at Huelva.*

53. *Conjectural model of* Santa Maria, *showing Columbus'* windlass.

54. Capitana, moored off Teneriffe, Canary Islands, as we waved farewell.

on the eastern shores of the Atlantic, Paul commuted almost daily, to Naples in the hydrofoil, to attend to her
welfare. On the island of Ischia we engaged rooms at the
excellent Hotel Regina Isabella in Lacco Ameno. We had
long heard much about the charms of the island, and Paul
was curious to sample the magic of the mud baths.
Whether he took them for his entertainment, his recreation, or his quite rugged health, I never discovered, but
they seemed to fulfill his expectations.

At Naples we boarded our old favorite, the American
Export S.S. *Constitution,* on July twenty-ninth and a
smooth and quiet voyage across the Atlantic gave us the
leisure to collect our thoughts and relive the past idyllic
months. We knew that the cross-currents of history, rif-
fling our consciousness during the last happy months of
sunshine and beauty, as we sailed in Greek waters from
island to island, had added light and understanding to our
lives and we rejoiced in the gain. Perhaps the pleasure
and profit derived by all of us were best summed up in a
letter from Marian Perkins that awaited us on our arrival
in Syosset. "Well," it read, "we're home again, but we'll
never be the same again."

PART II
Landfall—*Four Cruises, 1934–1937*

"That Greek Trip," 1934—
Diary of Richard Delano

INTRODUCTION TO THE 1934 CRUISE

Our ship's company during our 1934 cruise consisted of Helenka Adamowska, my daughter Lily Swann Saarinen, my cousin Nicholas Roosevelt, and Richard Delano.

Helenka's parents were Antoinette and Joseph Adamowski, lifelong friends of Ignace Jan Paderewski. The latter lived with the Adamowskis in his youth in Warsaw and Antoinette was his only woman pupil. In the early nineteen hundreds, she and her husband, together with his brother Timothé, formed a musical trio of piano, violin, and cello, that toured Europe triumphantly. They even went so far afield as St. Petersburg where they played before the Court of Czar Nicholas II. They later crossed the Atlantic Ocean and toured North America with such success that they eventually chose Boston, Massachusetts, for their permanent home.

Helenka grew up in Boston to be one of the most beloved girls who ever went to Friday evening dances or took part in Vincent shows. She later married a brilliant young lawyer in New York, Guido Pantaleoni, Jr. He enlisted in World War II and was killed by an enemy mine.

Helenka is now President of the United States Committee of UNICEF, the United Nations agency that is helping governments in over a hundred countries and territories to provide improved health, improved nutrition, and improved conditions for the children within their borders. It is a magnificent project that has gained by leaps and bounds with the conspicuous help of its "Master of Ceremonies," Danny Kaye.

Nicholas Roosevelt now lives in the beautiful country of Big Sur, California. For three years before this cruise, from 1930 to 1933, he had been our Minister to Hungary when that country was governed by Admiral Horthy, as regent.

Richard Delano is the son of the late William A. Delano. The latter was one of the two heads of the firm of Delano & Aldrich, both distinguished and honored names in architectural circles.

Dicky inherited his father's many talents but does not make architecture his profession. Fortunately, he kept a day-to-day diary of those six weeks on our cruise when he was twenty-four years old. We are grateful to him for permitting us to add it to these records as it has a youthful freshness and frankness; moreover, except for a few changes, it might have been written yesterday.

THAT GREEK TRIP

Friday, May 25th, 1934. Paris.

It was like this. One day I was sitting with my mother in her room at the Hotel Palais d'Orsay. She was reading aloud to me, and it was all warm and cozy. There was a knock at the door.

"C'est un telegramme pour Madame."

We opened it with trembling hand, as all telegrams seem to be bad news. This was a long one from Dad and read: "Paul Hammond offers Grecian island trip on his boat *Landfall* starting Athens, June 5th, arriving Venice, July 10th. Strongly advise Dick's going if he can get off from school. Opportunity exceptional. Writing explanatory letter—Dad." This was breathtaking: we had not dreamed of anything so extraordinary as this. We had to read it four or five times.

We waited impatiently for the letter. It seemed ages before it arrived, but finally it did. It was very clear about when I should meet Paul, and that was all. It was decided that I should go to Greece and see as much as I could and learn as much as I could. For a week I ran about getting all necessary papers (including a new passport) and clothes, etc. On Saturday, that week, I said good-bye to Mamma, who sailed on the *Bremen* for the U.S.A., and on the following Friday night I left on my way to Greece!

Saturday, June 2nd: Rome.

I woke up feeling very refreshed. It was a beautiful day, with not too hot a sun shining. I had my breakfast and walked down to the Piazza d'Espagna. (As I went down the long steps, I wished that I had followed my father's advice and learned Latin: there was so much to read on every plaque!) I saw the Fascisti Exhibition, as I was obliged to in order to have my railroad ticket stamped! But it was well worth the visit. On coming out I was held up some minutes at the door, because of a regiment of some sort or other being shown the exhibition. I was particularly impressed by how many people were in uniform and how smart they all looked.

I drove to St. Peter's in a horse carriage. It was a grand feeling to be back amongst such beauty—such continual beauty. I revisited St. Peter's and then installed myself for an afternoon's sketching under the Colonnade and made a water color of the fountains in the Plaza, and when finished I took the very good, quick and cheap bus home.

Sunday, June 3rd.

I woke up at eight and had my breakfast in my room, taking a picture of the event. Then I strolled into the Borghese gardens and made a water color of the little fountain of the two boys overlooking the circus. It took a long time and was not very good. I also made a sketch in pencil of the little tempetto.

A delicious lunch at the pension and then rested for two hours. It was so very hot and I felt lazy. At four I went to the steps of Piazza d'Espagna and made a small water color and a pencil sketch. At 8:00 P.M. I strolled into the cinema of the Planetarium and saw a very interesting film of elephants working in a lumber camp, plus some good newsreels and one on "cloud formations." This occupied the time till my train left, which I found very crowded. I had a hard time finding a seat but eventually shoved and edged my way in between three Greek sailors.

Monday, June 4th.

The train reached Brindisi at 10:51. Paul was standing on the platform, having spotted me from his train, which had met ours at the previous station! He gave me letters from Dad and Mamma, which put me at ease. We all had lunch together at the Continental, and after lunch Paul, Mrs. Hammond and I went for a sail. It was fun for an hour. The *Calatea* came in as we were sailing about. She is very handsome and modern. On boarding her I bought a second-class ticket, and was all settled, when I found to my surprise that Paul had paid the difference and brought me into the first-class, so I am sharing a cabin with Nicholas Roosevelt.

Tuesday, June 5th.

Paul woke me up at 7:30 and I went on deck. It was a beautiful day and we were in the Gulf of Corinth. It was rather misty and our visibility was impaired quite a bit. I wrote letters till very near lunch time, when we neared the canal. We entered it at noon and it was most interesting. A tug came out to meet us with two steel barges on either side. They made them fast to our stern in order to keep the sides from chafing in the narrow canal. There was only about three feet to spare on each side. The canal was a big cut, being some 25 meters deep. The strata formation is also very interesting. There had been two landslides eleven years ago and it has made little coves on the sides, which break up the monotony of the cut. The canal is about six kilometers long and it took us one hour and a half to go through. The lunch bell rang while we were in it and we *had* to go down and eat, much to my annoyance. After lunch we were in Megara Bay. It was very exciting nearing Piraeus. From a distance we saw the Acropolis with its temple, but could only see the Parthenon clearly from that distance through the binoculars. As we approached, the ships in the harbor loomed up and dominated the scene.

We came alongside the dock at about three in the afternoon. Mr. Lincoln MacVeagh, American Minister, came aboard to greet us. He is a charming fellow and I soon found out that his hobby was archaeology. He drove us up to Athens in his car. It was very swell. After a brief visit at the Embassy, Mr. MacVeagh and Nick Roosevelt and I went up to the Acropolis. It was very exciting driving up. The weather was damn hot but our enthusiasm made us forget everything but what we were looking at. After paying 50 drachmas we mounted the steps of the Propylaea, Mr. MacVeagh explaining everything as we went along. He was perfect. I asked a million and one questions and he always knew the answer. Having passed through the Propylaea, there stood the Parthenon before us, *not* against "a blue sky," as I had been told I would find it, but against a normal sky. MacVeagh explained that it was usually misty in the middle of the day in the summer, but that at sunset and dawn it all cleared off; and we have found this to be the case. It was very interesting and I marveled at the engineering skill. (He pointed out to me the six inch curve in the steps and the inward tilt of the columns and how the sculpture was carved deeper—in the case of bas-reliefs—at the top than at the bottom in order to make them look straight, etc.)

We then visited the museum with him and it was ten times more interesting to have him as our guide as he was so keen on his subject. We stayed about till sunset, and my, how lovely it was then! At sunset they pulled us out, and Nick and I went down to the sea to have a swim. Mrs. Hammond was waiting in a bungalow of a cousin of hers, Alexander Sedgwick. He is a great fellow, and gave us bathing suits and we swam in lovely water—quite warm although not too much so. Lily Swann, Nick and I tried some resinous Greek wine. I did not like it much, although Nick found it delicious. We then all went to a small Greek restaurant by the side of the sea and dined in the starlight to the sound of lapping water. We were

the only people there, and it was grand. The food was unbelievably good, I thought. I liked all their dishes. Nick
and I got away about 11:15 and drove down to Phaleron,
where *Landfall* was anchored. Paul was already in bed
when we arrived, but he got up to receive us and make us
comfortable.

Wednesday, June 6th.

Had breakfast on *Landfall* at seven-thirty and went
ashore. We drove up to the Acropolis again and I made a
lithograph of the Parthenon which took me almost two
hours. I also made one of the Erechtheum. I started a water color of the northeast corner of the Parthenon but the
bell rang before I was able to finish at sunset. The colors
were marvelous, though, and it was great fun to try and
catch them before they faded.

I returned to Athens with two ladies, one of whom is a
curator of the Metropolitan Museum in New York* and
the other a painter. They were both very kind in answer-
ing my many questions.

I dined alone with Lily at an open air restaurant in the
park, for all the others were dining with Mr. and Mrs.
MacVeagh. I went back to the boat at Phaleron and spent
the night there.

Thursday, June 7th.

I slept alone on *Landfall,* because all the others stayed
so late at their party that they did not want to drive all
the way back to Phaleron that night when they had shopping to do early the next morning. I got up at seven and
rowed myself out for a swim. It was not very clean water,
but still the swim was refreshing after a hot night. Break-

---

* Miss Gisela Richter and her sister. [Author's note.]

fasted and was cleaning my sneakers when a man came aboard and told me that a taxi was waiting to take me to Athens. On arriving there, I found to my disappointment that I had just missed the Hammonds, who had gone to visit something or other. However, I went for a walk in the small streets, and made a lithograph of the monument of Lysicrates, and was surrounded by a flock of small boys who gave me fleas! I went from there to see the temple of Olympian Zeus. I liked this temple very much because the columns are of such massive proportion. I found a fellow there who was about to be a guide, and he practised on me, which was very nice because he seemed to "know his stuff" thoroughly. The Arch of Hadrian is there.

Later we all went back to the National Museum again, and spent the rest of the morning there. At four Mrs. Hammond, Lily, Nick and I drove over to Sunium. It was a lovely drive and we passed many picturesque local farmers and their animals. The first valley we passed through was filled with grapevines; there seemed enough to supply the whole country's needs. Then we crossed a low mountain range and came into the wheat country: lovely golden wheat—lots of it. The farmers were cutting it and their little donkeys were laden with it. It seems that each farmer has been allotted a place in a big field where he stacks his wheat, and then later on a threshing machine comes and does the whole lot at one time. We got to Sunium about 6:00 P.M. and had a glorious swim in lovely limpid water, crystal clear and the bottom interesting to behold. I swam with delight for almost an hour—the temperature was just right. There was a beautiful cave too, but it was scary swimming in it, for I feared sea serpents. Of course, there were none but my imagination got the better of me.

Friday, June 8th.

Landfall is a ketch, 72 feet overall, with a 60-foot water line and an 18-foot beam. She is 90 tons, built by Abeking & Rasmussen in 1930—composite steel and mahogany framework. She has a three-cylinder, 30- to 40-h.p. Daimler-Benz Diesel motor. She has one double cabin having two wide lower bunks and two folding upper bunks— very smart; one single cabin and four additional guest bunks in the ward room, covered in Viennese red leather; two complete bunks in the deck-house, and a crew of four with accommodations forward.

The crew consists of four men: Captain Jariilo Walter, his brother Ahto (mate), Joe Fredericks (cook and steward), Ernest Fredericks (deck hand). As for the sails, she has a complete cruising rig with a liberal supply of light air and square sails and a set of ten flax storm sails, a loose-footed mainsail, a mizzen that brails into the mast, and two steering stations.

She has raced across the Atlantic, cruised in the Baltic and Scandinavian waters, and twice crossed the North Sea.

Saturday, June 9th.

We let go the anchor at Delos at 8:45 in the morning. The water was marvelously clear and we could see the anchor catch at six fathoms. We all went in for a swim; it was a great pleasure and woke us up properly. After breakfast we went ashore in a motor boat that came out to meet us. It has a lovely little harbor, blue as can be, an island very much like those in Labrador—except when one sets foot on it and sees all the ruins. It had been pretty well restored—one could see the plan clearly, and there were enough remains standing to really be interesting to those who are not archaeologists. We spent about an hour walking about with a guide, and then I left them and made a drawing of an old temple.

From there I went down to the museum. It is a modern structure, built along German lines, by the French, and has fragments of interest. There were some more ruins about the museum, the best of which was a row of lions. Lily made a nice sketch of them but I did not have time. I thought the best preserved and most interesting things in Delos were the mosaic floor patterns. Our guide wet them to bring out the colors more clearly, and I took photographs of them.

We went aboard *Landfall* at one o'clock and had lunch while under way for Naxos. Had a fine breeze and made about 7½ knots. I slept till 4:30, when we were coming into Naxos. We dropped anchor there at 5:15 and were met, in a most royal fashion, by the mayor and all his officers. I did not like this part much but the others did. When we arrived at the dock, the whole town was waiting there to greet us. They all thought Nick was the President's brother. This misinformation was gotten from a Greek newspaper which had an article with a photograph of Nick, labeled, "The brother of Franklin Roosevelt." I had to stand by Paul for a while to translate some of his queer questions, for they only spoke French. I hated this and was very embarrassed, but got out of it, thank God, soon, to make a water color. I was left alone on a breakwater for the rest of the afternoon and had a grand time. Went back to the boat for dinner at 7:30 and after that I was sleepy but had to stay and sing songs in the cabin with Lily, who played the so-called piano, and Mrs. Hammond the accordion.

Monday, June 11th. Kos.

We had a swim before breakfast and then went ashore. There was not *much* of a reception there, thank the Lord. Kos is all that I have read about it, and comes up to my most vivid dreams. I just loved it. I wandered about happily by myself, taking pictures here and there, and made two sketchy lithographs. The view of the inner harbor from the fort was the best. I would love to have had more time to paint there, but, of course, those not artistically inclined get sooner tired of sight-seeing and want to get back. I had to be back aboard at ten but we didn't set sail until almost eleven.

Kos struck me with its new energy. It seems that only three years ago the entire town was destroyed by an earthquake, and they are busy rebuilding it. Their mode of construction is of the latest, and their architecture seems good. On the other hand, I was delighted with the old Turks who were wandering all about, and there were many old picturesque spots left.

We weighed anchor at 11:35 and headed for Rhodes. There was not much wind and we had to use our engine all the way. I spent a peaceful, lazy day, and Mrs. Hammond read aloud to us about the medicine of the Greeks at the time when Kos was the center of the medical world. We dropped anchor in Rhodes at ten o'clock. I turned in on deck, where the mosquitoes would not bother me, and slept like a log. Turkish music came floating over the water to put me to sleep. It was like being in some strange dreamland instead of reality, and was delightful and exciting lying there.

Tuesday, June 12th.

I woke up on deck and saw a fortified Moorish town with walls much like those in Spain, with minarets sticking up all about. I hurried ashore, leaving the others, for I wanted to wander by myself and absorb it with no English voices about me. I walked for hours and my feet gave way by noon, but I'm sure I had seen much that many have not seen there—the Orient as it is—but the clean Orient, not the hot, dusty, dirty Orient. Mine was cool, smell-less and quiet! I had promised to meet the Hammonds at their hotel, so I went back to the ship to collect the bathing suits and we had a grand swim.

Later, the Governor's car came to drive us to Lindos. It was an open car, and we could see much better from it than from the one in which we had driven over to Sunium. The driver looked very snappy in a white coat with blue trimmings. The car carried an Italian flag on the radiator cap. Everywhere the people scattered to make way for us, and we made good time. The drive was exquisite: the country had much the same appearance as that from Athens to Sunium, in the way of grain and crops, but the mountains were higher and more cragged and there were glimpses of the sea every now and then, which looked superb from that height. We got to Lindos about five and immediately started up the hill towards the ruined Frankish castle.

The streets of Lindos were immaculately clean and were paved with river pebbles, in designs of black and white. The houses were all whitewashed, and there were many flowers about in old "Shell" oil cans, also whitewashed. It seems that in this part of the world everybody uses these oil cans for their flowers, and for many other purposes. They cut them horizontally and vertically and put them in rows. I walked up towards the castle, where the only smells were of incense, and flowers. There was literally no dirt anywhere: it was one of the cleanest places I have ever seen, even in Switzerland, Austria or Holland!

The walk up the mountain side was spectacular—many distant views of the bay, coves and mountains, and splendid cloud effects. On entering the castle I was confronted with an enormous flight of steps leading to the front door; there was a trireme carved in the rock and a semicircular seat beside it, at the bottom. They were beautiful, and I mounted them and entered into a sort of covered hall. This part had been restored to show what some of it must have looked like originally. The remainder was more or less in ruins, with here and there some columns that have been re-erected. The main thing was the views to be had from the top. It must certainly have been an impenetrable fort in its day. The stone they used looked to me like some sort of coral formation, and intermingled with it was black marble. This marble is what the hill is made of, and must have been obtained from the leveling out they did in order to build there. It gave the wall a nice play of light and dark. The coral stone is native to this part of the world and is very beautiful; it has a slightly reddish tint, almost a yellow ochre. It is very porous and could probably only be used in this climate—but it is effective.

We drove back to Rhodes late in the evening and I went back to the boat, while the Hammonds dined at the hotel with Nick and some officials.

Thursday, June 14th.

We sailed all day with a fine breeze and fair weather, and hove in sight of Crete in the afternoon, running along

its coast at a distance of a mile for six hours. It was beautiful and I saw countless windmills on the shore; they
were in clusters, like dandelion gone to seed. We were too
far away for me to take a picture, but I have seen nothing
like it anywhere else. We did not reach Candia until noon.
It was quite rough during the late afternoon and evening.
Both Nick and I felt ill and lay down in the cockpit aft.
Every time we came about Paul would shout "Ready
about," and then "Hard-a-lee"—and if we did not both
answer *each* time, he repeated the order until we both
did. He was just "training the boys," as he expressed it
later on!

Friday, June 15th.

At Candia I went ashore right after breakfast to see
what it was like. I had a hard time getting a boat to take
me in, but finally, after much shouting and whistling
through a megaphone, I attracted the attention of an old
fisherman. He was a great character. He landed me at the
dock and I started my walk. I went on to the quay and
started a water color, but I saw the Hammonds arriving
before I was through. They had obtained the best car on
the Island, which was a 1930 Studebaker. I must say it was
in fair condition, although it smelt rather badly and I am
sure was filled with fleas, but I was so covered with flea
powder that I was untouchable!

We drove to the palace of Minos at Knossos. It was a
most interesting, if not beautiful, excavation. I did not
personally like the way some of the buildings had been
restored, but we are lucky to have anything at all, for it is
all due to Mr. Evans and his money and work that it exists. I have a book about it. We walked about until I
dropped with fatigue, and having seen so much that I was

all mixed up. We drove over to a funny little town about 11 kilometers due west of Knossos. We had a hard time getting any food there, the natives had had no visitors for two years. We ended by getting bread, goats' cheese, boiled eggs and wine—strong wine, and those who drank it got rather drunk! We found a fellow who had once had a restaurant in New York and who now has a grape vineyard there. He took us all about his vineyard and explained the entire process to us. We stopped in at his house and tasted some of his wine. He gave us almonds with it, which made it taste very good, and he gave us a large bottle of it to take aboard. We then drove back to the museum at Candia about four, and were fascinated by it, and stayed on until 6:30. I feel that we have seen something that not many people have seen, or will see, unless they go to Crete. We went aboard tired and dirty at seven, dined, and went to bed.

Saturday, June 16th.

We stopped the boat at noon and all went for a swim. (We were then half way between Crete and Santorin.) The water was lovely and warm and we had a grand time. During the day I painted the oars of the dinghy white and blue (Paul's racing colors). The day had been pleasant and we were nearing Santorin.

We arrived at Santorin at 5:45 and made fast to a buoy with our bow line and carried a stern line to the quay. Paul sighted the boat of Conner O'Brien as we came in and was very excited to meet him. He has been corresponding for years with him—and had read his book, *Across Three Oceans* [1927]—but had never met him. We hailed him as we came to rest and he came aboard. He was a very nice Englishman, looking like King George.

He had with him a German, another Englishman who looked like Prince Albert, and his wife. We made a date with them to dine at a restaurant in the town and then all went ashore.

On the quay we were met by about thirty men with their donkeys and mules. I hardly had time to see that I was on the quay before I was bodily picked up and set on a mule. It was a strange sensation, but after I had time to look about I saw that I was mounted on the best animal in the place and had a saddle. This was quite extraordinary as all the other donkeys had, on their backs, a queer sort of pack-saddle made out of sticks. We were all mounted immediately, and started up the hill. Nick seemed to be left behind and it took some time to explain that we must stop and wait for him; but finally it sunk into them. He came along plodding on his ass. The road was terribly steep, a series of long steps all the way to the top. It was a climb of 980 feet and the road must have been a mile and a half long, winding back and forth. It was spectacular, as we rose rapidly. The yachts became mere specks before we reached the top. On arriving there, we found a completely white town, running along the top of the ridge. It was about three miles long and there was not one level spot in it all the way. I heard that it has ten thousand inhabitants and eighty churches. It *must* have eighty churches, because everywhere I looked I saw one.

I walked about for some time. The streets seemed to be built on other people's roofs and ran up and down haphazardly. They are all paved in rough cobbles but are not hard to walk on.

I met the others of our party at the only hotel at eight. It was a dirty place but that did not make any difference, since the company was so delightful. I sat on Mrs.

O'Brien's left and found her very interesting. She is a painter, and he is a writer, and they earn their living by practicing both their arts while cruising about the world. They live on a 30-footer, *Saoirse*, which is stoutly built but not handsome. He had been around the world in her, before he married, and ever since they have been married they have lived on her all the year round. The O'Briens seemed very distressed because their crew wanted to go back; and they were obliged to cut their trip short in order to take them home, as they had made a contract to do so. Mrs. O'Brien told me of many places and things she had painted, and I found her entrancing.

Dinner being over, we walked down the long flight of steps again, and our knees shook badly nearing the bottom. There are some 1500 steps, without a break in them. We all rowed out to *Landfall* and showed the O'Briens the ship.

Sunday, June 17th.

The O'Briens came aboard again for breakfast, and when that was over I left with Sis to go ashore. She and I went to make sketches. (Let me add that we had to work hard in order to get this day to sketch, as Paul, as usual, wanted to start at four in the morning and just *sail*), but we all got stubborn, and said we would desert, if he did not see our way of thinking. We are always five to one— yet he wins every time. This time, however, he had his dear sailor friend to talk to, and he *did;* he never left the ship all day. On shore we got donkeys and went up. It is great fun, this donkey riding, and it does not seem to be as flea-y as it *sounds* and *looks*. In fact I have had no fleas since I have been on donkeys.

We walked quite a long way before we settled down to

drawing, but we found a nice windmill on the summit, of which I made two water colors. Afterwards Sis joined me and we ate lunch. The farmers were so nice and set a table for us with all sorts of nice things on it, and we ate there in delight for some time. Then Sis left for one place, and I walked up to another with my nice guide-friend, and found an amusing little church that I made a sketch of. After that I walked up for another two miles and came to another town. I went into one of the many churches there and found, to my delight, that it was not ugly as I had imagined, and that behind the altar was a large, carved wooden screen, with paintings—a lovely thing—and I have never seen anything like it elsewhere. It may be a style particular to this island. The paintings were about 2 feet by 3½. The clothes of the figures were done in raised gold and silver, with holes cut for the face and hands, which were painted on the background. They were really beautifully done, by some master artist. Besides these, there were many small ones about 6 by 12 inches, done in the same manner. They had the look of Russian icons, but the subjects were not conventionally religious; there were men with flowing beards riding horses, and the like.

From here I walked rapidly back to the windmill, for I had an appointment to go with Sis to the volcano at three. We ran down the long flight of steps. It was easier this time; still my feet were all blisters by the time I got down. We were rowed out to *Landfall* and changed into bathing suits. Mrs. Hammond joined us, and we were rowed over to the volcano. It was weird. As we approached, sulphur fumes attacked our nostrils and the sea water became warmer. When we were very close, the water became very hot—almost too hot to put one's hand

into. There were lots of funny white things floating about.
I think it was some form of sulphur, for they were where
the water was warmest.

We landed, and climbed it. The formation was interesting—black, red, and yellow, no blue or green. We went
up to the rim of the crater and the ground there was very
hot, too hot to put your hand on with comfort. I fell down
once. As I was only in bathing trunks, the hot pumice and
my sliding were painful. I rolled down some distance, but,
fortunately, did not actually cut myself; but it was *sure
hot*. Having come down again we all went in for a swim
in the sulphurous hot water. It was very different from all
other swims. It was hot on top, but a few inches under the
surface it was much colder. The thing to do was to swim
as flat as possible, and get the full benefit of the heat. It
got so hot in one place that I had to change my course and
swim for cooler water. (This swim must have been good
for my many flea-bites.) Then we rowed back to the ship
and set sail for Aegina. I had the watch from one to four
and from eight to twelve and was good and tired by the
end. Paul *will* insist on sailing at night.

Monday, June 18th.

We spent the day on board until 5 o'clock, when we
dropped anchor at Aegina. There was a storm in the offing
but we decided that we would go ashore and see if we
could not get to the temple of Aphaia, which was about
one hour off in a car, or three hours on a donkey. A sailboat belonging to a fisherman took us ashore, and we
found a car on the quay, and what a car! It was in competition with those in Crete, a "tin lizzy" of 1929 vintage,
with an awful old torn top and smashed fender. Its tires
were so badly gone that they had put actual bolts and nuts

in the holes to try to hold them together. The inner tube was exposed in most places, and it seemed a wonder that it got over and back without a blowout—the road was simply marvelous! At times I could not see which was road and which was just barren rocks, or piles of dirt, but the driver was a great fellow, and certainly knew how to drive. We pounded and joggled over there, and got some asses to take us the remainder of the way. The approach to Aphaia was through a pine forest. The wind of a storm was howling through them and there were dramatic cloud effects everywhere. My camera gave out at this moment and I was unable to take any more pictures. I made one poor attempt at a litho, but a spattering of rain spoiled that.

The donkey-ride back was fun. I was enveloped in the blanket of my pack-saddle—it kept off the cold wind and rain which had now set in—and we arrived back at the car in a deluge. The car was not much better. The top leaked like a sieve, and we were all drenched. The road was now very slippery and we slid from side to side. The others were so nervous at one point that Paul ordered them "all out," but I refused, and rode on in style. The driver tried to take the same short cut that he had taken coming over, but had no success, as it was too slippery. (We slid down backwards and almost went over the bank, they said, although I did not think so, but anyway there was some cut stone before the embankment that would have stopped us.) After a very eventful ride back to the town we arranged for a boat to take us out to the ship. The only thing we could find was an open rowboat with a makeshift sail. They stretched a sun-awning over it, but it just increased the amount of water that went down our backs! We took turns standing up rowing, to keep us warm. It was a long row, about an hour, as *Land-fall* could come no closer to shore, the water there being very shallow. Aboard ship we changed and were soon warm again, with a coal fire burning in the grate; we dined and had a good long sleep, which was much needed.

Tuesday, June 19th.

We set sail for Corinth at 8:30 after a good swim and breakfast. The weather was rather more cloudy than usual, but made the scenery more beautiful; it was almost unbelievable. This sail up the Gulf of Aegina and into the Gulf of Athens is almost the best yet as far as scenery is concerned.

As we approached the canal of the isthmus of Corinth, we saw the *Calatea* emerge. We headed for her, as Helenka Adamowska was on board her, and came up close to her, but could not see Helenka until we had almost passed; then the figure of a woman appeared on deck and they all cried that that was she. She must have been nervous, for we were sailing in the opposite direction from her and apparently meant to have nothing to do with her!

We came to the mouth of the canal at 12:30 and had to anchor because a tug and barge were coming through it in the opposite direction. The authorities came aboard and arranged our papers, etc. (It cost 1000 drachmas for our boat—she is 90 tons.) Our lunch being over and the blue flag instead of the red one having been hoisted on the mast, we proceeded. It was fun going through. I always like going through canals. We saw some divers when we were halfway through and almost cut one of their air hoses with our keel (slight exaggeration). Otherwise it was not an eventful passage. We dropped anchor inside the breakwater at the northeast end of the canal at about

3:30. Nick went ashore to get a car, etc. The rest of us
worked on making *Landfall* fast to the breakwater. It was
a long operation with a bow line, stern line and anchor.
We got through about five and started for Mycenae in the
best looking car we have had while in Greece—a 1929
Buick touring car, in marvelous condition. The driver
made me nervous by turning off his ignition on every hill
we came to. He was a dumbbell, too. He never guessed
anything I meant with my sign language, as most of the
others had.

We passed one marvelous scene on our way to Mycenae
—a small town or village, where all the people were out
flaying wheat. One man and his wife were being towed
around in a circle by four horses. They each stood on a
thing that looked like a surfboard; it had steel knives on
the bottom, which cut open the chaff and liberated the
grain. Another man then threw up this mixture in the air
and let the wind blow away the chaff.

We arrived in Mycenae just in time for the sunset. The
entrance was most impressive with its huge blocks and all
such a lovely color, but the lion gate was too poorly lit to
see clearly. We wandered about for a short while, then
sat down and just *looked*—it was marvelous. The clouds
were black like the mountains but their fringes were pink
and rose. After this lovely sunset, that lasted a long time,
we went down to our hotel.* It was very small, and did
not look too good when we drove up, but when we went
in we found it to be a nice, clean little place. There were
iron beds in each room and one wash-stand, and that was
all, but it was immaculate! We dined out under the
trees and had delicious local food and wine. Nick and I

---

* Then called La Belle Hélène de Menelaüs. [Author's note.]

shared one room, and Mrs. Hammond and Lily the other.
We all slept like tops—no mosquitoes and no flies!

Wednesday, June 20th.

We had breakfast under the trees, but in the sun this
time. Then we got back in the car and drove up to Mycenae again, this time with a guide. He showed us about
and we visited the tomb of Agamemnon for the first time.
It is the grandest thing we have seen yet. It is a conically
vaulted, or more correctly, parabolically circular tomb,
with a smaller one connecting. The approach is a long
slanting cut in the hill leading up to it. It is built on the
same principles as the tombs of the kings in Egypt and
has very much the same look from the outside. The circular hall is 14 meters in diameter inside and is 15 meters
high. It is made of 33 stone courses and they are enormous
stones; but the lintel over the door is *the* extraordinary
thing: it is one solid stone—brought 6 kilometers, by
slaves and pushed into place by the sweat of men—meas-
uring 8 meters 50 long by 3 meters thick, 1 meter 22 high,
and weighing 120 tons. It is the largest stone in place in
Europe. On the inside, it is cut concave to fit the arc of the
tomb—a marvelous bit of engineering. I don't see how
they got it into place without block and tackle. Notice
that the column between the lions is inverted, like those
of Knossos. It was the first way of making a column. The
lions' heads, which were of bronze, are gone.

We drove back to Corinth, and what a road! Bump,
joggle, thump, bang, all the way, even in our *swell* car.
We got to Corinth at sunset. I looked up Mr. Stillwell.
He is a very nice young man with an aesthetic face. He
was playing tennis at the time but joined us later at the
museum. He made our visit most interesting and told me

lots I wanted to know. He was very glad to hear of Rowdy and van der Gracht: he evidently had been at college with them. He showed me the first attempts at a Corinthian capital, as I had asked how this capital got its name. It was much like the capitals at Knossos except it had channels cut in it with holes where there must have been bronze acanthus leaves attached. This, he said, was the origin of the Corinthian capital and the Romans, when they saw it, copied it and pushed it further and further until they reached what we know today. They gave or kept the name Corinthian, funnily enough. The temple here was badly shaken by earthquakes, but six columns still stand, and they are a lovely sepia. The sun setting behind them made them unearthly and beautiful.

We met Helenka Adamowska here. She had come down with Paul, who had gone to Athens to get her. She seems very charming. We all drove back to the boat, which was lying in the breakwater, having been repainted by fourteen men.

Thursday, June 21st. Delphi.

Once on shore we drove up to Delphi in two cars. We passed through some lovely olive groves on the way. They tell me that this grove produces the best olive oil in Greece; that nowhere else can they come near this in quality.

At Delphi the museum was full of lovely original things, and also many reconstructions of architectural fragments. The theatre was in a very good state of preservation, almost as much so as that of Epidaurus. We sat there for almost an hour without speaking—it was so lovely. I then made a rough sketch of the Treasury before we left. Coming down the view was beautiful all the way.

We went in for a swim and it was delicious but cold. It was dark by now and we had much fun.

Friday, June 22nd.

We weighed anchor at 6:00 A.M. from Itea for Patras. Sunny, without much wind, but later on we had a severe thunderstorm, with much lightning. Then later in the morning we had a fine breeze and calm water. It was a beautiful sail in the Gulf of Corinth. The gulf at this point is narrow and it is very much like sailing in a river. At the narrows there were forts on each side, which were most picturesque. All day we had lovely clouds, thick cumulus ones.

We got to Patras by 3:45 and moored off the end of the lighthouse pier with our anchor out in the harbor, with a stern line onto the pier. We had been previously informed that our train for Olympia would leave at 4:30 and had been reckoning on that, but as we tied up we heard, to our horror, that it left much earlier and that we had just ten minutes left to catch it; but we did, though it took much hustling on my part, as I was standing by the hauser when Paul shouted "Into the boat." I had only a bathing suit on and had to pack and dress in just two minutes. I acted quickly and did everything necessary except that I did not have a book to read on the train, which was a bore. Our train was a train, if ever I have seen one. The engine was a shunting engine of 1892, made in Alsace-Lorraine. It was one of those that have the engine and coal-car combined, and the cars were all four-wheelers, very short; a first- and second-class coach, two third-class coaches and about twelve freight cars. We all were in one first-class compartment and it was very hot.

We came to one station about an hour out of Patras,

where many men and boys came to the train's side with
chickens tied by their feet, hanging upside down. They
seemed to sell them to the passengers through the windows. It seemed a funny custom to be selling live chickens
and ducks to train riders, but it seems that it is quite an
ordinary custom in Greece. A conductor passed through
the train, after we had left the station, and collected the
animals from the various buyers and gave them, in return,
checks like hat checks. He seemed to have a car forward
where he put them during the trip. Funny people, these
Greeks! Coming back, however, it was not the same. The
people in my compartment kept their chickens on the
floor, and they cackled and crowed so much at times I
finally had to move out. The aisle was filled with them
too. It is lucky we caught no lice from them. The ride
down was eventful, with many stops where the engineer
and fireman had coffee, and the conductors saw their
friends. The train never exceeded forty miles per hour,
and rarely attained that. We arrived at Pirgos, where we
had to change trains, at about six o'clock. This train took
us direct to Olympia.

Olympia is entirely different from the other places we
have seen. It has many trees and is very green. The valley
it is in reminded me very much of the valley of the Seine,
near Vernon, but it has, instead of poplar trees, cypresses
and pines. It is a lovely spot but really not very characteristic of Greece. We had a fine dinner and then went
straight to bed.

Saturday, June 23rd.
Nick and I got up early and took another shower before
going to breakfast. Afterwards I went down to the museum. It is a charming little place, all done in the orig-

inal Greek style. In it are some of the finest pieces I have yet seen. I was all alone so could sit as long as I liked in front of each statue. There were two lovely pediments and, of course, the Hermes of Praxiteles. In the side rooms were many gargoyles, lions with their mouths open, in terra cotta, and griffons; also small bronze implements and treasures. Afterwards, I made my way into the ruins from a hillside, and not by the way one is supposed to enter. It was very nice because I had no guide bothering me or anybody else making remarks, and I found a nice place to make a sketch of the Heraion.

Nick, Helenka, Lily and I dined ashore at a small restaurant and went back to the boat to sleep, but none of us could, as there were many radios and much singing ashore all night. The Greeks seem to be much like the Spaniards in that respect: they stay up all night and keep up a big noise.

Monday, June 25th.

We weighed anchor at 4:30 and headed again for Corfu. It was a misty morning, with not a breath of air to fill our sails.

The wind freshened later on and we had a good sail. We got to the town of Corfu at 4:30 and dropped anchor. Once at Corfu we were rowed ashore in a small boat and hired the best looking car in the place, which was a 1932 touring Nash. It was nice and comfortable but the road, as usual, was very poor and dusty and it took us an hour to go 28 kilometers. The drive over was splendid and this island, above all the others, is the most beautiful. It is covered with trees and grass and is the first place that has had green grass, that we have been on, on our trip. It is rich in olive groves, tobacco and grapes. The peasants in their native costumes wear white cloth hats and white aprons and look rather Dutch. The women seem to do *all* the work, but I suppose it only seems so. We saw them, caring for the cattle and goats, carrying wheat on their heads, and breaking stones for the roadway. We passed one house that was under construction and all the work being done entirely by women—and always in their sweet costumes.

This island looks like Bermuda—full of little coves and bays that are tremendously deep, with clear water—sunny weather and not too dry. There is plenty of fresh water and it would be a perfect place for someone to come and spend a month or two quietly living on a small boat and cruising about. Every cove is worth exploring and painting: they are all different and charming in their own way. I should love to come back here.

On returning to the town of Corfu, the Hammonds decided to sleep ashore, but Nick, Helenka and I went back to the ship. It was a lovely moonlit night and Helenka and I went for a short row before swimming and turning in. There was an orchestra on the shore, which was playing sweet music, and it seemed very much like Venice.

Tuesday, June 26th. Corfu.

I met Nick and Helenka at the hotel, where we lunched together. We then drove back to the pier and went aboard and steamed over to Albania. At last I put foot on shore and it was at a lovely spot in a marsh that we had rowed to, and there was a great big fishery near there where I amused myself by rowing about until Nick got back. I also took a ride in a very primitive boat to see some fish. The boatman poled it with a trident. Things are primitive here, but the Albanians have a reputation to keep up.

Wednesday, June 27.

We started at five for Yugoslavia. The day has been perfectly calm, without a breath of wind. We have been keeping close to the shore of Albania all the way. It is arid, though beautiful, but seems to have no one on it. Of course it is so mountainous that it would be hard for anybody to live on the coast. There have been occasional olive groves, or what look like them through the binoculars, but no cottages nearby. We have passed several small towns high up on the hillside but that is all.

Thursday, June 28th. Yugoslavia.

Came on watch at 4:00 A.M. and took the wheel again for an hour after lunch.

At 3:30 P.M. we were off Fort Momula at the entrance of Topula Bay, on our way to Cattaro. It is a very impressive approach: green hills in the foreground and high, dry mountains in the rear. The weather is very hot in the sun but cool in the shade. On turning east in Topula Bay we saw the navy base and millions of brown men lying in the sun on the beach; also countless little sailing craft with young men and women in them sailing about the harbor. There are many villas on the shore; it is the most populated spot we have put into on our cruise. The houses are strung out here instead of being all huddled together as they have been in Greece.

On turning south in Cattaro Bay itself, we saw the most magnificent sight—breathtaking! High mountains on all sides of peaceful water, with many craft of all descriptions sailing about! Mrs. Hammond discovered why so many people were out; it was the celebration of King Alexander's assassination in 1914, a national holiday here. We

anchored a hundred yards from shore and were immediately met by the American Express agent and port authorities. All the people of this country seem to be
so polite—it is a pleasure to deal with them. In every way
this country seemed to me what Sweden or Norway must
be like.

Mrs. Hammond, Nick, Lily and Helenka went ashore,
and motored up the side of the mountain to get a general
view of the vicinity, but I stayed below and made two
water colors. The place hypnotized me: I could not take
my eyes off it. After making two sketches, I had a swim.
The water was frigid—so unexpected, as we had been
having warm water everywhere. It was only 65 degrees
here. I could not account for it until I had gone ashore
and then the reason was clear. On shore all along the
waterfront were springs of cold fresh water bubbling up.
In one place, at a distance of about 50 feet, an entire
river sprang up. I have never seen anything like it before.
This is the only place we have seen that has so much fresh
water at its disposal, and yet they have no fountains!

Cattaro, as I soon found out, is a town built close against
the mountain, with a marvelous wall all around it. The
wall is built right on the side of the steep slope and looks
like the great wall of China. The town itself is Venetian,
picturesque and unspoiled. On entering through an
arched gate, you are confronted with a clock tower. The
place in which it is, is like an opera set—small buildings,
colorful. Some of them look as if they were made out of
cardboard and had painted stone joints. Most of them
have nice stone balconies and green shutters. The lettering on a great many of the shops is Russian, but the remainder is in Roman script. Helenka spoke Polish to them,

and they seemed to understand readily. I walked about for some time alone. It was lovely in the lamplight, snooping about the little streets, all quiet, for the better part of the populace was promenading on the waterfront. I went into one little church, but it was not very rewarding. I watched the folk walking up and down the esplanade, and was impressed by the great majority of young girls there were between the ages of twelve and sixteen. Some of them were pretty but most of them not. The men, on the contrary, were very handsome—all fairly blond. This may have been only the action of the sun on their cropped heads, but I think not.

We had an excellent dinner of wienerschnitzel and beer. Nick loves this beer but I confess I don't. I have had better beer in all other countries, except perhaps France.

We all went out to *Landfall* at 9:30 and turned in. I slept on deck and it was delicious. I tried Nick's idea of an old stocking around my eyes and it worked beautifully.

Friday, June 29th.

We weighed anchor at 10:15 for Ragusa. Going out of the harbor was just as beautiful as going in and the water in the outer harbor was all lovely and warm again. We have passed many steamboats; the place seemed to be full of them and these Yugoslavian boats seem very clean and shipshape. Outside again we headed north for Ragusa. It was pretty as we hugged the coast of Yugoslavia. The rocks were highly colored—and sometimes it was green on the mountainsides. As we approached the port of Ragusa, we saw the S.S. *Homeric* anchored there. She looked huge lying in such a small port. There were many small boats and launches milling about and we searched through the glasses hoping to recognize somebody, but saw no one we knew. We dropped anchor 300 yards off the inner harbor, dressed and went ashore.

I came across a church procession on its way up to a small chapel. It was interesting to see the natives in their costumes. Some were very beautiful. This procession was in celebration of All Saint's Day.

Sunday, July 1st. Ragusa.

We set sail for Korčula. We had gusty winds all day and got to Korčula at 4:00 P.M. and anchored in a small cove next to the town of Korčula itself, about one mile overland. This little cove was completely protected from winds and waves—a sweet place. We all went ashore with raincoats, for the weather looked ominous, and had a walk of about a mile to the town. I found the town charming. You mount a flight of steps to the town gate and come into a little 2 x 4 place with a silly little church and a tiny column with a broken lion on top of it. Going on up the street one sees many sorts of gargoyles projecting from the houses, which must have supported balconies at one time. The stone of the buildings is a lovely color—rich orange and brown tints. I only made one drawing, but every corner of this town seemed worth exploring. I started into the big church, but I made such a noise in opening the door that the whole congregation turned around to look at me, and as I had a pack on my back and my old raincoat on, I was too embarrassed to enter further. Then I could not shut the damned door and that made it worse. I was so frightened that I just left it open and fled down the street.

Korčula's main industry is boat building and almost everywhere you look you see boats on ways.

Helenka, Nick and I met for dinner. The food was good and we had music but *what* a price! We screamed like peahens, but to no avail, and we had to pay.

Tuesday, July 3rd.

We got to Trogir at eleven and I immediately started making a water color. Trogir is lovely, a 15th-Century town, in good condition, with good architecture and picturesque views. The chief industry is almonds and going down one street I saw hundreds of women and children cracking them by the thousands. The street was literally covered with nut shells. The other big industry is making barrels to ship the nuts in. One half of the townspeople make barrels while the other half crack the nuts. Seeing this nut cracking, though, was just luck, because they only crack nuts for three days a year, and we happened to come on one of the three days. They crack so many in the three days that they don't need to do any more for a year. Trogir is the center of the almond country of Dalmatia, which is the largest almond growing country in the world. They supply 80% of the almonds of the world from this small acreage. The women earn about 25 dinars a day cracking them, and if one has ten children working for her the family makes 250 dinars or $5.00, which is very good for this part of the world. They collect the nuts in September and keep them until July, letting them dry thoroughly. They sell some green ones to France but she is the only country which buys them green.

I made a drawing in Trogir and then took the boat back at 4:00 P.M. with Nick and Helenka. We had a swim before a lunch of fish fried over charcoal.

All Yugoslavian boats seem to be good. When we got back I visited Diocletian's palace, which is an enormous

place with a town inside it. In the center is the mauso-
leum or tomb of Diocletian and from its portal I made a
picture of the arches. There is a large statue by Mestrovic
in the place; it seems to me out of scale, but he is a marvelous sculptor and we have seen many splendid things of
his up and down the coast.

We dined together in a small restaurant inside the palace walls—a nice little place in the open air, and drove
back to *Landfall* afterwards.

Wednesday, July 4.

We sailed for Zara (a free port) at 6:30 A.M. It was a
fine day, with not too much wind. We could not swim at
noon because there was too much wind to stop here, but it
died out; at four o'clock, however, it suddenly picked up
astern and blew at about ten miles per hour, just to the
white cap point, and we heeled over beautifully. It was
the best sail we have had on the whole cruise, and the only
time it has blown abaft the beam. (When a sailing ship in
these waters is taking this same route at this time of year
—June and July—she should start from the north and
work southwards, and then west and back, as the prevail-
ing winds blow that way. We have had head winds all the
time except when there has been a local thunderstorm in
the offing.) Paul ordered down the mizzen and jib and we
were all disappointed, but we saw that it was a sensible
precaution. We still went at a good rate and came into
Zara at about 5:30 and dropped anchor, dined aboard and
then rowed ourselves ashore, that is, Helenka, Nick, Lily,
John and I. We walked about, Nick acting as guide, but
Zara is not a beautiful place, though it's a good place for
shopping because there are no taxes. We bought quanti-

ties of American cigarettes. One can get them cheaper here than in New York.

July 5th, Thursday. Zara.

Got up at seven and set sail under power. While under way we pulled out all the extra gear, which is to be stowed on shore at Lussin Piccolo. There has been a light head wind all day. Everybody has had a whack at the Dulcitone, which is our swinging table, ballast and musical instrument. It did not sound right to me, and the pedal didn't work, so I decided to take it apart. I found that it was made up of a series of tuning forks and by moving a rubber strap on each, one could get more or less vibration out of them. I also repaired the pedal and put it together again and it was much improved.

We got into Lussin Piccolo at seven and had dinner before going ashore. We hired a car and drove to a lovely spot but, unfortunately, there was no music. We had a good time, nevertheless, and drank beer and posed riddles to each other.

July 6th, Friday. Lussin Piccolo.

I was wakened by the laundry being taken away from under me and my head; it had to go ashore early so that was the reason. I swam before breakfast and found the water warmer than ever. It is strange how the farther north we go the water and air become warmer, especially the water. I finished my final packing and rowed my baggage over to the pier in the dinghy, had my passport put in order, etc., and came back, said good-by to all the crew and then to everyone else except Paul, who came down to the dock to see me off. It was the best send-off I have ever had, I think.

The *Francesco Morisini* is quite a swell boat. It would seem that all these Italian boats are good, they are new and clean. I am on my way to my beloved parents in Brioni now and hope to find them well and have a good time with them there. I am very sorry to leave *Landfall* and her crew. It has been really a marvelous cruise and I am grateful to have seen much and learned lots.

So ends "That Greek Trip."

Athens to Istanbul, 1935

Unlike the previous chapter, the cruise of 1935 is not an on-the-spot account. None of us kept a day-to-day diary that year so I am now relying on my goddess Mnemosyne to hand me threads that may have some tie-in with what is happening today.

That was the year that we made Istanbul our objective. We found it hard not to forget and call it Constantinople in those days, for that had been the name used by the non-Moslem world for 500 years, and Constantinople it had stood, in every book we read. To Mustapha Kemal it was a matter of nationalism and pride to bring back the vocabulary of the Ottoman Empire, and though he moved the seat of government to Ankara in 1923, he preferred to recapture the Turkish name of his famous seaport; so Istanbul it then was, and still is.

Our friends Rachel and James Stuart joined us in Athens. He belongs to the type of Scotsman who is tall, handsome, fair, charming, and does not take himself, or anything else, too seriously. He is a direct descendant of the Earl of Moray who received his title at the hands of his half-sister, Mary Queen of Scots.

James's wife is one of the daughters of the late Duke of Devonshire. Her pretty fresh English complexion speaks eloquently of the healthy outdoor life she has always led. Training dogs and horses and sailing in small craft were

175

her constant recreation in her girlhood, and she was always the best of sports when it came to putting up with any kind of discomfort, as we soon learned.

The Earldom of Moray, which is the same as Murray, just as Stuart is often spelled Stewart, is one of the seven original earldoms of Scotland, its dominion roughly corresponding to the present counties of Ross and Inverness.

Some time after John Randolph, the third Earl of Moray, who was childless, was killed in battle in 1346, Henry Plantagenet, Duke of Lancaster, was made Earl of Moray by King David II. In 1372 the title came into the Dunbar family, who lost it when James Dunbar, the last of that family, was murdered in 1429.   ,

James IV later bestowed the title on his natural son James Stuart, and in 1562 Mary Queen of Scots bestowed it upon her half-brother, son of her father, James V. This James Stuart was murdered in 1570.

One of the two murdered Morays, the second Earl (also James Stuart), and known in a ballad as "The Bonnie Earl of Moray," is honored in a strange and macabre way in Darnaway Castle. One of the family's many and great estates is this handsome castle in Forres, Morayshire. Built of great gray blocks of stone, it stands in a lush, green, hilly countryside and must have been the silent witness to every kind of medieval stratagem and counter-stratagem.

We spent an interesting and delightful twenty-four hours with the Stuarts in their then homelike fortress, in 1938. It contains a great hall that, in former times was used for banquets, and for the holding of courts, for the administration of justice during the periodical visits to the North of one or another of the Stuart Kings. The room was almost empty of furniture when we were guided across its waxed and polished floor to be introduced to the murdered Moray mentioned above. He lies recumbent, a sort of painted effigy stabbed with many bloody wounds, in a lidded coffin, locked behind closed doors recessed in the wall. The painting was commissioned by his mother, to be used as a banner to be carried through the streets of Edinburgh to rouse the people against Huntly (a Gordon) who had murdered the "Bonnie Earl." It bears the date and the words "God revenge my Caus." The reigning Morays of the twentieth century seem to guard it as a family skeleton in the cupboard—to be venerated with averted eyes, and avoided at all times, except when foreign visitors must be entertained. Today, James's brother John bears the title of the nineteenth Earl of Moray. As for James himself, he served his country long and faithfully in the House of Commons as "whip for Scotland," and for seven years during the War and after, as chief Conservative whip to Winston Churchill, before becoming Secretary of State for Scotland from 1951 to 1957. In 1959, he left the House of Commons for the House of Lords when Queen Elizabeth honored him with the title of Viscount Stuart of Findhorn.

My husband has made many British friends, over the years, and in two world wars, and this is one of his oldest friendships, dating from Cowes Week in 1921. In that year, Paul was largely instrumental in starting the six-metre boat races, which have been one of the most competitive sailing events of every season. He took his Burgess designed *Sheila* over to Cowes that summer, but was unsuccessful, and Gerald Boardman won the series with *Grebe.*

As our little Italian steamer made fast one sunny May day in 1935 in the harbor of Piraeus, Paul and I looked over the side of the ship and were happy to find the Stuarts waiting to greet us. They waved gaily and James shouted, "We've been to the museum, but I can stand just so much sight-seeing and then I have to make for the nearest bar." As he is an epicure, and therefore our food suspect, we soon discovered that he had brought along a jar of Savora mustard, with which to make it more palatable.

After renewing the delights of Athens, and making a short trip to Delphi, we sailed around Cape Colonna, as we were on our way to Istanbul. At no other cape in the world, I suppose, have such countless sailors either fought adverse winds with fierce determination, or given up hope of ever sensing a breeze again, in the kind of tantalizing calm that kept Agamemnon's fleet in despair as they wallowed in the doldrums, and their leader conceived the sacrifice of his daughter, Iphegenia. Since time immemorial, and even today, a ship passing Cape Colonna, on which stands the beautiful Temple of Poseidon, dips her flag in tribute. In 1935 A.D., we were better treated than were the Fleet of Agamemnon in the second millennium B.C., or perhaps this was one of those occasions when our engines propelled us and the sails were auxiliary.

The next day we found ourselves in the narrow strait between the mainland and the island of Euboea. We steamed past the site of the battle of Marathon, contended with the swift currents of the Channel Euripos, and signalled for permission to go through the swing-bridge of Khalkis. Proceeding north through the Atalanta Channel, we left the site of Thermopylae on the mainland unvisited this time. Instead, we entered the Oreos Channel, where there are traces of interesting historic scenery on both shores, and took advantage of the usual afternoon sea breeze that springs up in that area. We then rounded Cape

Artemisium and headed directly for the peninsula of Khalkidiki. With its three-fingered hand grasping the northern waters of the Aegean, this peninsula has a curious resemblance to the three jagged headlands of the southern end of the Peloponnesus.

After a wonderful night sail, Paul called me on deck at daybreak to watch the deepening silhouette of the seven thousand foot Mt. Athos against the blaze of a splendid sunrise, but the Holy Mountain forfeited its charm for me, sunrise or sunset, knowing that I would be unwelcome there at any time. At this point, in Mrs. Lars Anderson's admirable, *A Yacht in Mediterranean Seas,** she turned her authorship over to her husband for two chapters, because he, not she, would be allowed to land on that sacred shore.

As Tom Whittemore had written about us to one of the high dignitaries, we were joined soon after our arrival by four picturesque monks with long black cassocks, long black hair, and long black beards. Three of them came smilingly aboard, but the fourth, the oarsman, sat on the thwart, head averted, back to, face down, the picture of misery, and acting as if everybody on board *Landfall* were the heretics that he believed us to be.

The other three were nice, happy priests, who accepted us (even the women as long as we stayed put) in their stride, and assumed that our men, heathen though they might be, could be accorded the hospitality of the voyager.

Paul, who loves to play the heathen whenever given a chance, dived below and came up with my accordion, saying that I must play "The Sidewalks of New York." I compromised by playing "Silent Night," and the three

* Boston: Marshall Jones, 1930.

black priests gallantly applauded, but the fourth remained in his boat, head averted, back to, face down, and
probably prayed that both he and we might be forgiven.

Then Paul and James were conducted to the St.
Panteleimon. This is the largest of the monasteries, with
beautiful inner courts and gardens, and where the "Guest
Master" receives the favored traveler. A great ringing of
magnificent bells was ordered in honor of the visiting foreigners, and they were shown all that was permissible, and
finally dispatched back to the wicked world. Athos is the
haunt of many a recluse, and here and there, against the
backdrop curtain of the dark, high mountains, you can see
a tiny, thin, wisp of smoke rising to the heavens from the
lone place of worship of one of these solitary hermits.

From Athos we proceeded to Troy. It was Emil Lud-
wig's *Schliemann*,* that had prepared us for what we were
to find in Troy, and we were so fortunate as to be able to
go there while our American field archaeologist, Professor Carl W. Blegen, was still engaged with the Turkish
archaeologist, Dr. K. Kourouniotis in discovering the nine
cities of Troy.

It would be difficult to overestimate the value of the
contribution that Professor and Mrs. Blegen and Professor and Mrs. W. T. Semple made during the thirty years
when they devoted their time, energies, and support to
this area of archaeological excavations, in the name of the
University of Cincinnati. Imaginative leadership, inexhaustible patience, and financial assistance, with the aid
of dedicated scholars of all ages and nationalities, have
achieved triumphant results. Many of their findings
brought facts to light that strengthen the belief that
there is an historic basis for the *Iliad* and the *Odyssey*. To

* Boston: Little, Brown, 1932.

find the proof that Homer's epics are founded on history has been the dream of scholars long before the astute Schliemann verified his inspired intuition.

We asked Professor Blegen if Schliemann had not caused a great deal of damage when he slashed through earth, enriched by the artifacts of eras of culture. Had Schliemann not irretrievably destroyed priceless works of art that could nowadays be saved by the technique of modern archaeology?

"Yes," he said, "many important and beautiful things were undoubtedly destroyed, but on the whole, I am glad he went ahead and did what he did, because I really believe that through his passionate determination to find what he was seeking, he brought much to light that might otherwise have escaped the timidity of the trained and reverent archaeologist."

The first city of Troy, which lies at the greatest depth of the excavations, dated about 2700 B.C., is primitive, and roughly hewn and little is known of its inhabitants. The second city, on the other hand, is five hundred years later in development and shows a far higher state of civilization. The progress from city to city is uneven, but somewhere along the level of the seventh city is a solid wall of the Greek Bronze Age, and that great wall, it is now believed, is the wall that surrounded the city of the *Iliad*.

It was during the fifth century A.D., that the last of the ancient Troys lost its grip on life and succumbed to the overgrowth of thyme and asphodel that sooner or later buries the treasures of antiquity. With a profusion of wild flowers come the bees—tiny indefatigable symbols of fertility worshipped through the Near and Middle East. With the bees come more wild flowers and with the wild flowers more nectar for food and more pollen to be scat-

tered. And as the bees produce more honey than they
need, man takes over the surplus, and one of the eternal
cycles of nature is re-established. Then comes the archaeologist, giving acquisitive attention to the green mound
of Hissarlik, and down goes the dig, and away fly the bees
to find another area in which to begin a new cycle.

At one time that morning, as we stood at the edge of this
great disorderly dig, we saw for the first time in our lives
the strange and colorful flight of a Jay-like bird known as
a Mediterranean roller. Out of the sunny sky above us suddenly dropped a succession of infinitesimal Nattier blue
apparitions tumbling head over heels as they fell chat-
tering—down, down, till they skimmed the white marble
herringbone-patterned pavement of the second city of
Troy. Having their own built-in lifting apparatus, they
righted themselves at will, without making a landing,
and soared up again into the blue, dropping in noisy and
ecstatic descent, for repeat performances.

Also indigenous to the Bosporus, is a less happy little
bird that was just as novel to us. It is a tiny black Petrel-
like sea bird that flies in flocks. They too come out of the
blue, this time horizontally, skimming the surface of the
water with excessive speed, and they never seem to reach
their destination—at least we never saw them rest on land
or sea. To the Turks they are the souls of the women of
the harem, paying for their sins; but Paul, who is less familiar with harems, christened them "The New York
Business Men," remembering his busy days in New
York.

Our next port of call was Istanbul.

We were eager to arrive in order to see our old friend
Thomas Whittemore, then engaged in his great work of
removing the plaster from the early Christian mosaics in

St. Sophia. Harvard University was once proud to claim both his father and himself as their number one and number two Byzantine scholars. He it was who had persuaded Atatürk to convert the largest and most impressive church in Christendom to another kind of place of worship—a museum. In point of fact this was not at all unsuitable as the Turkish University had formerly permitted the great scholars of Mohammed II to give their first courses in certain mosques. Tom was now hard at work, with many young assistants, using tools as large as a hoe and instruments as small as a dental chisel. One day when he came on board *Landfall*, inspecting every gadget with the close scrutiny of the artist and savant that he was, he whispered, "I feel as if I were in the inside of a watch."

I quote from a delicious description in *Europa Minor*,* by Lord Kinross, that awakens recollections of our own happy hours spent with the immortal Tom.

St. Sophia owes much to an American, Professor Whittemore, who became, as it were, its familiar spirit. Through his friendship with Atatürk he ensured its maintenance as a museum, and devoted some twenty years of his life to uncovering its mosaics. The Professor was a slow-moving sprite with a deep, sonorous voice and a skin as pale and as crinkled as tissue-paper, who lived in imagination in the Byzantine Age. . . .
It was the Professor who took me to stand, for the first time, beneath the dome of St. Sophia. Its serene expanse, together with the immaculate symmetry of the colonnades around us, absorbed the profuse decoration of the sculpture and the marbles to achieve a masterpiece of grandiose simplicity. Here, embodying treasures of pagan architecture from temples throughout the classical world—from Rome,

* London: John Murray, 1956, pp. 140–43.

from Athens, from Delphi, from Ephesus, from Baalbek—
is the apotheosis of classical art, given a new illumination
and a new continuity by its translation into Christian terms.
We stood for a few moments in silence. Then the Professor
intoned, with a broad sweep of the arm:

　　'*It's volu-metric.*' . . .

When Justinian first saw it completed by his two architects from Miletus and Tralles, he exclaimed: 'Glory be to
God, who has thought me worthy of accomplishing such a
work. Oh Solomon, I have conquered you.' His emotions
may well have been shared by Fatih (Mohamet II) the en-
lightened conqueror of Byzantium, who ordered its preservation, together with all the mosaics, and maintained its
continuity of worship as a mosque. The mosaics survived
until the nineteenth century, when they were covered over
with plaster, and with an inferior decoration in the ara-
besque style. Professor Whittemore had uncovered all that
survive, and was now expounding to me, with fervor, their
peculiar '*con*-ceptual' quality, as opposed to the mere
'*per*-ceptual' creations of the Latins.

　　'You do not *see* the figure of Christ. You *react* to
him.' . . .

　　'You do not look at the Virgin,' the Professor whispered
slowly. '*She* looks at *you.*'

She looks out also from above the altar, a long slim seated
figure, all robed in black, with the slim child on her lap—
a pair at once human and Divine whom the Angel Gabriel,
in resplendent white with enfolding wings, protects. The
mature Christ, bearded and grave in demeanour, presides
over a gallery with the Virgin on one hand and a mournful
John the Baptist, clad in green, head bowed, on the other—
figures achieving in mosaic the refinement and depth of
painting.

This was the gallery designed for the ladies of the court
of Theodora, whose praises the Professor was now chanting: 'A woman as great as the dome . . . as great as the
Law . . . as great as Belisarius.' . . . 　　　　　　　　,

I knew that the Professor's appetites were frugal, for I

had seen him by St. Sophia in the luncheon hour, sitting on the edge of a fountain, taking a lump of bread and some olives from his pocket, nibbling at an olive and throwing the bread to the birds. Thus I was hardly surprised to see, placed before us, not one of Pandeli's famous mixed grills, but a modest portion of steamed fish, divided into two. There was at first nothing to drink. But when we had eaten half our fish, the Professor recollected himself, called for the waiter, and consulted him earnestly over the wine list. Presently the waiter reappeared with a bottle. The Professor took a taste, and nodded with approval. The waiter poured us out two glasses of an excellent brand of water. . . .

Afterwards the Professor led me to the Museum of Antiquities. . . . Scorning classical masterpieces, he then hurried me through the Alexandrine to the Byzantine rooms. Here we wandered for an hour. . . . Finally we came to a small Byzantine pulpit, built of green porphyry, austerely simple, yet a living piece of sculpture. The Professor stood for a long time before it, in silence. Then he murmured:

'It *looks* at you. It advances towards you, like . . . like . . . like a *tank!*'

Shortly after our 1935 cruise, the formal unveiling of the mosaics took place in Istanbul, and Thomas Whittemore wrote:

A thousand years and more before St. Peter's was consecrated at Rome, Justinian had built his great church at Constantinople and dedicated it to Divine Wisdom, the title of the earlier church on the same site. Until yesterday it was a mosque and had been a mosque during nearly five centuries, since the Turks conquered the city and ruled Istanbul. Today it has been converted into a museum of Byzantine Art. St. Sophia was incomparably more richly built than any other church in Christendom and was more richly endowed with treasure. Into it poured the wealth of an empire to adorn the imperial place of worship, and everything combined to make it the most illustrious of Christian shrines.

Legend has gathered round this building. It has been the theme of poems, the subject of history, the object of architectural study; but it also excited the greed of Europe. . . .

One of those fascinating glimpses of cross currents in history came to our attention through Sir John Forsdyke, the distinguished British archaeologist, while we were in Istanbul. He was staying with Tom when we arrived and he undertook to be our guide on several occasions. Being an Englishman, and at the head of the British Museum in London, where the Greek works of art known as the Elgin Marbles have long been jealously guarded, he was happy to meet James Stuart and the daughter of so well-known a patron of the arts as the Duke of Devonshire. He gave us the benefit of his vast classical knowledge at every turn, and we were delighted when he accepted our invitation to return to Athens with us.

One day he took us to the Hippodrome and showed us the proud bronze serpentine column that was a votive offering from Plataea to Attica, commemorating the Battle of Plataea in 479 B.C. It had stood on a modest pedestal near the Delphic Oracle in Delphi for upwards of 700 years. It was a beautiful monument topped by the golden heads of three serpents once carrying a golden tripod and inscribed with the names of the thirty-one contingents that fought in the decisive victory over the Persians, begun at Thermopylae. Ever since Constantine the Great transported the Serpentine Column to his Hippodrome in Constantinople, leaving only the pedestal in Delphi, near the

Temple of Apollo, it has remained alone and unadorned, with only a guidebook to record its former renown.

With our prize classical scholar on board, we sailed (stopping only at Skyros) quite straight for Delphi, Mycenae, and Corinth. It was a chance in a lifetime to have such a guide, counselor, and friend as Sir John along, and both the Stuarts and we benefited greatly through his talk and companionship before we parted in Athens.

We had one more great treat awaiting us in Malta. Admiral French was then the Flag Officer commanding His Majesty's dockyard and he had courteously arranged a winter berth for *Landfall*. Lord Mountbatten was then Captain D. of a flotilla of Destroyers, based on Malta— the youngest Captain in the Royal Navy.

Dickie and Edwina Mountbatten had spent a few days of their American honeymoon ten years earlier with Paul in Syosset, as they were friends of old, and we were overjoyed to see them once more. We dined with them that night in their attractive little town house on the water, and enjoyed their delicious ice cream so much that the next day when they came on board, to speed us on our way, they presented us with a large thermos full of it. This was being carried by Edwina, because it is beneath the dignity of an officer of the Royal Navy to carry anything whatsoever.

They were, in those days, the romantic young couple of your dreams—the prince and princess of a fairy story. Dickie was conspicuously handsome in his whites, and Edwina, graceful and beautiful in an enchanting abbreviated dress of pink and white liberty silk—both equally full of the zest of life and the spirit of adventure, and enormously proud of one another. When Dickie had long terms of sea duty, Edwina would snatch the opportunity to see the world and travel on her own. They profited by this way of life, and together grew in stature and dignity. Twelve years after our meeting in Malta, when Dickie was Viceroy of India, King George VI bestowed on him the title of Earl Mountbatten of Burma. It was appropriate that the hour of Indian Independence was eventually struck during that reign of mutual understanding and good will.

"Sailing to Egypt," 1936*

The coastline of every port of the world varies as much
as do the cities and the people, and it is with eager interest
that sailors make their landfall—the zenith of all sea passages. It is the exchange of a watchful routine, now peaceful, now hazardous, for the familiar, more even pastimes
of life on shore. In former years we had approached the
grim austere grandeur of Norwegian fjords, the smiling
slopes of the Bosporus and the unrivaled beauty of the
Greek Islands and Dalmatian coast. We had smelled the
pitch of the Maine pines, and become familiar with the
rocks of Plymouth and the bristling spars of sword fishermen nested in Block Island. But this was something never
seen by us before. An endless gleam of shining gold lay
outstretched between sea and sky. No rocks, no hills, no
green trees, no houses, no boats. In the sunset glow it was
gold, gold, gold that heralded the approach to Alexandria.
"All is not gold that glitters," sighed the wind through
the shrouds as we gazed spellbound at the treacherous,
parching, threatening Libyan Desert that today beckoned
us on, promising only beauty and sunshine.

It was because of the significance my husband attaches
to that happy moment in a sailor's life, that he had christened his ketch "Landfall." She is seventy-two feet over-

* This chapter is reprinted by courtesy of *Harper's Bazaar* in which it
appeared as an article with the same title in the March 1937 issue. Our
departure was from Malta and our landfall at Alexandria.

all, was designed by L. Francis Herreshoff and built in 1931. Her first year she crossed the Atlantic in a race from Newport, R. I., to Plymouth, England, cruising the following summer in the Scandinavian and Scottish waters, and during the last three seasons has done about ten thousand miles in the Mediterranean. Certain improvements in the conventional ketch rig make her an ideal craft for cruising with a crew of four professional hands forward, and an afterguard of about six persons with one or two good sailors among them. The mizzen sail brails in to the mast (a job usually handled by the ladies) and is consequently never lowered during the summer. The loose-footed mainsail has been used most successfully for four seasons. The yards are kept aloft permanently, and for running and reaching, support the triangular squaresails known as the Gish Sisters. Each yard can be trained well forward and both squaresails rolled up on reels, like a window shade on end, when not in use, as does the working jib. The sheets and halyards are all wire, secured directly to the drums of the winches, thereby saving one man on each job, as there is never any need of taking in slack and belaying and coiling down lines.

Below, an 18-foot wardroom with natural teak trim, red morocco cushions, an open fire and a small piano, forms an inviting retreat from a summer shower or a burning midday sun. On deck there is a cuddy with two comfortable day bunks, also a large cockpit where most meals are eaten beneath an awning, even when underway.

Early last May we took our departure from Malta, starting our voyage with a week at sea which offered us all kinds of wind and weather. Seasickness was not entirely unknown and, contrary to tradition, not much helped by some nice little pints of 1929 champagne purchased in

Malta at the famous Saccone & Speed. However, smooth
waters often come surprisingly quickly after a lump of a
sea and our "Bright Star Miss Lillian Gish" (as our
dragoman called her) proved herself to have a talent for
sportsmanship quite as great as her many other talents.
She assured us that it was a most perfect "rest." Later on
we realized that when one has myriads of devoted
admirers in every corner of the world, as she has, a small
boat on a large ocean, seasick or not, is the only sure way
of getting a rest. Our other delightful companions, Clover
and Buff Chace,* were sturdy young travelers, who
turned from work to play and from play to work with
equal ardor.

May 11th, 1936.
   "We have had a fair wind a third of the way—eight
hundred miles from Malta to Alexandria—and a northeast wind the rest of the time, with an old lump of a sea
and a good deal of motion, but comfortable corners to
wedge ourselves into, and an air mattress, now here, now
there, and hot meals on deck. The sun's rays illumine
every part of the sky, air, land and water, and bore their
way into our skin. Delicious to the nth degree and satisfying beyond words."

   Why is it that life at sea is so much more enchanted than
life on shore? The friends of land are warm, clever, generous, but within this limited compass, with the flags of
all nations in our locker, the rapport of the small circle is
so much greater. The give and take is more necessary,
the reliance and the sense of comradeship deeper. The
esprit de corps of the crew takes on noble proportions.

* Clover Chace Nicholas and her brother Arnold B. Chace.

The extravagant comforts, distractions and interruptions on land are numbing to our bodies and minds. At sea, and especially on the Mediterranean, the years that have brought us to where we are drop away. The virgin soil, physically and intellectually, that confronted the builders of the pyramids and the prophets of Israel, becomes understandable.

Last night we gave ourselves a short lesson in astronomy. We followed the arc of the Dipper's handle to Arcturus and Spica, and found the diamond of Virgo and the other small diamond within it; and also the bright little irregular quadrilateral of Corvus.

Now, as we approach Alexandria, with our long-cherished dream of seeing the masterpieces wrought by the first great center of civilization about to be realized; as we look for the Nile, the Desert, and the Sphinx, we are haunted by the question of whether it is to be War or Peace. We have seen no American paper for two weeks, but we know that the British battleships left Malta in March and preceded us to Alexandria, Haifa, and Cyprus, the three places that we have been planning to visit this month. It will be a comfort to find the white ensign in all three places.

We have been carrying our squaresails. Two glorious masses of Egyptian cotton that cut up into the canopy of stars as do the pyramids into the blazing sky. Last night the skipper called me at two, when the waning moon was high, and I took the wheel while the great squaresails were being set. It was a delicious night of infinite beauty. Yesterday an Italian liner, the *Marsala*, sighted us and came close to investigate. She pleased Paul by coming up to leeward, "A sailor, by gosh," said he.

The port of Alexandria, with its semicircular sweep of

white sand, is a superb setting for conjuring up memories
of Antony and Cleopatra, and for the site of one of the
Wonders of the World—the first great lighthouse of antiquity that cast the rays of its open fire from a height of
four hundred feet. The situation of Alexandria speaks
eloquently for the ambitions of Alexander the Great, and
the scarcity of its *monuments historiques* reminds one of
the burning of the most precious library the world has
ever known, as well as constant, destructive fires of recur-
rent wars from the dawn of civilization.

The presence of the greater part of the British fleet did
not allow us to forget the predatory instincts of Hittite,
Persian, Roman, Turk and human nature in general. In
fact, our own newspapers, just before we sailed, had carried such headlines as, "Italians Smash Foe in South and
Close in on Addis Ababa," and "Eleven Killed, Fifty
Injured in Palestine Riots—British Troops on Guard—
Curfew Law Is Invoked," and the President stated that
"Americans who travel abroad, do so at their own risk,"
and friends looked dubious. But it seemed to us that until
a state of war exists, it is better to assume that we are in a
state of peace. The tragedy of the beautiful Mediterranean basin is that the horrors of war are never absent and
are as close to its people today as they have been through
the ages. The Rock speaks of it, Rome testifies to it. The
scars of Sicily, of Alexandria, of Athens, of Istanbul, can
never be forgotten. Most of all do the nine cities of Ancient Troy repeat the oft-told tale of Destruction and Resurrection, Victory and Defeat.

When a clever person returns from travels abroad, that
is your opportunity to get a quick, sharp, living impression. And when Alice Duer Miller returned from Egypt
two years ago, I asked her what one thing struck her most.

Her answer was, "What no teacher or traveler ever before sufficiently dramatized for me—that Egypt is nothing more or less than a tiny green strip of land about two hundred miles long and about ten to thirty miles wide, bordering each side of the Nile." With this concise picture in mind, we looked toward the Delta.

It is too late in May to sail up the river. The foreign archeologists—British, American, French, German—have already packed up their new-found treasures and their masses of data, and have returned to their centers of learning where they will spend a tantalizing summer putting together the pieces of a gigantic puzzle. But almost as interesting as a sail in a dahabiyeh is the train trip along the border of the Nile. My idea of trains is derived from trips between New York and Stockbridge, Massachusetts, or to Thomasville, Georgia, where the trains whiz past back doors and through dreary back alleys filled with the bones of dead automata and enlivened only by the billboards of the enemy. But in Egypt, because it is so narrow and so fertile, and because every inch of it is arable, the train window offers a ringside seat for one of the finest human dramas ever produced on any stage. Little brown settlements of mud brick appear here and there, mud walls, mud roofs, mud streets. Tiny one- and two-room houses. Who cares for a house in Egypt when the sunshine is always everywhere? So they sleep indoors only, and take refuge there during the hard rains, and for the rest of the time, year in and year out, they are in the field or in the garden.

The precious water of the Nile still often irrigates the rich fields by means of the shadoof, the oldest well-sweep in the world. The grain is still winnowed on the threshing floor, and the produce is still loaded on dahabiyehs that vary little from the beautiful bas-reliefs of boats to be seen in tombs belonging to the Pharaohs of the sixth dynasty. Most amazing of all is the fact that this primitive people had worked out a 365 day year in 4221 B.C.

The phenomenally early flowering of Egypt was due partly to its natural geographic protection from enemies, and partly, as Breasted puts it, because, "A genial and generous but exacting soil demanded for cultivation the development of a high degree of skill in the manipulation of the life-giving waters." It was this rich soil that enabled the early Egyptian to get his food so easily that he had the leisure in which to think and create.

If you go to Egypt, don't fail to take a ticket on one of the trains from Alexandria to Luxor, or the little Diesel-driven duralumin rail-car between Cairo and Suez that runs so close to the road along which Joseph's captors took him to Egypt; along which Moses led the Children of Israel back to the home of their forefathers; and along which Mary and Joseph fled with the infant Christ when they were threatened by Herod.

We spent a night on the desert. A motor at dusk and then a short ride on loping camels brought us to a spot facing East from which we could watch the lights of Cairo and dimly see the great forms of the pyramids on our left, between which we would later see the sunrise. A Lucullan feast had been prepared for us:

Menu

Arabian consommé with native bread
Fried sole with lime
Lamb chops and string beans
Entrée of vegetable marrow filled
with rice and mutton

Chicken with peas
Turkey with potatoes
Tomato and lettuce salad
Caramel custard with fruit
Stewed apricots containing raisins and nuts
Fruit
Coffee

After dinner came a pretty crude entertainment of songs and dance—men and boys only, of course, as the Koran decrees that women may not dance. Then, under a perfect starlight night our dragoman became communicative and told us much of the habits and customs of Arabians. His great-grandfather had been one of a wandering tribe in the desert, and his grandfather had settled near the old city of Memphis and had become its sheik. He is a devout Mohammedan who bears the title of Hadj, as he has twice made pilgrimages to Mecca. He is a middle-aged, kindly man with an intelligent face and the graceful manners of the East.

We were interested in the women, and he gave us a grim picture of the wife who disobeys her husband by doing nothing worse than leaving the house without her lord's permission. He may divorce her on the spot, in which case he returns her small dot to her father, and the bride returns with it, a dishonored woman. Arabians must marry within their tribe, and often when a man wishes to find a mate there isn't more than one eligible girl for him in existence. He may dislike her, but his father says, "Very well, it is she or no one." And he marries her, and both live to regret it. A friend of Hadj's had had a wife who displeased him by ordering her clothes, on one occasion, shorter in skirt- and sleeve-length than usual. He said nothing, but gathering the beautiful new em-

broidered linens and dresses in a heap, he lit a match to
the pile. And that was that.

Hadj's own wife he took us to see in his own apartment
in Cairo, and there he served us a delicious lunch. If she
is a slave she is a very happy one, and to be envied even by
spoiled American wives. Fortunately our men were not
permitted to look upon her, so they don't yet know how
happy an unspoiled woman can be.

We separated to our various tents, and all night the cool
desert air blew over our faces like refreshing waves from
the sea. In the twilight before dawn, shadowy forms
passed back and forth outside our tents and we heard
strange and unfamiliar accents in prayer and parley. Hadj
called us at 4:00 A.M. and we wandered away from the
tents and sat down on the sand to watch the coming of the
great god Re.

I am not as gullible concerning the art of the Near East
as were my forebears when they hung bead curtains in
doorways and furnished their Victorian drawing-rooms
with stuffed ottomans, nor am I mosque-minded, nor did
we frequent Chez Rameses and the Tutankhamen Bar,
but there is a fascinating colorful pageantry in every part
of Cairo that I have never seen equaled in any other city.
The old bazaars consist of myriads of tiny box-like shops,
one side opening on the artery of traffic, forming a cellular
tissue that is quite unique. All day long the shopkeeper
builds up his stock with his own nimble fingers while he
trades with his customers. Silks, perfumes, cottons, spices,
and everything that can be grown or made in that fertile
land are displayed and bargained over, and the sale encouraged by an infinitesimal cup of thick Turkish coffee.
If your time is limited, it is better to accept the price, high
as it is, swallow the coffee, and shoulder your wares before

the spectators roughly involve you in further complications, and the eternal cry of "bakshish" from men, women and children swamps your activities, and dampens your enthusiasm.

Some of the mosques are very beautiful, but if I had several weeks to spend in Cairo they would be divided between the Desert and the Museum. Speaking of the Museum, Meyer-Graefe says in his delightful "Pyramid and Temple," "Here one can get to know the faces of people who lived fifty centuries ago. . . . These are the people of the pyramids. . . . So long as the stone is alive, we snap our fingers at everything else." Later on he says of the Pillars of Luxor, "We pass them every day, hurrying or loitering, irritated or contented; and they stand there without bothering us. . . . The pyramid, on the other hand, is ideally accessible for all its abstractness, even if it needs the desert as a background and if the beings with whom it converses intimately are the sunbeams."

Diary of Jane Nichols Page, 1937

INTRODUCTION TO 1937 CRUISE

Jane Nichols, who was then eighteen years old, had been schooled since her earliest years to be a sailor, by her father, George Nichols. George and his wife are among our oldest and closest friends, and he was throughout his lifetime, one of the outstanding racing men on Long Island Sound. Between 1914 and 1930 he took an active and important part in the Class J sloop races that kept the America's Cup on this side of the Atlantic Ocean. When his three children, Jane, Rita, and George, Jr. grew old enough to become racing enthusiasts themselves, they won many a race together; first in their sixteen-foot Herreshoff fish-boat, *Volador,* then in their atlantic, *Cowslip,* and after that in their deservedly famous six-metre, *Goose.*

In April 1937, Jane and her mother went to England for the Coronation of George VI on May 12, and after that Jane traveled south and joined us in Naples. She kept a day-to-day diary on this trip and has kindly allowed me to include it in this record. Her vivacious and telegraphic style is an amusing contrast to that of Richard Delano, and I might add, my own.

The "Mike" of her story was our sailing master that

year. He was the son of Rear Admiral C. L. Cumberlege, R.N., who distinguished himself in World War I.

Michael Cumberlege was full of zest and the joy of life. He had lived at sea so long that he never knew what it was like to live ashore, and he had every expectation of following the sea, as had his father, through a long and happy life. Because of his unconventional upbringing, his education had been in some ways neglected, a deficiency which he himself overcame by an innate superiority of mind and heart. As he traveled, he observed, he studied, he made the most of every opportunity, and his infectious gaiety charmed everyone who crossed his path. The day we first saw him he was neatly dressed and wearing a gold ring in one ear as naturally as he wore his tie. When England met the challenge of war in 1939, he parted with his young wife and two small children, and enlisted in the most dangerous of services and the one for which he was best qualified, espionage. After a few tragic and dangerous months he was taken prisoner and shot. All of us on that cruise will long remember how much, and in how many ways, he added to the pleasure of our voyage.

The "Kim" of the diary stands for one of Paul's young ocean-racing crew, Charles McKim Norton. He was with Paul on *Niña* in the race to Spain in 1928, and on *Landfall* in 1931 in the race from Newport, Rhode Island, to Plymouth, England. He is one of the keen and proficient enthusiasts of the sailing world. Kim has unselfishly dedicated his life's work to a greatly needed service, that of city planning; and on the side, perhaps because cooking is another essential, he became co-author with Russell K. Jones in one of the most successful and satisfactory books of its kind ever published, *The Cruising Cook Book*.

DIARY OF JANE NICHOLS PAGE

May 12th, 1937. London (for coronation of George VI).
In seats in window on second floor of Swan and Edgar
at 6:45 A.M. having walked from Grosvenor Square. Grey
and foggy, but not actively raining. Could see length of
Regent Street. Some of people lining the street had
camped there all night and were cooking over sternos, very
orderly but cold and wet. Umbrellas and raincoats everywhere. When carriages started to go by it was hard to see
in because of height of seats. Princess Elizabeth with her
nose flattened on window, and Stanley Baldwin only ones
clearly seen. Royal coach just like Cinderella's, equally
gilded, shone in dark! Crowd very patient, cheered when
notables passed, and just as last of royal escort went by us
the rain came down. By 4:30 P.M. the crowd was so thick
people couldn't move, and they broke through restraining
troops. Everyone perfectly amiable.

Later that evening walked through packed parks, jubi-
lant crowds. Six or eight people on top of most taxis.
Everybody unflustered and amazingly pleasant. King and
Queen and Queen Mother seemed permanently on palace
balcony. When did they eat?

May 16th.
Joined Hammonds in Naples, having been chaperoned
down by Gregory from travel department of Morgan,
Grenfel. Perfectly amiable gentleman, but galling. Was as
glad to shed me as I him. Did Pompeii and Herculaneum,
took off for Alexandria in SS *Esperia*. Two volcanos in one

day, Vesuvius and Stromboli. The latter, seen from *Landfall* at midnight, looked like fireworks.

May 19th.

Alexandria. Small horses pulling huge loads with
drivers in flapping white shirts on top. Lateen-rigged
small craft all over harbor, with one, two and sometimes
three masts. Can't tack, jibe by taking whole sail round
forward of mast.

May 20th.

Beirut and Baalbek. Dined with Dodges. Temple of
Baalbek so huge it was beautiful in spite of ornateness.
Nice yellow-brown colour with bright green weeds and
pink hollyhocks between the stones.

May 21st.

Drove from Beirut to Jerusalem via Sea of Galilee. On
way up from Sidon and the coast saw my first Bedouin
tents, low and black. One settlement of expatriate German Jews in *lederhosen* very tidy and military looking beside gypsy Arab camps. Jewish settlement fenced with
barbed wire. At the watering holes were flocks of sheep,
goats and camels. Small, badly cared for, but Arab-looking
horses.

Sea of Galilee at lunch time looked like Ghirlandajo's
painting in the Sistine Chapel. Blue water and steep yellow hills. Lunched at hospice kept by Father Tabagh close
to Capernaum. An elderly German called Gauer was
building a church over the spot where the loaves and fishes
had been divided. Country rough and half desert on way
to Jerusalem. Every village full of children, goats and

camels—scattered by horn. Jackals or coyotes came out with the dusk.

May 22nd.

Spent morning floating high in Dead Sea. Paul, in topee, smoked a cigar and read the paper! Felt like mercury, you couldn't sink! Bought camel and horse harness and saddlebags in Jericho. P.M. in Bethlehem. Incredible number of different churches built over presumed birthplace of Christ. A funeral in process; mourners, mostly women, in tall Bethlehem headdress; two major domos with staffs that came down bang on the pavement every other step, and chanting like howling dogs.

May 23rd.

Walked through old streets and markets to the Dome of the Rock. Streets dark and smelly, crowded with most diverse people. Huge Abyssinians, very negroid with gaudy turbans and white Arab shirts, thumbing rosaries; women like black bundles with veiled faces. Must say the veils of the younger ones are pretty transparent. Beggars asleep in the doorways, men looking like Dulac illustrations for the Arabian Nights working in their shops, carrying loads, talking and eating in doorways. Shafts of light slanting down full of dust. From that, one comes out onto the Dome in a big open space full of colour and light, and Moorish shapes. The Dome and the Mosque behind it are spaced well with a fountain between. The whole space around the Dome surrounded by a square with eight arched gates built by the Crusaders.

A bit of the Via Dolorosa, then the pools of Bethesda, kept by a group of French White Friars from Algeria. Then through more crazy streets to the Church of the

Holy Sepulchre. Several Christian sects keep it and have
their own altars and parts of the Church. From the bright
sunlight you go in the south door into inky blackness, up a
flight of steps and suddenly on to the Armenian altar,
silver gilt and blazing with candles. Beside it the wax figures of a Catholic altar. You buy tapers and go down
through a series of corridors to the supposed location of
Calvary. As we got to the bottom a group of Franciscan
friars armed with tapers and hymn books moved past
chanting. Behind them a group of female orphans in
dark and white uniforms, and behind them a group of
wizened old women. Each group carried its own light with
it, in the thick darkness.

May 27th.

On board *Landfall* for three days. In harbor at Limassol, Cyprus. Drove to Famagusta. Venetian fortified town
still there though no longer lived in. Looked like perfect
sand castle or block fort. Spent all afternoon exploring
walls. Ruins of Crusader churches or chapels inside walls.

May 28th.

Visited ruined castle of St. Hilarion on an eyrie; was
Berengaria's, they say. Hillocky country on the way there,
small farms with donkeys carrying huge loads, oxen to
plow or thresh grain on stone floors. Three kinds of dogs:
mastiffs (yellow with curly tails), greyhounds, and mutt-
dachshund types with feathery tails and legs. Nicosia for
lunch, then on 'round the island via Vouni, the ruins of a
Hellenistic villa. Back to Limassol across the mountains
where the houses are suddenly peak-roofed instead of flat,
and the air is cool and there are pine trees.

May 30th.

Sighted Turkish Coast. Mt. Adratchan and Cape Khe-lidonia. Abrupt high mountains down to the water's edge with clouds settled along the ridges. Only sign of life a lighthouse on the cape. Wind SW and freshening, and sea making up when we went between Cape Khelidonia and the islands off it. By the time we got into Phinea Bay the wind was so strong that we took two reefs in the main, took the mizzen off altogether and doused the foresail. The sun went down slowly behind the rollers and the mountains looked cut out of dark grey and blue paper. Finally we decided it was too uncomfortable to go on to Rhodes that night so we turned back into the Gulf of Adalia and came into Adratchan Bay about 9:30.

May 31st.

By daylight Adratchan Bay was even nicer, very small, hemmed with high mountains. The clouds lifted for a moment early and showed another range behind them snowcapped. There are pines on the lower slopes and banks of wild pink oleanders just back of the beach. At the head of the harbor were three rough huts and a couple of fishing boats drawn up on the beach. No one paid any attention to us; a woman went back and forth from the huts to the boats, a herd of black sheep and goats were driven along the beach, and three camels came out of the woods and lay down. We sailed out through bright blue water north along the coast to a little harbor, Tekrova (ancient Phaselis). We got there just after lunch and anchored in a little harbor. There were the remains of a huge sea wall, and blocks of stone tumbled out into the water. We landed on the north side under the wall beside a broken pediment with a Greek inscription. The whole beach was covered with bits of broken earthenware worn smooth by the sea, and under the tide mark were columns of various lengths. The wall must have been built after the column era, because its foundation was made of columns laid lengthwise like logs. On a tiny peninsula between two harbors are the bare traces of a very complete city buried in a jungle of pines, catbriar and thorn bushes. We explored the theater, cisterns, and the remains of an artificial harbor on the other side from ours. There was no sign of life on shore except for a fisherman's hut and sheep droppings all through the ruins. As we sailed away for Rhodes two smoky fires appeared on the beach. Off Cape Khelidonia the wind died, and the engine also.

June 1st.

Little wind, big sea. 10 P.M. Hypsili light abeam, ruins every point or so.

June 2nd.

Strong wind ahead, humpy sea. Tacked towards Rhodes, finally made Lindos at 4 P.M. Some argument about going ashore to hire car and drive to Rhodes, as Lindos is not port of entry. Paul prevailed, and we went to explore the castle, plus stacks of washing. Took donkeys so small they bent in the middle.

June 3rd and 4th.

Rhodes. Hotel on the beach very Italian and pleasant around the point from the harbor. Colossus replaced by two very sophisticated columns; artificial walled harbor. Old town surrounded by Crusader, with 15th-century walls. Trying to circumnavigate on them proved quite difficult, and we ended up climbing down a powerhouse ladder to the great amusement of the caretaker. Gloomy couple from New Zealand in a rotting sailboat. Had been going for three years! Mike lost the registration papers of the *Landfall* on the quay, but a kindly Ala-Litoria employee hired a native boat and brought them back to us. Typical of relaxed, pleasant town, clean due to Mussolini.

June 5th.
　　Night in Episkopi.

June 6th.
　　Good sailing breeze, though head. Made Kos. Still no engine. This is Hippocrates' island, and his plane tree still stands in the town.

June 7th.
　　Strong north wind. Not much 'summer sea' about the Mediterranean so far. Started for Delos, changed course for Naxos, and finally ran in between Apano-Kupho and Kato-Kupho where there was some lee. A couple of sponge fishermen gave us a lift ashore where we were greeted on the beach with song by the local school. Climbed through the town up onto a bluff to stretch our legs. Accompanied by the school and half the town in fits of giggles. Explored a local windmill—primitive, but with roller reefing gear on the sails.

June 8th.
　　Still blowing great guns. Paul has most of the local population on board shining brass. Went ashore in P.M. and walked to weather side of the island where the surf

was big and lovely. Herbs of all kinds grow in cracks of the rocks, the ground looks dry and hard to work, houses built of dry stones and whitewashed, fields walled with dry stone walls. Sea is turquoise and sapphire against the barren yellow islands.

June 9th.

Went out in usual gale as far as Antiparos. Anchored between it and Despoticon. This was second day we'd been double-reefed.

June 10th.

Still blowing, went out double-reefed. Tried harbor at Seriphos but it was foaming with spray, so we went on. The wind gradually let up, and by 6 P.M. we were off Cape Colonna with Sunium right ahead and Athens and the Acropolis in the distance. Six miles from Phaleron the wind died, and we didn't get in till early morning. All evening in the fading light we might have been back in the *Odyssey.*

June 13th.

Kim and I went off with Charles Bird, an old friend of the Hammonds, and his daughter, on a converted Italian caique, the *San Marco.* Sailed across bay of Athens to Epidaurus on Peleponnesus with intention of getting inland to ancient Epidaurus from the modern town on the coast.

As we landed in New Epidaurus, we were firmly absorbed into a double wedding festivity by two retired Greeks from Chicago and California. The bridal couple were kissed, and kissed everyone in sight, and were showered with sugar almonds to the detriment of the paper crowns they wore. Everybody danced in circles, including us. Finally acquired a boy as guide and three mounts, two minute horses (mine had a foal that kept stopping us to lunch), and a donkey, to climb the hill to old Epidaurus. Distance variously reported as from two to six miles. The path was a track with stream bed that wound up between orange and olive orchards, lined with oleanders and daphne bushes in flower, but as we rose it got more barren and wilder, with rocky sides and coarse pine trees. Finally we topped the hill onto a wide plain of cultivated fields and hedgerows just as the sun went down in a blaze of silver and pink clouds. Goat bells tinkled everywhere and a shepherd played a little round-noted tune on his pipe.

The theater and stadium were reportedly a mile from where we came out, so we got off and ran the rest of the way on the modern tarred road from Nauplia. The theater when we came to it was silver grey in the twilight, and almost complete. It was very steep-sided, and from the round stage at the bottom a whisper could be heard in the topmost seats! By this time it was 9 p.m., and as dark as it could get, and beginning to rain. We and our mounts trotted along the road to a village that turned out to be a New Epidaurus proper, where the local pub provided beer and some food; then down the pitch black track again to the shore. It was 1:15 when we got there; even the wedding was beginning to peter out, we were almost sound asleep, and to our relief Mr. Bird was relaxed, not worrying.

June 14th.

Left the *San Marco* regretfully about noon, and Kim and I took off for Delphi in an ancient but shining touring car with a marvelous round chauffeur, Popandreau. After the slums of Piraeus we were glad to stop for a minute at Daphne, and later to lunch by the side of the road on the top of the divide between Eleusis and Thebes. All the hills smelled heavenly of thyme and pine, it was broiling in the sun, but almost cold in the shade, and we sat and ate very comfortably indeed. Down in the gullies between the hills are hectic little brooks and streams with huge plane trees at intervals over white houses.

About 3 o'clock we came down into the wide flat Theban plain, as well watered and lined with poplars as Belgium. It is easy to see why Cadmus Dragon's teeth grew, anything would! As we came across, a thunderstorm banked up on Parnassus to the southwest and the rain came sweeping down the valley. The people who had been working in the fields crouched in the lee of hedges and sun-tents while the grey rain poured by them. First view of shepherds in white smocks, short, pleated kilts and turned up shoes—looking like evzones.

Down the valley to Delphi, and an uneducated look at the ruins, but mostly at the heavenly view down to Itea. Did notice the curve along the base of the Temple of Apollo which made it look straight to the eye when the columns were standing.

At 8 P.M. we headed down to Itea where *Landfall* was supposed to meet us. No sign of her. We tried to trace her by having Popandreau phone Corinth, but when that failed we settled down in a local restaurant to a well earned and welcome supper. As it got later and darker, and still no *Landfall*, Kim went over and tested the local hotel, and we settled into three rooms to the horror of the landlord who considered us extravagant. Bed sagged in odd places but was clean, and I was dead.

Suddenly there were terrific thumpings on my door and

yells of "Jane, it's Mike." It was past midnight and *Landfall* was in. I struggled out of bed into the hall to find Popandreau in the loudest striped pyjamas on record, and Kim and Mike. *Landfall* was aground half a mile down the coast, and the Skipper, who had been strong for a chaperone all along, thought we should be aboard, so we went.

By 3 p.m. we had been hauled off by native boats, and placated the tug pilot and diver, both of whom had arrived too late, and motored 'round beyond Itea into a tiny harbor, Vithavri, for the night. The engine is finally running due to 'Germany' an engineer from that country taken on in Athens. This just added another language to our babel of English, French, Maltese, already on board. No common communication beyond essentials.

June 18th to 22nd.

Levkas, of Sappho, with her cliff; the site of the battle of Actium on the Albanian coast. I am told the shooting is lovely in the fall, but the marshy land looked better for its other specialty: ague. Left in the stifling heat and made Corfu at midnight. Lunched in a lovely bay on the west side of the island off Langouste. Whole feel suddenly very Italian, lusher than the bare Greek islands. Came back by the harbor with the island reputed to be Odysseus ship. Good breeze as we left at 4, but it died before night, and as engine had died again, we worked into small, dull Albanian harbor for the night. Drifted out along the coast for a day until 'Germany' mastered the engine, and we made Brindisi in time to catch the train for Naples and the steamer home. Last view of *Landfall* with the crew lined up on the rail with 'Germany' in the middle doing Nazi salutes.

PART III
Capitana
Harvard Columbus Expedition,
1939

On Sept. 1, 1939, a few hours after Germany's invasion of Poland, the Harvard Columbus Expedition headed out of New London, Conn., for the Azores. For five months and for 10,000 miles, we retraced routes that Christopher Columbus followed over unknown seas four and a half centuries ago. Our aims were to verify by actual observation, ancient accounts of his four great voyages, to identify the capes and coastlines he first described and to determine finally whether America's discoverer was just a lucky Baldwin or truly a great master of the sea. . . .

Our vessels were the 140-ft. barkentine *Capitana*, a steel three-master, named after one of Columbus's flagships, and the 45-ft. ketch *Mary Otis*, which served as our tender. All told, including wives, daughters, seamen and volunteers, we were 24. . . .

We brought home enormous respect for Columbus as a dead-reckoning navigator and for his caravels, which by and large made better time before the wind than we.

SAMUEL E. MORISON
from an article in *Life* (March 25, 1940)*

* Courtesy *Life* Magazine. Copr. 1940 Time Inc.

Capitana
Harvard Columbus Expedition,
1939
*(from the author's diary)**

Departure from Seawanhaka Corinthian Yacht Club, Oyster Bay, N. Y. On board *Capitana,*

Monday, August 28th, 1939, 7:15 A.M.

We had thought to be off before the chicory was in blossom, but the gay flags of goldenrod lined the roadside and the horror of World War II already clouded the warm August days with fear and dread.

The departure had been scheduled for August 1st. We had been packed and ready with food, cleaning materials, clothes, all the necessities and some of the luxuries of life, to last us about six months.

During the period of preparation, to have more time meant to think of more things to do, more things to get. I wished my mind could exclude the continuous trickle of possible wants. I needed to learn more about Columbus, to study Spanish, to practice on the accordion so that I could play on a slippery deck. I had said goodbye to my children and grandchildren and couldn't keep on disturbing them with more goodbyes. It would soon be time to

* The author and her husband returned to New York in December, 1939. Therefore the diary does not include the last two months of the Harvard Columbus Expedition, which terminated early in 1940.

go off on probably the longest and greatest adventure of my life, and yet the details and the business of living seemed more than ever to take first place. What had soap and Bon Ami and blankets to do with Columbus, and beautiful islands and changing seas? Alas, drudgery had everything to do with them. Men who follow the sea, in particular, are always working against time, always concentrating on the necessities of existence, preoccupied by details dictated by the apprehension of possible dangers and a care for safety. Weather is still often unpredictable. Distance must be covered between seasonal upheavals of nature.

I woke this morning to hear the hum of the engine and then presently that indefinable sensation of motion in protected waters—not speed, but just the knowledge that we were really off. August 28th, 1939, and what of the war cloud in Europe? We were putting on a bold front and trying not to think about it.

We are twenty-one all told, and the afterguard are:

Samuel E. Morison, Commodore
Paul Hammond, U.S.N.R., Commanding Officer
Susan S. Hammond
James McG. Byrne
Dwight W. Morrow, Jr.
Margot Morrow
Elizabeth Morison
Clifton Anderson, Ship's Surgeon
Richard Colley

Our Sailing Master, Jariilo Walter, is a splendid seaman. We know him well because he has been with us on former cruises in the Mediterranean. He and his three sailor brothers are known in many parts of the world. They are named for the Finnish pagan gods: Ahto, the god of the sea; Kou, of thunder; Uku, a sort of benevolent Jupiter, and Jariilo, the god of wisdom.

August 28th, 9 P.M.

Put in at New London, Connecticut, because of the following radio storm warning: "Disturbance off North Carolina coast, will move slowly northward and cause fresh to strong northeast winds and rain along the middle Atlantic coast today."

So we put into harbor and given this opportunity Moir, Little, and Philip and Richard Howison, overworked and discontented, announced that they would leave the ship. It is sad and serious to have those boys go. Life at sea, as I understand it, always means overwork, because it means working against time, and if there isn't sufficient compensation in work well done, or in pride, or in excitement, or in financial gain, then some men will always quit. These four may have had personal reasons for regretting their decision to sail with us, and those reasons coupled with the fact that they had had long hours under an Estonian taskmaster, and perhaps too little liberty, was enough to justify them in their own eyes. The boat had been outfitted in Brooklyn, where none of us lived, and much was done over the telephone when face to face talks would have been better. These four boys were living, and were going to live, under far less comfortable conditions than they would have at home. Moir had been a quartermaster on an ocean liner, Little has a naval architect's degree; they are college men. Shipping as hands isn't good enough for them.

Our mascot, the black kitty, also left, by mutual consent. But not till she had gone overboard between *Capitana* and the launch—and not till the launch (taking it and the French-leave crew ashore) had died for lack of gasoline, and signals to the Coast Guard rescued them. An episode that inspired the first creative expression from our historian:

The Cotter-Pin Cruise

The Doc and the pussy-cat went to sea
　　With a couple of cotter-pin oars
And the Commodore too with his French-leave crew
　　And the Chief Engineer and the big mutineer
While the No'theaster loudly roars.
They set sail for the far Azores.

Dick Colley he stood on the Barkentine's deck
　　And a salt tear stood in his eye,
For the Doc had stole off with his kitty by heck
And he feared he would wring its doggone neck
　　So he heaved a deep, deep sigh
　　And wished his bedfellow was nigh.

A black kitty they say brings luck to a ship,
　　But the sailors must have lied,
For this one drew blood to the Doctor's lip
　　And the engine sputtered and died
And the cotter-pin oars gave the oarlocks the slip
While the time and the gale whirled her round like a chip.

As the bold mutineers turned blue with fright
　　And each seaman thought of his Polly,
The Coast Guard cutter steamed down into sight
And rescued the launch from her dangerous plight

And ended that unequal cotter-pin fight
　By towing the kitty and shipmates so jolly
　Back to the arms of their good papa Colley.

Tuesday, August 29th.

Kept ashore because of the necessity of filling the four places and also because of continued storm warnings.

Much scrubbing and cleaning today. Augean stables will follow us for some time because of the hundreds of dirty shoes in and out, up and down; dirty hands, shredded materials, lack of time to keep up with the accumulating dirt. Lack of time to stow things away, lack of time to prepare, lack of time to repair, pressure of work on engine, on rig, on the necessities and safeguards of navigation, pressure of work. I come across an apt quotation in Washington Irving's *Life of Columbus.*

Let those who are disposed to faint under difficulties, in the prosecution of any great and worthy undertaking, remember that 18 years elapsed after the time that Columbus conceived his enterprise, before he was enabled to carry it into effect; that the greater part of that time was passed in almost hopeless solicitation amidst taunting ridicule; that the prime of his life had wasted away in the struggle, and that when his perseverance was finally crowned with success, he was about his 56th year. His example should encourage the enterprising never to despair.

Wednesday, August 30th. New London.

Headlines in the Herald Tribune: "Britain Studies Hitler's Reply in Midnight Council. London Hears Germany Stands Firm in Its Demands. Poland Warns Slovakia; U.S. Still Holds Bremen."

Yesterday, shortly after dropping our anchor, four little

girls in a small boat rowed around us. "What war news?" we called. After a short huddle. "Averted" their shrill voices answered. Their sea code was good, but were they correct?

Thursday, August 31st.

Rapidly learning that you can't follow in the wake of C.C. without accumulating all of his troubles brought up to date.

As with Columbus, by his own account, "all kinds of obstacles were thrown in the way, by these people and their friends to retard or defeat the voyage. Some men employed upon the vessels did their work in a careless and imperfect manner, and on being commanded to do it over again absconded. Some of the seamen who had enlisted willingly, repented of their hardihood, or were dissuaded by their relatives and sought to retract." Many of the troubles complained of by Columbus at Palos in August 1492 were re-enacted at the foot of Hubbard Street in Brooklyn; and again at Oyster Bay, and again at New London.

Friday, September 1st, 1:50 P.M.

Weighed anchor, proceeding to sea under power. Just one month after our scheduled sailing date. Columbus's sailing date was on a Friday, August 3rd.

The question most frequently put by those on land to those who go to sea is "What do you find to do all day?" And the only answer is "We never find enough time in which to do it all."

We are to find that our course will be charted by two compasses. One, the direction finder, the other the compass of human nature. Dr. Richard Cabot has called the

four points of the compass, "work, play, love, and worship." We are to discover the necessity for limits of work
and play and the impossibility of keeping to the limita-
tions. We are to learn the fine adjustments necessary for
interdependence in a small space and consideration for
others at all times.

Our Commodore is the historian and scholar, the guiding mind who dictates our general course, because he has
a large number of definitive objectives to study and to follow through. He is our teacher, our historical navigator,
our intellectual god. When monotony takes over, he will
remind us of the drama of the indefatigable pioneers and
all that they accomplished and endured. He has known
them since boyhood, studied their charts, followed each
voyage, and, because he has lived their lives vicariously,
he must stand a watch himself, check their navigation
himself, be ready at any hour to seize the chance of re-
living one of their immortal moments.

Sam is an enigma to me because I haven't known many
great scholars near to. We all hope and expect to learn
much from him, for he is extremely generous with his
precious time.

He is very handsome, has a youthful figure, and presents
an impression of self-confidence and the manner of habit-
ual command. He has some of the British quality of reti-
cence and aloofness, and the critical faculties of the
scholar are always there, but a liberal attitude and an
open mind are naturals for him. He wrote to me, last winter, in a light vein, "Bessie and I live by the Morison motto
praetio prudentia praestat—good judgment is better than
money. But then Bessie and I never had any money!"

His family is of the best in the New England tradition,
which means, I suppose, that he has a pirate or two in the

family tree. His inherent interest in American history was early fostered and stimulated by the fact that his grandfather and great-grandfather were intimate friends of our historian William H. Prescott.

Sam spent his childhood summers on Mount Desert Island, and his friends of those years were the intrepid fishermen of the Maine coast. He raced small boats in hot competition there, and later as a grown man, he made many an adventurous cruise for pleasure or research. Among the latter, and quite recently, were long ones in the West Indies for the purpose of checking on the sources of all four of the voyages of Columbus told in the original languages. Latin, Italian, French, Spanish, Portuguese and also, of course, the various English translations. Thus, the Harvard Columbus expedition is to be the culmination of all those researches.

Sam's form of relaxation comes to him in a keen appreciation of the pleasures and amenities of everyday living. The enjoyment of beauty, the sparkling salt sea air, the sensation of the warm sunshine, the refreshing breeze, the painted sunset, the path of the moon, are all to him a part of the happiness of life at sea. He loves the sensuous swing of the Portuguese epic and the stark power of the prayer of Thomas Aquinas. He also enjoys good food and good wine, but he equally enjoys moderation.

His mental powers are deeply occupied with the vast fund of information that he has stored up during his industrious life, and with performing the intellectual flights and speculations that are required of an historian. His preoccupation with these mental gymnastics leaves him less time for the awareness that is required of a man of action. The scarcely perceptible rise of the wind, the dim and distant approach of the fog are sometimes observed too late for the easy shortening of sail. But perhaps this thought comes to me because I am Paul's wife and not Sam's!

The Skipper, on the other hand, is essentially a man of action, which means that his every thought is almost immediately translated into something done. His momentary rest simply means the gathering of his forces to be catapulted at the next objective.

Having a superb physique that has been developed with a colossal energy, and groomed by the most temperate of habits, he has fitted himself equally well for a life at sea or on land, and his resourcefulness and inventive powers would stand him in good stead on a desert island. But he would not thrive as well on a desert island because his motives are largely bound up with human beings.

He loves to think that his voyages kindle the imagination of boys and girls, and therefore help to develop the qualities he most admires—courage, resourcefulness, integrity, love of nature, being useful to others.

One of his greatest qualities, not usually associated with men of action, is intuition. An awareness of everyone and everything about him, and a keen consciousness of what should be done about each one at any given time. Jay is overworked and needs a rest; the mate and bosun are misfits and should exchange places; the cook is homesick and should be replaced; one of the able-bodied seamen is not able bodied and will have to be put on the beach. The lead for the mainsail sheet forms a throat in the traffic, that wire must be seized; wind is rising and sail must be shortened. All this is no sooner perceived than acted on. Jay may protest, the seaman may protest, but in the end the Skipper usually proves right.

That awareness of all minutia must be part of the great

illusive quality of leadership that is so hard to define. A command at sea requires an intuitiveness in emergencies, directing one man here, another there, having a knowledge of which thing must be done first, and how it can best be done.

Being aware of space, and objects in space, means being aware of time. It means a place for everything and everything in its place. It means punctuality and impatience with the unpunctual. It means exacting a great deal from everyone and frequent correction. But it also means, with him, great praise where praise is due and encouragement where encouragement is necessary, and kindness and reward at the needed moment.

No one is idle on the Skipper's boat and least of all himself. There is work to be done in the watches and, when not in your bunk, there is work to be done off watch— the deck to be scraped and sanded, baggy wrinkle to be made, the lifeboats to be got ready to the last detail, ropes to be limbered out, painting to be done, cleaning, polishing, and always the inevitable tidying up. It is endless, endless, the work on a boat—all more compactly done than in our cottage at home, but what if that cottage had a way of rolling and plunging, and throwing spray all over the terrace, and in at the front door? What if there were no nearby shops to buy food or clothing or household articles of any kind? What if we had to forego washing in fear that the water supply may give out? What if the house catches on fire?

All these and many more hazards had to be guarded against by the Skipper, while on the other hand numberless conveniences had been provided for. A hospital bed in case of serious illness; a sea captain's swinging bunk for me; the Mackay Radio sending and receiving set; the ship

of steel to keep off the toredo worm, the square sails designed for the trade winds; a Diesel engine, an aga stove;
loops in the yardarms as an insurance for the men who
were to set and furl the square sails—and all provided for
while working against time, trying to outwit the march
of the seasons that, sooner or later, would herald a hurricane.

A great zest for life is what makes the Skipper fun to do
things with. A zest for work and for play, usually indis-
tinguishable to him and to those about him. After a long
vigil on deck, he will come below at 2 A.M., have a short
sleep and then dawn will find him on deck again, planning, directing; and then, finding me awake, he will make
a comfortable corner for me on deck, bring me a tray
with a hot breakfast and go below and make up our bunks.

I won't try to describe each of the twenty-one souls on
board. But from our wonderful Estonian Captain Jariilo
Walter, the efficient engineer Emerson, our lovelorn mate
Herbert B. Hosmer, Jr., the clever navigator and radio
operator Jack McElroy, our cook Kenneth Spear, right
through the whole group, every man adds much in his
own individual way and several add very greatly to the
general welfare and harmony on board.

Saturday, September 2nd.

A cloudless sky, warm and delicious with a gentle swell
and *Capitana* riding it majestically. "She acts like a big
ship," says Jay in a satisfied key.

Sight a pair of pomarine jaegers and skuas, and several
small flocks of Mother Carey's chickens. After my first lesson in W. B. Alexander's *Birds of the Ocean*, discover that
they are Wilson's stormy petrels, the commonest member
of the family. In the late hours a large white steamer with

two smokestacks approached us from Europe, circled around us and disappeared in the north.

Sunday, September 3rd.

At about 9 A.M. sailed through enormous school of whales blowing and shaking the barnacles off themselves; a large flock of forty or fifty Wilson's stormy petrels follow the boat, rarely lighting, in continuous flight.

Over the air we hear that Chamberlain stated in the House of Commons today that "the time of the ultimatum having elapsed a state of war exists between Germany and England." This news was announced at lunch by Dwight and received in silence and gloom. What next for Europe—and what then for *Capitana?*

The ocean no longer gives that lonely sense that the Ancient Mariner once haunted us with. It has been destroyed by the radio. It is remote, yes, with only a few sea birds and possibly the distant smoke of one vessel in twenty-four hours; always a sense of placing one's future at the mercy of an all-powerful Providence, but loneliness and complete escape, no longer.

1:15 P.M. Small flock of stormy petrels seen bunched and riding the waves. As we approached they became more and more disturbed, till they scattered widely and gradually fell in at the wake of the vessel.

On Sunday, October 7th, 1492, Columbus made this entry:

Towards evening seeing nothing of the land which the *Niña* had made signals for, and observing large flocks of birds coming from the North and making for the S.W., whereby it was rendered probable that they were either going to land, to pass the night, or abandoning the countries of the north, on account of the approaches of winter, he determined to alter his course knowing also that the Portuguese had discovered most of the islands they possessed by attending to the flights of birds.

A good part of the day the men have spent in provisioning the lifeboats. They filled watertight tin cannisters with hardtack and condensed milk, according to marine law, but first burned a candle inside of the cannister so as to make the required vacuum.

Then a drill for Lifeboat No. 1. Two Morrows, two Morisons, Doctor Anderson, Hosmer, the Chef, the Steward (all in life jackets) climbed into the boat swung out on the davits. "Look out for your hands," shouted the Skipper as the boat swung towards our bulwark and would have crushed unwary fingers. Down they were lowered with all the sensations of abandoning ship; it was so exciting that I did everything wrong with my Leica. After drill was over we sailed through a tremendous school of porpoises and I wasted much film trying to get them on the wing.

Everything in our nice little cabin has a place. The bookshelves, the folding table that forms a desk beside the minute stove, the bench at the table, the swinging bunk, all have their lights and shelves conveniently nearby for reading, dressing and odds and ends. The accordion fits exactly across the right of one closet, the Linguaphone and Victrola opposite, while between lie two dress suitcases that need not be unpacked till we get to Lisbon. A folding wicker chair and the wastepaper basket have a place under the desk. In case the electricity must be conserved each of us has a lamp, and an electric torch and a candle.

Monday, September 4th.

Soon after midnight we woke to a surging of waves and rushing of wind, the thud of running feet on deck, hoarse shouts, with an occasional quiet command from the Skipper or Jariilo. Noisy activity and then, with the taking in of the sails, that sudden letting up of stress and strain, the ceasing of tremendous effort, and the knowledge that the driven creature is no longer forced to do more than her powers permit.

This is a hot, turbulent Gulf Stream day. Bright sunshine and beautiful lights and shadows. A warm southeasterly breeze on our quarter. Pictures painted in the colors of Winslow Homer. The tempers of the men might well be frayed by last night, but today they are as cheerful as ever.

Tuesday, September 5th.

Another hot, sunny, but quieter Gulf Stream day—we have only seen three or four stormy petrels, and three or four other birds in the distance, of which I was uncertain. At 9:30 they took in the forecourse. Four diminutive figures high against the sky, clinging on the yard, furling, furling. An almost invisible footrope under their insteps; their bodies leaning against the yard trying to smother the topsail, and nothing but their own sense of equilibrium and co-ordination between them and the deep sea. A beautiful blue sky in the day and starry evening, followed by another squally and turbulent night. A frightfully noisy night it was. Bang, bang, shouts, then running of feet—thud, thud, and a great quiver the full length of the ship as she met the oncoming breakers.

It is tremendously hot, considering that we are making eight and nine knots and the southwest wind blowing hard. I have only a play suit on with nothing underneath, and I'm still hot. Everyone on board is angelic, no cross words, constant offers to help, no criticism. There are several quite indispensable companions. One of these is Jimmy Byrne who is charming, intelligent, considerate and endearing. He contributes enormously to our pleasure and interest.

Wednesday, September 6th.
Frightening war bulletins are being received at night.

Thursday, September 7th, 10:40 A.M.
Another day of making about nine knots. Southwest breeze, suddenly a "chick-achick-achick" and a belted kingfisher flew on board and perched on a rope for a few seconds, then away.

Then Sam read to us from *The Portuguese Pioneers*, by Edgar Prestage, and told us of some of the things that he hopes to find when we reach Corvo, the tiny westernmost island of the Azores. What remnant or reminiscences shall we find? Will there still be echoes of a fable, or even signs of a statue of a man on horseback with his left arm extended and pointing to the West, which was one of the early legends that proved to believers that a new world existed in that direction? Shall we, like Columbus, hear of, and see driftwood that has followed the tides and trade winds from the West Indies?

In the natural course of events, relating to history and biography, one shining figure for hundreds of years will capture the imagination of writers and collectors, will drain wise men of their wealth and energies, and will even ride roughshod over capricious and arbitrary fashion. Amerigo Vespucci pretended to have discovered America in 1497. Both continents are even named after him, because at that time our hero had fallen upon evil days. But the honor of Columbus has been restored, that of Vespucci repudiated, and it is now believed that it was John Cabot, in 1497, who was the first of the three to stand on the new world continent.

Though Columbus himself belittled and destroyed many of his own writings, he guarded with his life's blood the *Codex Diplomaticus*—documents that proved his title to the discovery of the new world and secured to his heirs and assigns land and titles to the new world.

Here again is one of our inconsistencies. What the man himself belittled, we covet; what he cherished is to us insignificant. It is his colossal ambition and courage, his dramatic personality, his cruel end, darkened by failure and despair that grasp and hold our sympathies. Perhaps it is the picture of the wandering stranger holding his little son by the hand, begging for a drink at the gate of the Monastery of Santa Maria de la Rábida (whether this be fact or fiction) that still holds us enthralled in 1939. Then it was that Columbus won the ear of Fray Juan Perez de Marchena in 1484 and the holy father listened attentively to the persuasive arguments that convinced him of Columbus's sincerity.

Perhaps Columbus even then drew from his pocket his cherished Baedeker for India, the little volume of Marco Polo with its minute marginalia in his own Spanish lettering that is to be seen today in Seville. And because this stranger at the gate lived to find a new continent (though not the one he sought) he returned to Seville in such triumph that Ferdinand and Isabella rose to greet him and remained standing while he reviewed the sum of the treasures he could lay at their feet.

Because he returned from his first voyage in triumph, from the second under suspicion, from the third in chains, and from the fourth to die a broken and impoverished man—because of this great human drama, a certain stream of humanity will always follow in his wake, searching for pieces of the puzzle and paying huge prices for rare items of memorabilia.

Friday, September 8th.

Another noisy and sleepless night. Crashes occasionally, and great shivering lurches from end to end of the boat as she plunges into the waves; or sharp slaps on her deck. With the usual vigilance, the forecourse had been furled, while it was still light, and then the topgallant sail soon after. Today they have fastened safety loops to the yards so that the men can put them under their arms when they are furling. We are very proud of our able-bodied seamen Jim and Dwight.

And then in the evening, the stars. All day our attention is riveted on the ocean bed, the whitecaps, the direction of the wind, the angle of the boat, the smoke of a distant steamer, or the stormy petrels now flying, now walking on their little webbed feet. But as darkness approaches, our attention changes to a wider field.

We have each brought with us our old friends and are introducing them to each other. Some of mine are the stars that I learned about in the Planetarium. The Great Dipper and Polaris, Vega the brightest star of the summer, now just over our mast head; Denebola in Cygnus, Altair in Aquila, and in the south, Scorpius gracefully stretched out and showing the full beauty of his long curling tail. And Mars, nearer this summer to the earth than it has been for twenty years, has touched off the war, and

now is receding with a bright mockery. Shooting stars
skim across the sky much as the white flying fish skim the
waves by day.

Those who sleep at night know only a seasonal pattern
of the kaleidoscope in the heavens, but those who stand
watches at sea have almost the full glory of the yearly pageant in twelve hours.

I am so glad I brought along *Star Names*, by R. H. Allen. Someone asks, "Why Sirius?" and then we turn to
Allen and find that—

> Two lovers, Zulamith the bold, and Salnic the Fair
> Straight rushed into each other's arms
> And melted into one;
> So they became the brightest star
> In heaven's high arch that dwelt—
> Great Sirius, the Mighty Sun
> Beneath Orion's belt.

And from John Minsheu's polyglot dictionary of 1617:
"Some thinke that the Dog-starre is called Sirius, because
at the time the Dogge-starre reigneth, Nilus also overflow-
eth as though the water were led by that Starre." This,
I suppose, explains the belief that the Temple of Sak-
kara, dating from about 2700 B.C. was erected in honor of
Sirius.

All books of reference are particularly valuable at sea.
Motion and travel stimulate thought and there is some
leisure in which to think. An hour at the wheel is an hour
when all sorts of questions come to mind, Who first used a
compass? What kind of navigational instruments did Columbus have? How does Columbus compare with other
early explorers? etc., etc.

Sunday, September 10th.

This morning dawned after quite a frightening night. We rolled and we rolled far over, further, further again, and then bang, as my swinging bunk brought up hard against the locker. Great long lunges into the waves and a rotary motion in pulling out of them. Crashes on deck, seas surging by us, wind whistling. Too much noise to allow sleep for more than a few minutes at a time—and then in the early hours of the dawn when Paul had come below for a much needed rest, knock, knock, knock.

"Yes?"

"Skipper, the lifeboat has carried away."

Sleepily, "Which lifeboat?"

"No. 1, sir."

"Enter it in the log."

The thought of what suspicions that lifeboat adrift, sighted and reported, might awaken, sent an added fear through my head. Perhaps Lily, sailing on the *Rex* from Naples yesterday might be told that the *Rex* sighted a capsized lifeboat, and imagined that it was all that was left of *Capitana*!

Divine Service again today, with added significance. Sam gave me copies of my three favorite prayers to add here. They are as follows:

Prayer for Those at Sea

O Eternal God, who alone spreadest out the heavens, and rulest the raging of the sea; who has compassed the water with bounds, until day and midnight come to an end; be pleased to receive into thy Almighty and most gracious protection the persons of us Thy servants, and the ship in which we serve. Send us favoring and not too violent winds, spare us from calms, variables, fog and hurricanes; make us watchful and vigilant that we may escape the violence of the sea, and when near land, avoid the shoals and find the deeps; help us to be considerate to our shipmates, and diligent in our several ratings; grant us patience under any delays or other afflictions that thou shalt see fit to lay on us; grant us a prosperous and pleasant voyage, that we may the more enjoy the blessings of the land, fortified by the health-giving bounties of the ocean, and strengthened by a lively sense of thy watchful protection. Withdraw not thy watchful care over our dear ones at home, and extend the strength of thy right arm to protect all ships and seamen.

A Prayer for Peace

Eternal Father, we pray thee to forgive the blasphemies daily committed in thy name by the nations now at war, and not to abandon mankind because of their provoking cruelty and folly. We beseech thee so to rule and govern rulers and people alike that this conflict be brought to a speedy and just conclusion. Save our nation from being involved; or, if thy will be otherwise, make us thy instrument for securing a just and lasting peace, and for lifting the scourge of war from the shoulders of mankind.

The End of the Prayer of St. Thomas Aquinas for Students Beginning a Task

Thou who makest eloquent the tongues of children, polish our speech, and on our lips pour the grace of thy blessing. Grant us acuteness of understanding, sagacity of interpretation, facility of instruction, and abundant beauty of expression. Instruct us commencing, direct us progressing, perfect us concluding our task, through Jesus Christ our Lord.

The same wind and heavy seas have prevailed all day, with wind velocity increasing to gale force in the middle of the afternoon, when we were hove-to under storm trysail and fore topsail for a couple of hours. The latter was made by Jay out of a Vanitie mainsail kindly given to

Capitana by a former Commodore of the New York Yacht Club, Gerard Lambert. Mr. Lambert has always been a generous and unfailing friend to the sport, and himself a fine helmsman. Then, slowly, haltingly, while we watched, the wind began to abate. Fear gave place to rejoicing, tension to relief. Sam brought out some of his Ms concerning the Azores, and read it aloud. He repeated the story of the stone horseman carved in the cliffs of Corvo, pointing with his left arm to the new world. Again we were looking forward to Corvo, that tiny volcanic island that we were hoping and expecting to see; Horta, where we would get our mail; Ponte Delgada, where we would have a bath; Santa Maria, where Columbus carried out his vow of penance in the face of Portuguese abuse. All these and more we would see and add to the treasures of our memory, and not "Heaven Too"—as yet! We opened a bottle of port for dinner and my Maillard box of candy that Lucy and Lily had given me, and we had a merry evening.

Later the engineer made a little petitioning speech, begging us to forego using electric lights. As I started to go to bed by the light of a votive offering candle I suddenly heard the sharp repeated cries of someone in distress. Louder and louder, the shrieks came down the gangway and went into the wardroom. I threw on a dressing gown and dashed after the strange sounds to find Dick Colley holding in his hands a young tropic bird. It had flown against the sails and fallen stunned, and Dick had him in his hands before he recovered. None of us had ever before seen a live tropic bird so close and we checked his characteristics in *Birds of the Ocean*: "A black line before and over the eye; a black band on the wing; tail of 12 feathers, the central pair very long, bill yellow, legs and

base of toes yellowish, rest of feet black." W. B. Alexander
says, speaking of the North Atlantic Ocean "in this region,
skimmers, gannets and tropic birds are each represented
by a single species," and that species he states is the red-
billed tropic bird. So our tropic bird should not be found
in this latitude, but it was.

*Tuesday, September 12th. Six hundred miles due west
of the Island of Flores.*

Yesterday the jib carried away in a continued blow, and
last night was another hard one for the men. At about two
o'clock the gaff carried away and all hands were on deck
most of the night. I feel very useless, lying comfortably in
my bunk while such stress and strain is going on overhead,
with sleeplessness the only thing I can complain of; but
also very thankful that nothing is expected of me.

Wednesday, September 13th.

The last twenty-four hours have been perfectly heavenly. The most beautiful of all; almost no motion. Last
night in my bunk nothing could be heard but the gentle
trickle of running water against the outer skin of the boat.
No longer the fierce Atlantic Ocean that forty-eight hours
ago had seemed to be on the verge of tearing its way
through our strong steel hull; now just the gurgle of a
little meadow stream that I once waded in as a child in
Europe, with bluebells growing on either bank. Everyone
had a good sleep. The sun is shining, and spirits are high.

We are also very thankful that Jariilo is better. He is
our indispensable mainstay and he has been having what
was probably an attack of appendicitis. The thought of
Jay with a possible attack of peritonitis has been a night-
mare for all of us. We remember the grim story of Wil-

liam Robinson. The vigil of his heroic wife and the ice packs from the nearby fishermen that eventually saved his life after eight days of torment.

But today is no day for dark thoughts. Today is the kind of a day that all seagoers dream of—sunshine, warmth, beauty, rest. It can only be felt, not written about.

Thursday, September 14th.

It was five o'clock in the morning when I heard someone knocking at our door. The mate, Hosmer, was letting me know that Orion was riding high in the sky and just about to make his spectacular exit as the first rays of dawn were appearing. I slipped on a coat and ran up on deck to find an imperturbable calm on the face of the sea. Dull and heavy, it was like molten lead.

"An Irish hurricane," John the rigger said.

They gave me the wheel and I said goodbye to Orion, Betelgeuse, Rigel, and finally Sirius, while the clouds of dawn ahead staged a set for Olympus.

Only three hundred miles from Corvo and another beautiful day.

Friday, September 15th.

Ever since the end of the storm that carried away our gaff, we have had absolutely ideal weather. Sunshine, warmth, and a serene calm. Not enough wind to carry us to Corvo, and the engine has been running for forty-eight hours. Now it is off again and we are almost attaining the rapid speed of two miles an hour. A little barn swallow flew on board and perched on the span between the davits of our lost lifeboat and took a short rest, during which we plied him with crumbs. Then off again, ignoring us and our food. He must be a Florian swallow. This fine weather, we have scarcely seen a bird, only perhaps a dozen Wilson petrels. Whenever refuse is thrown overboard, one or two petrels will appear from nowhere, and make the most of it. It seems as if birds only seek ships in bad weather, when the wake offers them small organisms to eat and possibly also a slight protection from the storm. When the weather is fine they prefer their magnificent solitude.

Our Dr. Chanco is the greatest success. Though he had had only a moderate experience in small boats on the Sound, he has stood his watch, and climbed the rigging, and furled the square sails, and does it better than any, except the professionals. He is a gentle, even-tempered, and agreeable companion at sea. He takes his surgical duties very seriously and sleeps with a stretcher above his bed and a hypodermic needle under his pillow. But he is not an alarmist and has thus far been able to make light of small ailments. If he takes his surgical and medical duties seriously, he also does justice to every other possible duty that presents itself to him. He sanded the deck yesterday for many hours, and is doing the same today, and does it all in a modest and unassuming way. We are extremely fortunate in having him with us.

Saturday, September 16, 2 A.M.

Corvo, the smallest of the Azores. Dwight's sharp eyes picked up a light on the island of Flores and the silver dollar nailed to the mast is his. The only landing is a small cleft in a natural jetty of lava. A native boat (almost the only one) ferried us in on the crest of an incoming wave.

Though the scene, in travel, is always changing, the people and their ways are strangely familiar. A beautiful sunshiny day on a tiny speck of an ocean island in mid-Atlantic, about twelve miles in circumference, and there before us in New England terms is Thornton Wilder's "Our Town." Older, of course and poorer, and shabbier and dirtier, but the same happenings, the same eternal quest. Some of the young men had left the island at an early age, for Portugal or the United States, and had later returned with a family, to retire and eke out a minute fortune during the evening of their days, by means of the fertile nature of their lava-covered homeland. You often hear, "Oh yes, I've been in New York, in Boston, in Detroit; my brother works in Vanderbilt Garden in Newport."

Wee Villa Nova, with its 760 inhabitants, the only community on the island, nestles in the lee. "Have you a penknife?" asked one old man as we trudged along accompanied by a bodyguard of old men, women, and children. "That is something we need on this Island." It is easy to be Santa Claus on an ocean island, and the gratitude is always very sincere.

The little native boat took us all ashore, in relays, the two young rowers bending on their enormously long and heavy oars with colossal strength.

A gentleman to whom we had a letter from Mr. Bensaude, the head of a well-known Portuguese family, told us that he had been on the island for the last twenty-two years and had never once seen a yacht anchor. Can it be that none had actually come here since Charles Wellington Furlong in the *Kitty A* about twenty-five years ago? They added that the last steamer had stopped there in July, and the next one was due to arrive in November. One difference between Corvo and the Greek Islands is that the women are all about in the streets; there is none of the Eastern hiding away.

The anchorage was very poor. Later Paul said, "Jay, I never was happier to get away from an anchorage than I was at Corvo."

"It was like being anchored on glass," was Jay's picturesque rejoinder.

Wednesday, September 20th. Fayal, on the Island of Horta.

On Monday we explored the crater and saw from there a Yankee Clipper glide gracefully first to the smooth surface of the outer harbor, and then into her mooring within the breakwater.

Yesterday, Paul and I had some shooting. After a drive of about three quarters of an hour, we picked up a native who guided us down one of the steep lava cliffs that practically surround all of the Azores. Huge black boulders of lava hang or perch on one another, looking as if a push would precipitate the whole tremendous mass rolling down into the sea. We found a wedge between the high boulders about one hundred feet below the top, where we could see the approach of pigeons on either side or overhead. Very easily they became aware of us and veered off out of gun shot. It was the most beautiful natural butt I have ever shot from, and the most spectacular; the blue Atlantic stretching off towards Pico, St. George and Graciosa. The blue sky with fluffy clouds, the black boulders of lava all around and about us, and the steep decent to a harsh coast of continuous surf and spray, is very fascinating.

I have never seen so many beautifully patched clothes.

Often two old trousers or two old shirts will be converted into one whole one, most ingeniously, with the finest of stitches. The shoes are very generally absent or else sandals made of a piece of a tire are worn. Our guide saved every empty shell to fill and use again. There is no word for "Bakshish" here. A most untouched, unspoiled people. Pleased to hear our stumbling "obrigado" when they do us a favor, and always ready to do another.

The old oxcarts are beautiful with their solid wooden wheels. Great massive yokes and an oval base with basket of wicker woven to form the body. Sometimes you see a pair of oxen in front to pull, and a pair of cows aft, to act as brakes.

After our descent from the crater on Monday we got to the quay in time to watch the Yankee Clipper take off. There was a good deal of a swell. Not ideal conditions, and we watched for half an hour while she taxied to and fro, warming up her engines and trying to get the right momentum. At last she was away with roaring open throttle and four great propellers invisible to the naked eye.

There is a great variety and profusion of growing things on all of the Azorian islands. Evidently both northern and southern plants and trees can grow here. Many cryptomeria, tamariolus, eucalyptus, poplars and the tall tropical axacaria. Hydrangeas flourish in vast profusion, edging the roads, and they even plant them to act as boundary walls. Oleanders, blue morning glories, genesta, camellia, azalea, fuchsia, nasturtiums, portulaca, roses, cosmos are all growing in the garden of the Dabney House on the Consul Dabney Street.

Dabney was from 1870 to 1890 our Consul who thrived on the ingenuous simplicity of the people and was also

kind to them in times of trial. When the day for the retirement of the old man came, he was found in the garden
with his arms affectionately encircling his favorite tree.

Wednesday, September 20th.

We had heard that there was a museum in Horta and
were given the name of Mr. Dionysus. Shortly after arriving, a short, dark, middle-aged man with a scholarly look
approached us and asked very politely in French, with a
Portuguese accent, if he could take us to his home. We
thought that this was a little gesture of hospitality that
would be followed by a trip to the museum, but his home
turned out to be the museum. Hand-hewn wedding chests
and bureau drawers were filled to overflowing; tables
were covered with innumerable artifacts and a collection
of stuffed birds stood on numberless shelves. The prize
pieces were some tiny models that Curator Dionysus had
made with his own hands. One was of a little family in
early Neolithic days. When wound up, the man in the
family shot an arrow from a bow at a mammoth; the
woman hung a skin up to dry, and another woman prepared the next meal over a fire. The solar system, the
Pleistocene Age, the Megalithic Age, the Lake Dwellers,
a sailing vessel of the time of Henry the Navigator when
Portugal was in the heyday of its glory, were all represented, and all were wound up and did stunts. There was
also a small replica of the creation of the Azorian islands,
as they burst, irrepressibly, through their ocean bed to
find a volcanic existence in the sunshine.

Mr. Dionysus was a school teacher, and in bad odor with
the Board of Trustees. Too leftist, they said, and too many
impossible notions. Mechanic, historian, archaeologist,
geologist, astronomer and artist, he was so obviously a

modest Leonardo da Vinci that we asked him where he had received his remarkable general education. His answer was that he had never left the island of Fayal except to visit the island opposite—Pico.

Sam left at 6 A.M. to go to Terceira on *Mary Otis*. We are to meet again at Ponte Delgada on San Miguel.

Thursday, September 21st.

We should have sailed for San Miguel at noon today, but poor weather forecasts are keeping us in harbor till tomorrow. We are here in a very significant time of the history of the Azores.

Years ago, when the cargoes of the world were being carried by myriads of sailing craft, this was a great stopping place for water, wine, and stores. In those days the whole ocean was dotted with white sails, and a day rarely passed without a foray, a race, or a gam, with pirate, competitor or friend. The isolation, such as ours now, was then unknown.

Aeons ago, the nine volcanic Azorian islands were violently ejected from the depths of the ocean and have remained protected bulwarks ever since. By grace of industry, sun, and shower, and the rich fertility of volcanic ash, their undulating highlands have granted a livelihood to their scattered 250,000 souls. They have formed their own natural defenses against the continual onslaught of the sea, and still bear the scars of volcanic upheavals, when lava poured down the steep mountain sides, and ashes reached Lisbon, eight hundred miles away.

The winds and waves have left few harbors, always wearing away the tiny beaches that are covered with large round pebbles as smooth as eggs, and the steep overhanging lava above offers no refuge. Even pieces of driftwood, brought in now and then by swirling ocean currents, are soon carried away again on the ebb of the tide. Frequent wrecks there may be, but salvaging yields no man a livelihood.

Though fires of destruction may have created these islands, the blessings of Heaven and the arduous industry of the natives have kept them alive with vegetation. Crater deeps and shallows, in sharp or gradual undulations, are the natural demarcations of terraced vineyards, terraced fields of grain, and little pockets of exuberant green, bright as emeralds, that tell of sunshine and showers and the long labors of man. The farmers live together gregariously in the villages, owning the terraces here and there about them, and driving their livestock daily to and from their land. Huge masses of hydrangea that match sea and sky border every roadside, line the paths, fill the empty spaces at the bases of trees, and take the place of stone walls. Along the highways, dozens of restless wagtails add their flashes of yellow and blue.

One garden on San Miguel, of about twenty acres, is bordered and crossed twice by a cryptomeria hedge of trees forty feet high, footed by hortensia. The garden is filled with tea plants, and is bordered alternately by camellia, azalea, and oranges. This is a garden of industry. It is overrun with small workers aged eight to sixteen. No time for them to play or make mischief.

Thomas Hickling made a home and planted a garden at Furnas on San Miguel, which acquired the title of "Yankee Hall," and to which his nephew William H. Prescott, the American historian, came in 1806, when he was a boy of ten. In this cradle of maritime pioneers, the young Prescott must have received much of his inspiration concerning the early Portuguese and Spanish mariners.

With the coming of power and the consequent decrease of stopovers in small ports, the Azores were no longer steppingstones in the Atlantic crossing. Their communication turned chiefly towards Portugal and occasional north and south voyages. Now, however, they are again steppingstones. Charles Lindbergh chose Horta as the first refueling station for the trans-Atlantic Yankee Clipper. The islands are being relied upon for valuable information concerning weather forecasts. They are being visited by more and more people. They are becoming a part of two continents. They are receiving the publicity that seems to be necessary to support life in this era, and they will once more reap some of the riches that used to be theirs. One of Henry the Navigator's captains, Diogo de Seville, came upon the Azores about 1427, when in search of the legendary island of St. Brendan, much as Columbus discovered America in his search for India. By 1439 the seven easterly Azores were known. The two most westerly, Corvo and Flores, were discovered by Diego de Teive, with the aid of a Spanish pilot from whom Columbus later received information and encouragement.

Sunday, September 24th. Delgada.

As soon as we landed yesterday afternoon Margot and Dwight and I came to this nice little comfortable modern hotel at Furnas. We had a swim in a hot sulphur pool and afterwards a delicious omelet, *vinho cheiro,* and pineapple, and a hot bath in a real bathroom. Here we found one of the survivors of a submarine attack. The submarine scare is everywhere. Dwight wanted to introduce the sur-

vivor, an Englishman, to Jay, but Jay said, "No, I would
rather not know just what is going to happen when we
meet our submarine, it would spoil the fun."

Dwight, "Have you painted the American Flag on our
hull, yet?"

Jay, "Better we paint the British flag, then we might
have some excitement."

Our survivor is from a British freighter which was carrying coal from Cumberland to Montevideo.

In February 1493, on his triumphant return from his
first voyage, Columbus was driven, after a frightful storm,
onto the island of Santa Maria, most southerly of this
group. Here he fulfilled his vow of penitence by sending
half of his crew to the little church to offer up prayers of
thanksgiving for their salvation, and here the Portuguese
showed their jealousy and anger by attacking the men
while at their devotions.

That accidental stopover, induced by a great storm, was
the first suggestion of the Azores as a steppingstone in the
route between Europe and its western continent. Soon
the pioneer mariners of Portugal, Spain, England and the
Scandinavian countries were using them for their cargo
fleets north and south, east and west.

At Horta, we had found an opportunity to shoot pigeons
(the woodcock and quail seasons being closed) and that
took us quickly into a fascinating wilderness of black
lava. Now we again are seizing an opportunity to pene-
trate beyond the ordinary tourist line.

We left our motor on the highroad and with our guns
and a strong young Azorian guide descended a beautiful
ravine, through a half-finished tunnel where men and
boys were building a roadway that will, before long, con-
nect the primitive fishing village with a highroad. The

youngsters, from nine to twelve years old, were gaily shouldering baskets of earth out of the excavations as the men filled them with the heavier spading, and they greeted us with welcoming "Bons dias."

The tiny village stands only a few feet above the high-water mark. There were almost as many boats on the stony beach and runway as there were houses on the shore, and as we approached, it was moving day for one of the families. Grandmother, father, mother and babe, children, bureaus, beds—all were starting out on their only highway, the ocean. Friends and neighbors were giving a hand to the head boatman, who took the initiative in choosing the moment of an onrushing comber for launching the heavy native boat.

There we found a boat awaiting us that was to take us under the cliffs, in search of wild African pigeons. They put me in the bow while our boat was still high and dry, and with Paul's help they ran her down on the next comber and all jumped aboard. The sun shone warm, the blue ocean rocked us to and fro on big gentle swells, we loaded our guns and held them ready expectantly while from behind a distant cliff a cloud of pigeons assured us of their presence by taking flight.

"Hsst—madame," and our guide showed me a little firecracker that he proceeded to light with his cigarette and then throw at a cave in the wall. Bang—and several birds left their hiding places and with startling swiftness disappeared into the distance. For about two hours, pigeons circled tantalizingly about, towards and above us, or flew ahead, but always out of gunshot. The combination of towering bird and rocking boat was too much for my shooting. I wondered how I had ever missed a dove while standing on level ground on my own two feet, but Paul brought his down almost every time. We returned on donkeys up the steep hill to our car and that afternoon we drove back by the northern road. At times it was so like a Scotch moor that we looked for a line of butts.

We stopped at a tea factory, where a dignified and attractive owner of the property, a man of about sixty, showed us about. He wore a small red ribbon in his buttonhole which I thought was a badge of the Legion d'Honeur. "No, madame," he said, "I have twice been governor of this island." The tiny church on his property bore the date of 1701 and is the oldest in San Miguel. We signed our names in his guest book and we were delighted to recognize a picture of *Aloha*, signed by Harriet and Arthur Curtis James, when they sailed across the Atlantic in 1921. And here are we in the Azores, beautiful *Aloha* junked, and *Capitana* carrying some of her blocks and yards. The former governor of these islands might have been our old friend Jo Alsop, San Miguel exchanged for Connecticut and "cha" for tobacco.

Then we went on to a linen factory where we bought yards of linen for sheets and huge bath towels at a dollar apiece, and where the factory workers, mostly girls and women, looked happy and healthy.

The night before our last, September 29th, Sam shoved off with Bill Stevens and others on *Mary Otis* to see the island of Santa Maria. Sam wanted to place a wreath in the old church where Columbus, on his return voyage in 1493, sent his men to offer a prayer of thanksgiving for being saved from the great storm, and he was anxious to recreate and verify for himself the scene of the savage attack.

The Morrows, Jim Byrne, Elizabeth, and I have come back to luxuriate in this nice little hotel in Furnas while

Paul and the Doc and Dick Colley are staying with the boat, and making necessary purchases ashore. Last night we saw a movie of Yvonne Printemps as Adrienne Lecouvreur, ten cents admission. A confusing story, between the Portuguese captions, French diction, and watching the charm and play of emotion of Y. P.'s entrancing features.

Saturday, September 30th.

Fully expected to sail for Lisbon at noon today. Suddenly from out of the blue came a radio report to the effect that the *Mary Otis* had carried away her rudder. Could it be a coincidence, or were they joking? From the diary of Columbus, Monday, August 6th, 1492: "The rudder of the caravel *Pinta* became loose, became broken and unshipped."

We immediately weighed anchor and in about two hours saw a tiny speck on the horizon ahead which in another hour turned out to be the little yawl lamely limping back with one of the huge native oars rigged so as to form a jury rudder, and fortunately, no contrary winds or high seas to endanger her. Wonderful luck that the rudder snapped before they set out on a far longer passage.

Thursday, October 6th.

This afternoon Sam read to us about Columbus' storm-driven, and unwelcome arrival at Santa Maria on the return from his first voyage. He read the chapters from Irving, Winsor, and Charcot and then followed with his own account just written. The comparison was absorbing, and to our delight we all agreed that S.E.M.'s account proved beyond doubt the value of his three dimensional history.

Irving is the story teller with human interest, but long-winded and verbose; Winsor has the more concise and scholarly approach; Charcot's history is the one-sided account of a sailor; but Sam's has a happy combination of the best of all three, plus the sure touch of experience. He is a historian and story teller, *sans peur et sans reproche.*

Tuesday, October 10th.

Lisbon, like Rome, like San Francisco, is built on hills. A beautiful city dominated by an ancient Moorish citadel, that was almost completely destroyed by an earthquake and fire in 1755. Fortunately that date was early enough so that it was rebuilt with taste and on a good plan, and has a little Champs Elysées cutting through the center. The populace, either living at or sauntering along the water's edge, still seems to strain its eyes for the absent explorer, about to return from another discovery in the East, or from the new world. Prince Henry's picture in the Museu Antigo shows the courage, tenacity, and strength that Portugal knew so well in her great day of explorers.

Sam and Elizabeth are at the Embassy, and others at various hotels. We are in the Aviz, a sumptuous palace, once privately owned, but now a luxurious hotel.

Thursday, October 12th. Lisbon.

Lunched at the Negrisco and had a delicious sole mornay, with vinho verde—the best restaurant in Lisbon. Dined last night on board the U.S.S. *Trenton* with Admiral Courtney where we met the Italian Naval Attaché Bimelli, and his wife. He had already heard about our expedition and said, "Today, I wrote to my minister, yes, really, to my minister, and said 'I am going to meet Capt. and Mrs. Paul Hammond who have sailed across the Atlantic on *Capitana.*' If more people would take such voyages there would be no wars because such a voyage teaches what life is, and the voyagers learn to love the people they meet along the way."

We dined at the Legation with the Herbert Pells (Our minister to Portugal, and his wife), Elizabeth, Sam, the Bensaudes, Jim and Dick Colley.

Friday, October 13th.

A lazy morning writing and reading. Another delicious lunch at the Negrisco, after which we took the ferry and went to Mrs. Herbert Scoville's Quinta Palacio da Bacalhôa.

As Mrs. Scoville had returned to her home in Connecticut, her nice little secretary, Miss Eloisa, showed us about, and it was perfectly beautiful. Originally old enough to have a Moorish feeling, it was bought from a princess by Albuquerque, the second viceroy of India, and through him elaborated, with an Indian influence added. When Mrs. Scoville and her husband bought it, it was roofless and practically floorless, only walls and foundations standing. She has transformed it into a comfortable and livable home, adding interesting ideas of her own—ingenious, tasteful and dramatic. A great white bathtub is a magnificent circular piece of marble from Cintra, sunk in the floor of the round tower room, giving off her own bedroom. White, white walls throughout, with absolutely nothing on them, everything simple and restful. The only ornaments are small colored tiles outlining every door and window. Tiled or stone floors everywhere, with dark Queen Anne furniture and the general effect beautiful, dignified, and imaginative.

A formal garden of box-bordered flower beds fills the enclosure, and as you open the Moorish window, the heavy scent from the boxwood rises up through the shafts of sunlight as it would in South Carolina.

Saturday, October 14th.

The Bimellis and an Italian Naval Attaché called for us at 9:30 and we went aboard *Capitana*. They were much interested. At 4:00 Mr. Webb came for Dick Colley and us, and we all drove to Evora, a fascinating old town with Roman and Moorish influence. We are staying in the stronghold of the Inquisition and having our meals in the Judgment Hall. Our rooms are at the end of miles of chilly corridors where there are arrows to show us our way. Very clean and quite comfortable enough. The Cathedral, or *Sé*, is an interesting example of fourteenth-century architecture. The town very higgledy-piggledy in its formless growth. It was the early seat of many of the kings. The peasants are picturesque in their native costumes. The men wear a coat of sheepskin with short sleeves, and sheepskin chaps; no buttons in front, and swallowtails behind. The women are very gay in yellows and reds, and they have a superb carriage as they balance heavy loads, supported by doughnut shaped cushions on their heads.

Food seems always to be plentiful and always good. Quinces grow wild everywhere, and quince jelly sells in every shop. Sheep cheese is something new to us, in dairy products. Portugal has all sorts of traditional delicacies and native dishes that continue to be passed on from one faithful generation to another, and the *vinho verde,* meaning green, or new, wine, accompanies many a delicious meal.

Sunday, October 15th.

I wandered about the town (Paul away shooting) and saw the Romeos addressing their Sunday courting to the Juliets on the balconies. Yesterday we found, and were fortunately able to buy, three peasant bags of beautiful native workmanship. They were the only three we have found anywhere in Portugal. Little flat, woven and embroidered purse bags, worn on Sundays and fete days over the left arm, and worked in fascinating designs and colors, no two alike.

Monday, October 16th.

Another day of shooting for Paul, with Mr. Sillem, the Dutch Minister, and Mr. Reynolds, a collateral descendant of Sir Joshua. Mr. Reynolds married an American girl. He was born in Lisbon and has lived here most of his life. They have a large cork factory and large farming estates in the Allenteyo country. He took us to his house, near Setúbal, the next day. His wife and two children are charming, and gave us tea.

While Paul was shooting, the rest of us attended a ceremony at St. Jeronimo, the beautiful monastery in which Vasco da Gama, and the great Portuguese poet Camões are buried.

During the ceremony Mr. Antonio Ferro stood near me. He is the Propaganda Minister who organized the Portuguese Exhibit at the New York World's Fair two years ago. Bertie Pell read a speech and Sam placed a wreath on the tomb of Vasco da Gama while I placed one on the tomb of

Camões. They lie opposite each other across the aisle, the honors equally divided. Afterwards we repaired to the hotel Aviz for a sumptuous lunch. Pretty little Portuguese dolls of wood, painted in bright colors in various native costumes stood at each place. There were a great many distinguished Portuguese present, but the language difficulties were great and even the names are already forgotten.

Wednesday, October 18th.

Returned to the ship at 4 P.M. Sam told us about Columbus's meeting with John II at Valparaiso on the return from his first voyage.

Columbus, triumphantly certain that he had discovered the land of his dreams, at the first opportunity sought out the king who had formerly refused his support. The arrogant assurance with which he announced his success nearly cost him his life. When the interview was over, and Columbus had taken his leave, John's courtiers begged to be allowed to follow and destroy him, but John refused his permission, and Columbus lived to make his three later voyages.

Thursday, October 19th.

Back in our little cabin, bathed, shampooed, manicured and in clean clothes. We brought back with us Portuguese foods such as sole, red mullet, pineapples, cake, coffee, and sheep cheese. We are now prepared to cast anchor off Sagres, the rugged point of cliff jutting out into the Atlantic just south of Cape St. Vincent.

At about 9:30 Sam and Dwight went ashore in the dory to determine whether the base of the "school of navigation" of Henry the Navigator had been on the Promontory of Sagres or the Cape St. Vincent. Sagres means sacred and is referred to by Azurare, the Portuguese historian, as the site of the school and town founded by Prince Henry in 1421.

Sam and Dwight landed shoulder-deep in breakers and we watched through glasses the two bedraggled figures giving their passports to the uniformed police with one hand, while they tried to rearrange their wet clothes with the other hand so as to feel less wet. They then started off on a five-mile trek to the Sacred Promontory. They found in the floor of the old fort a circular ornament, possibly once a rude compass, about 100 feet in diameter, that might have been placed in the center of Prince Henry's seacoast town. It was Mr. Dionysus who told Sam about this circular formation of stone.

They are bleak, bleak spots, these two westernmost points of Europe, jutting out into the Atlantic Ocean with great breakers perpetually throwing their spray a hundred feet high. Here Prince Henry waited and watched. Here he organized and inspired expeditions to explore along the African coast. For, as his chronicler says, "Above all was this Prince bound to attempt the discovery of things which were hidden from other men, and secret." *

Saturday, October 21st. Spain.

It was raining as we entered and steamed slowly up the Odiel River to Huelva where we anchored. Huelva is an Arabic word meaning frontier, and it was there that Columbus fitted out for his first voyage. We were beginning to get a magnificent view of Gertrude Whitney's colossal statue of Columbus. He stands about two hundred feet

* Azurara, *The Chronicles of Conquests and Discoveries of Henry the Navigator* (London: George Allen and Unwin, 1936).

high, assuming the form of the crusader that he believed himself to be, and proudly facing the new world that he discovered.

Sunday, October 22nd.

At 10:00 A.M. a Spanish delegation came on board. They arrived in a launch in which they would escort us to several nearby sites of everlasting fame. Sam had brought a wreath all the way across the ocean for this particular occasion. Inside of the huge base that supports the statue are two oversized seated figures of Ferdinand and Isabella. We entered and stood around these statues reverently while Sam spoke a few words of dedication and placed the wreath at the feet of Columbus' Queen. When this was over, we all boarded the small model of the *Santa Maria.* It is only a conjectural model, because nothing exists to describe the original accurately, but the details are carefully thought out, with desk, chair, bed, arquebuses, astrolabe, hourglass, etc.

Then we crossed the Odiel River to the church of La Rábida, where we reconstructed the famous scene of Columbus stopping at the gate with his little son Diego, begging for bread and water. Fray Juan Perez, impressed by the commanding stranger, and himself versed in cosmographical lore, listened sympathetically to his eager story and eventually pleaded the cause of Columbus with Isabella. La Rábida is a simple and handsome example of fifteenth-century architecture and looks as if it might not have been changed since Columbus lived there. In the very same refrectory where Columbus and his young son ate many meals, we opened our picnic lunch which was designed for ten and eaten by seventeen. The pious monks gave us wine, but refused all food for themselves.

Then we were driven to Palos, which is about two miles up the Tinto River. All of this region, though deep water five hundred years ago, has since then silted up and is now mere shallow mud flats. You can still see, however, a small trickle of the stream from which the mariners drew the water for their caravels in 1492. Not far away was Santa Clara de Moguer, the church where Columbus said his last mass before sailing. The little madonna before which he prayed is still there, and another sacred spot is the place where he did penance in accordance with a vow on his return. Palos is the place where the Pinzon family came from, the brothers who did so much in equipping and sailing the vessels, but who failed Columbus on that Christmas eve when the *Santa Maria* settled on a coral reef, off the island of Hispaniola, and were never again to be trusted. To this day, there are descendants of theirs living in Palos.

Monday, October 23rd.

Such a wonderful drive from Huelva to Seville; why is Spain so distinctive and why are Spaniards such individuals? Every landscape suggests either a painting of El Greco or Goya or Zuloaga, every mounted horseman one of a thousand different Don Quixotes, every donkey rider one of as many varieties of Sancho Panzas. On account of the hot sun and the cold shadows, men and boys wear either a native cap or a huge sombrero. Every man and boy carries an extra loose garment thrown over his shoulder. It is unfitted and comfortable, and adapted to every need. It may serve as protection from the sun or as a warm blanket at night.

Except for the peasants in the fields, the women are always in black and they wear it with grace and dignity. They put me in mind of Oliver's query to his father in

George Santayana's *Last Puritan*. Why, asked the boy, did his father paint his beloved yacht black, and christen her the *Black Swan?* Because black, came the answer ". . . is the ultimate background of space and of consciousness, satisfying intrinsically, and by contrast a source of precision and liveliness in other colours. It tires less, it protects more . . ." * Half Spanish himself, Santayana must have been thinking of the women in Spain.

Guidebooks and natives tend to keep our eyes close to the ground and we forget that the sky and cloud effects of every country shape the character of its people as much as do their rivers and their mountains. Only in Scotland can you find the vivid colors and rainbows that come and go with swift passing showers over Wuthering Heights, and only in the Holy Land do you see clouds of the Resurrection. Only in New England does the lighthouse stand out against the blue sky like the pictures of Edward Hopper. Only in Spain does one see the gray curtain of Zuloaga's landscapes forming a background for the attenuated figures, and long pale lean faces of El Greco.

Here at sunset, there is often a dark, threatening, leaden grayness that fashions the western clouds in a flat curtain falling short of the horizon. The sun's rays behind the curtain fall lightly, shining on a grove of olive trees or a Moorish mosque, or a church low-lying on a green hilltop.

Our great stone hotel, Alfonso XIII, offers the dignified service of a reduced gentle lady. Fine linen sheets and pillowcases, bed spreads and blankets, coronet-embroidered. Marble floors with the expensive rugs in storage. Down to a dinner without butter and a little notice at the end of

---

* George Santayana, *The Last Puritan* (New York: Scribner, 1936), p. 177.

the menu—"No postre"—politely apologized for by the amiable but inefficient head waiter. We ask for "café complet" for the following morning, and the waiter advises us to take tea as "there is no coffee in Spain."

Thursday, October 26th, 9 A.M.

We met Sam and Elizabeth and John McElroy at the Columbian Library and saw, among many interesting things, Ferdinand's copy of Seneca's *Medea*. Sam pointed out the following quotation. "There will come a year in the series of centuries when the ocean will loose its chains, and a mighty continent will lie revealed and Tiphis will discover new worlds, and Thule will no longer be the last of lands." In the margin beside this quotation is, in Ferdinand Columbus' handwriting, "Haec prophetia impleta est par patrem meum Christoforum Colon Almirantem anno 1492." I took some pictures of pages of books and maps and passed on to Sam the film that the Marquis of Mérito had kindly given us, of every page of the Marco Polo or Christopher Columbus on which were marginalia.

This collection of books is what remains (and there is still a substantial remainder, though years of neglect did much damage) of a superb library collected by Ferdinand Columbus. He built himself a beautiful house in Seville, but there are no remains now of either his house or garden.

After that we went to see the Archives of the Indies in which are all the documents to do with the West Indian or South American colonies—a very handsome and elaborate building with rooms and rooms full of archives.

Friday, October 27th. Madrid.

Arrived two and one half hours late after a comfortable night. Searching for breakfast on the train, we climbed over and around seething, half-sleeping humanity in eight cars that reminded me of "the hard" in Russia. They had been sitting up on the benches, five in each seat, all night. Mostly soldiers, some old people and a few babies. There was one prostrate form, lying in the aisle, completely covered by a blanket. I thought it must be a dead child, but as it had vanished when we returned, it may have been just a sensible person very full of courage, attempting a somewhat risky rest.

Madrid is frightfully crowded because everyone who has been driven out by the civil war has now returned, and people who have lost their homes, or had them damaged, are all staying at the hotels. The Ritz greeted us with "no rooms at all," but we just stood there looking dejected and presently we were ushered up to a nice one. Even at the Ritz you find on Thursdays a menu at both lunch and dinner, offering a "plato unico" only. On Mondays "no postre," and no butter on any day of the week.

Don Luis Bolin, the head of the Tourist Bureau, a branch of the ministry of information and tourism, has been very helpful in taking us to the Royal Palace (where no one is allowed now) to see a painting by Alejo Fernandez (1470-1543), called "La Virgen del buen Aires, Patrona de los Navigantes," by the Spanish; by the English, "Our Lady of the Fair Winds." According to Sam it is the only contemporary portrait of Columbus, and he asked us to get a photograph of it and also see it, so that he could describe it in connection with the frontispiece of the two-volume edition of his *Admiral of the Ocean Seas*.

It was fortunate for Sam, and the Harvard Columbus Expedition that, because Paul had won the Queen's Cup in the ocean race from New York to Santander in 1928, he had made some powerful Spanish friends who now came to our rescue. Don Luis Bolin was one of these. We are among the very first tourists to visit Spain since the end of the civil war. During those three years, all works of art had been carefully hidden away by both factions, and these are only now slowly coming to light again. The portrait in question had last been heard of in Seville, in the private suite of King Alfonso, but according to Sam's telegram, it was now supposedly in Madrid—where, nobody knew. Paul did a most intricate Sherlock Holmes detective stunt in first finding a photograph of the portrait, by canvassing every shop that sold reprints of famous paintings, and then sending it to Don Luis, who in turn unearthed the portrait in the cellar of the Royal Palace—all within forty-eight hours. He then telephoned us that it had been brought to a reception room where we could see it, and I was able to photograph it myself.

We have twice been to the Prado, which is thrilling; they say that the paintings are hung better than ever; not everything is yet to be seen—no sculpture, no Goya's "Maja."

Don Luis drove us out to University City where I had been with the Morrows and Murat Williams yesterday, and his story was terribly interesting. He was the man who was in England and arranged for the famous flight to the Canaries. He had been in prison the three years of the war. But he said, "We have been very lucky, we have lost no one; my mother and two brothers and three sisters are still alive. I have no car because it was stolen; we lost everything, but that is nothing." Most vivid of all the earthly wounds in Madrid are the network of trenches in the heart of the city that carry signs on which are written *Ellos* and *Nosotros*.

The women are all in black, with many silver fox capes in the evening as it is extremely cold, but no décolletage. The Falangists are in a serious mood of thankfulness that they are alive, and are interested in the work ahead of rebuilding the devastated areas and restoring the morale and spirit of the people.

Sunday, October 29th. Toledo.

Don Luis Bolin provided an interpreter, Señor Carlos de la Lastra, and the Marquis of Mérito procured a car, and we drove the beautiful straight road to Toledo in about an hour. At the Alcázar, we were met by one of the commanders who had defended it during the great siege. He walked painfully but successfully with a cane.

Toledo is a fascinating city on a high hill surrounded by the Tagus River. The colors are of untinted olive greens, browns, blacks and whites, unrelieved by brightness of color, as it seems to me, are all Spanish towns.

When we were introduced to the commander, Julian Cuarto Sanchez, "Serreño Commandante de Infanteria, mutilado de guerra por la patria, Conservador del Materiel del Alcázar del Toledo," he proceeded to show us the greatest picture of destruction and heroism imaginable.

We met the Governor and he was very gracious and nice. After lunch we saw the wonderful El Grecos in the house that he lived in, and most wonderful of all was the "Burial of the Count of Orgaz," in the Church of San

Tomé. It is one of the most interesting and beautiful large canvasses I have ever seen.

Left on the 8:30 train for Seville.

Monday, October 30th.

Arrived at 8 o'clock.

Don Luis Medina had very kindly spoken of us to his brother the Duke of Alcalá who lives in the Casa de Pilatos, the impressive palace in the Mudejar style, that we saw as tourists the other day. The Duke has 36 titles, but has married the Duchess of the House of Pilatos and none of his 36 titles are as high as hers, so he has to take his wife's name of Alcalá and renounce his own of Medina Celi.

The Duke came around to see us and asked us to drive out to see the Roman ruins and have tea with them afterwards; he is also going to try to arrange some shooting for Paul. He was extremely nice with the invariably good manners of Iberians.

At four o'clock the Duke and a little friend of the Duchess's came for us in a 1928 Buick, borrowed from a garage, and they took us to see the Roman ruins called the "Italica." We were driven by his own chauffeur and Paul remarked that he was a careful driver. "He ought to be," said the Duke, "he was trained by a bullfighter who kept telling him that if he was going to be killed he preferred the bull ring to an automobile accident."

The ruins, of about 200 B.C. are well preserved and the guide enjoyed describing the bloody gladiatorial combats. He pointed out the gates through which the wild lions had come plunging toward the gladiators, the high wall to protect the spectators from the wild animals, the pool in which fights were held with large and dangerous fish, and the small room with mosaic floor where the wounded gladiators were killed. "Very strange," said the Duke with a shudder.

Later, they drove us back to the palace for tea, after first showing us about. In the entrance hall of the intimate apartments of the Duke we found a series of pictures painted by a Spaniard, the subject being somewhat like the "Cries of London," but with rollicking sadism instead of sentiment. One was of a bull tossing the two halves of his matador in the air. Another showed the bull as having killed horse, matador, picador, and toreador and about to jump the fence to end it all. They were not my idea of jollity and I was glad to hear the Duchess say, "Honestly, I don't like them, I think they are very grim." She is young and charming and looks just like a Goya. She is the youthful and sporting Duchess, speaking her own mind and acting on impulse. They told us of the death of the Duke of Veragua, the direct descendant of Christopher Columbus. "He was just a simple, gentle old man," said the Duchess, "who enjoyed living a quiet country life, who loved his dogs and horses, and was without political ambitions of any kind. But one day, without trial, he was summarily shot."

Now that the war has been won by the Nationalists the Loyalists are falling in line. Chaos has given way to order and patriotism, and they say, "There is no truth but the truth of church and state." So Franco's picture hangs at one end of the Ritz dining room, and José Antonio de Ribera's picture at the other end. Franco's picture is at every street corner, in every theater and every station, etc. "Viva España" is written in great letters wherever it can be seen, on the walls of houses, on billboards in the country, on shop windows, on the little pieces of paper that are wrapped around the sugar with the "té complet."

Thursday, November 2nd. Cadiz.

We left the Andalusia Palace in Seville at 4 P.M. on Tuesday in a good car and were driven in a rainstorm down to Jerez. The greatest sherry merchants in Spain are the family who own and manage the Gonzalez, Biass Company in Jerez-de-la-Frontera. The Duke of Alcalá had given us a card to Manolo Gonzalez Gordon. A Spanish custom adds the mother's name to that of the father, and the Gordon belongs to the distaff side of Manolo's family.

Manolo and his brother Hernandez conducted us through the *bodéga,* where the numerous gigantic hogsheads are embellished with the signatures of distinguished visitors. One hogshead is for royalty: Alfonso XII, Alfonso XIII, and "Jaime." One is a blank in respectful memory of the dead. The name of Queen Victoria Eugenia came next, then Juan Belmonte the great bullfighter, then Franklin D. Roosevelt, Jr. But perhaps the most venerated of them all is the hogshead dedicated to the Defenders of the Alcázar at Toledo, and signed by many of the commanders. All the while that we were being shown through the *bodégas,* we were constantly being offered sips of delicious sherry by an old retainer, who dipped a little silver cup with a very long handle, first into a dry sherry, then into a less dry one, then into the famous "1847," and lastly into a very sweet liqueur tasting of raisins.

The brothers were very gay, spoke perfect English and we drank to Spain in many tiny tastes of sherry. To our delight Manolo invited us to come there the next day at eleven and have a day of shooting with them. We returned to Cadiz in the drenching rain and spent the night on *Capitana.*

The following day we drove to Jerez and met many of the Gonzalez family: Señor and Señora Gonzalez Gordon, two more of the latter's sisters, and their husbands, their mothers, and a lot of children—all at a nice little shooting lodge. The four men that had married five of the sisters were there. One of the sisters had died and her widower had married another. The Italian husband, a lively amusing tough guy, enjoyed saying, "What do they say about what is left on a bargain counter? Oh, yes, the remnant—the remnant is the one I married. She was the only one left."

We all set out much as we should for a day of shooting in Thomasville, Georgia, only the series of short drives was within walking distance of the house. One horse and four or five beaters were assistance enough. In our last drive, as the sun was setting, our improvised butts were strung along under and between huge, beautiful umbrella pines. There was a little corn field behind us and a small green rise immediately in front of us, over which the partridges flew towards us. Each drive was a changing scene of olive trees, corn fields, distant mountains, and umbrella pines.

After three drives we came back to the house for a very good lunch in the sun (only the six shooters, me included); the wives and children all had a separate lunch. We had a cold omelet with fried potatoes in it; a cold Wiener schnitzel, another cold meat, rolls, *pâté de foie gras,* and almonds. Sherry of two kinds, of course, and then off for three more drives. Lots of mosquitoes, but as we were well covered they didn't bother us very much, they were not as virulent or as swift-flying as ours—somewhat lethargic and easy to kill. Going out we saw some of the white egrets perched on the cattle, eating the lice, but they are quite wild and made it difficult to get close enough for a picture.

At the end of the afternoon came a sumptuous tea, with a delicious meat loaf with a sweetish jelly, accompanied by a sort of doughnut called *charros*. Flour and boiling water are combined to the right thickness. Then the mixture is put in a pastry bag, and the dough pushed in snakelike patterns into a frying pan with sizzling olive oil. When served it is very hot and crisp outside and soft inside; then you sprinkle granulated sugar on it and it is the tastiest tea cake imaginable.

Spain leads all other countries in the production of olives, and after tea they showed us the oil press where they squash and squeeze the olives. The first pressing extracts pure oil, but subsequent pressures yield only an inferior quality. During the season of production, which is short and high-powered, they have two working shifts of eight hours each. Mr. Gonzalez Gordon told us that they had turned a church into a school for the children of the employees. They then drove us back to their house where we saw a pleasant drawing room with a bowl of zinnias that might have been arranged and painted by Redon. After which they very kindly lent us their car and chauffeur to take us back to *Capitana*. We drove to the boat first, but finding she had been moved out to the stream for a safer berth while we were gone, we drove to the Atlantic Hotel where we spent the night.

Friday, November 17th.

Bound for the Canaries after a week in Madeira. There we found once again the Portuguese to whom we said goodbye in Lisbon. Again the gentle, pretty manners, the ready smile, and "muito obrigado" from shopkeeper and farmer. The daintily wrapped package in fine striped paper with the little handle of wood to hold it, and again the good food. The poor man's fish, *espada,* is a filet, fried in olive oil and is as good as the best sole meuniere to be found at the Ritz; added to this are little chunks of veal en brochette, topped off with Madeira and a piece of *bola de miel,* a dark, fruity gingerbread that improves with time and is not too sweet.

The Portuguese are a gentle, pious people, with native humility. Their bullfights are not orgies of killing. Fine-blooded horses are used and neither the horses nor bulls are killed. Capital punishment has been abolished. The rent laws are entirely in favor of the tenant, which seems to be a successful attempt to protect him from losing his home. Provided he pays his rent during the first week of the month he can stay there forever, and the land-lord cannot raise the rent.

Natural piety thrives, like the flowers, on the sunshine of Portugal and her islands. Strolling among the hills where the vineyards are plentiful and the poorer people live in a tiny spotless one-room house of white plaster, thatched roof, and no windows, you are a welcome stranger. Have no fear of annoying the peasant owner. Push the gate gently a little wider and you will see him sunning himself on the flower-grown terrace a few yards square. Through the open door between the bed and the ward-robe will stand a pretty painted bureau, the shrine of this little home. In the center, there will perhaps be a tiny statuette of the Madonna and child standing beside a cru-cifix. Small vases of roses and violets are the only orna-ments to be seen. The only pictures are of Scriptural subjects, cut out of the colored sections of newspapers and magazines and nailed on the walls with loving care.

One day in looking for Mr. Hinton's house we rang the wrong gate-bell and a pretty maid led us through a lovely garden to the front door of the home of an English couple who had heard of the approach of the Harvard Columbus Expedition, a Mr. and Mrs. Lee, related somehow to General Robert E. Lee. From their flowering terrace we could see *Capitana* riding at anchor. Mrs. Lee is the daughter of Mr. Cossart. He and William Hinton were the two great pioneers and promoters of Madeira. They were two Englishmen who bought the Deserta Islands at auction, and several heads of the original wild goats that then roamed unmolested, hang on the wall. Messrs. Cossart and Hinton made fortunes out of sugar, wine and other enterprises. The house is full of the most beautiful things. The high white Portuguese ceilings with elaborate mouldings, a wonderful collection of books on Madeira, a great variety of beautiful pieces of furniture, all add to the interest and charm of the interior. Mrs. Lee, herself, does the finest miniature embroidery ever seen, and she gave me an exquisite little Columbus window she had embroidered, that has ever since acted as my paperweight. They also had a book of the genealogy of the du Pont family, as a Cossart married a du Pont. Mrs. Lee's aunt had married Lord Kelvin, whose lifelong work in thermodynamics and electricity led to a theory of undersea signaling that resulted in the laying of the great transatlantic cable.

Later, when Sam joined us, we all went there and had a delicious English tea. A Mrs. Camera came too, most attractive, and said that her great-great-greataunt had been Columbus' wife. This because the Perestrello family "live forever," one member having lived to be ninety-nine

years old. This would be a lovely place in which to settle
down for a while.

The truth about the progress of the war is very difficult
to discover. The news is either obviously garbled or entirely lacking, and the future is anyone's guess from day
to day. Paul is getting anxious about what is happening at
home, and it looks to me as if we might soon be returning.

Saturday, November 18th. Las Palmas, Canary Islands.

Sighted the Canaries early in the A.M. and went on shore
at Las Palmas in time to spend an hour at the bank. Signing, signing—everything in duplicate. Two men writing, sorting, putting papers here and there; bothersome
work in the subtropics, all to cash two ten-dollar Express
checks. It isn't only Spanish bureaucracy at work in the
banks, but Hitler bureaucracy as well. Since the civil war,
the Germans have a strangle hold on the currency, and
some of it goes straight to Germany. They tell us
that hundreds of Germans have come here in the last few
months. The first girl we spoke to in the bus was a German. They run pensions, and are in every firm as well as
the hotels and banks.

We lunched at the hotel and found a Spanish woman
knitting on the terrace in the sun. Later she and her husband, Señor Torro came on board for cocktails and he
turned out to be the best friend of Don Rafael Medina,
and the Duke of Alcalá. Sam says that Señor Torro knows
more about Columbus than almost anyone he has met in
Spain or Portugal. He has been sent by Franco to repre-
sent him here and to keep order, so he is the head of the
Falanges in the Canaries. There is evidently a good deal
of discontent over the red tape.

We motored up into the country for a short drive. A heavenly, warm, cloudless day. Not a breath stirring. Apparently all the weather, rain, and wind is around Teneriffe. Here in the Grand Canary there is nothing but sunshine and warmth. An extremely heavy dew keeps the green things from getting too parched. To the cocktail party came the McKellars and a pretty daughter, conducted by Jim. They met at the party the night before at which everybody stayed till three, and Dwight made witty speeches in Spanish and covered himself with glory. The Millers, Señor and Señora Torro, the Mayor, a Spanish beauty and her husband, and two Pilchers formed the dinner party.

Mrs. McKellar is very much of an artist and she has several interesting pieces of wood carving done by a native carpenter. Book ends in the shape of the dogs or *canes* that the Canaries are named after, and a clever owl. We were also very much struck by a beautiful carved head of a negro girl in the museum, obviously done by a native artist, who had apparently just presented it to the museum. There seems to be a distinguished school of art and a great deal of native talent here, and I am much disappointed not to have seen more of it. There is also a very beautiful opera house with frescoes by the man who painted the bar in the Pilchers' house, and who died two years ago. I imagine that art flourishes in this climate— so warm, so sunny, and yet not enervating.

Mrs. McKellar has been here on and off for the last seven years, and lived here through the terrific strikes that harassed everyone beyond endurance soon after the monarchy fell, and until the civil war began. She said that during that time she didn't dare let the children and governess out of the house as there were continual threats against them by telephone, etc. And yet in spite of all this she believes that the Spaniards could have worked it out without the civil war.

Tuesday, November 21st. Teneriffe.

We are staying in such a nice little hotel, Piño de Oro, run by an Englishman named Lewis who has been here for twenty-five years. Nice old retainers for servants; good and sufficient food, though of course lacking butter and cream; a perfectly lovely garden, well kept up, even if the furniture is threadbare and the woodwork needs painting.

The Island of Teneriffe was originally the seat of the Guanches, who later spread to the other Canaries. Guanches is said to mean "Son of Teneriffe." The island is not very well formed to make many beautiful drives because the great peak, 12,000 feet high, rises up nearly in the center of the island and high mountains are on several of the shores. This means that there are very few beaches, and road building is difficult, and it is also almost impossible to find distant views of the peak. There are still many of the Guanches caves in use, as at Las Palmas. You can see here and there houses decorated in an Oriental manner standing out against the mountain. Cupolas and towers are decorated with coats of arms, and just a few hundred yards up the mountain are cave dwellers in rags, with chickens and goats, attending to the business of living in the most primitive kind of condition. The handsome banana plantations are all over the mountains, and are one of the main sources of income, as are also tomatoes and oranges. In Teneriffe is a building on which is a plaque stating that Franco began the war there.

Friday, November 24th.

Now I am doing nothing but packing those horrible possessions that gobble up so much of our precious time.

Very regretfully we are turning our steps homeward. The *Dominie* has arrived in port and we are going down to see her, and expect the worst. Behind her stands a British boat just starting for England with a cargo of oranges and bananas. The *Aquila* is painted black from bow to stern, even the lifeboats are black. There are sandbags around the pilot house and against the afterdeck and bulkheads, where they probably have stowed ammunition, and there is a four-inch gun on the stern. She is on her way into the dangers of the English Channel.

A very good cabin on the *Dominie*, and an extremely comfortable trip of three nights and two days in spite of all the ominous accounts of these boats from various people.

Manolo Gonzalez with two Custom officials, very kindly met us at Cadiz with a large car and helped us get through. Then we went back to his "Sans Souci" just being built, with swimming pool and tennis court and had some "1847" sherry. He gave us a bottle of it, and sped us on our way.

Then a drive to Seville, and after lunching there, a most beautiful drive from Seville to Badajoz, of about 200 kilometers. Very curving, very hilly with glorious mountains in the distance—a most uninhabited district. In all the 120 miles, we passed only two or three tiny towns. Just miles and miles of olive trees—probably great private estates—we could only guess. At one bend of a high hill we came on an overturned truck, and we had the feeling that if we overturned it might be days before anyone would be the wiser. The full moon rose at five, and for four more hours we drove in this wild, remote, beautiful part of Spain.

When we finally reached Badajoz the border was closed, so we spent the night in the Hotel Majestic between sheets that oozed so much cold clamminess that we kept on most of our clothes. The hotel was full of soldiers. Uniforms everywhere. Food shortage everywhere. Pictures of Franco, of Antonio de Ribera, of Moscardó. The hotel keeper compromising with his loyalties. The usual well mannered, soft-spoken, efficient German, running the border hotel.

Año de la victoria!

Ariba España!

Spain is a cold country with a hot sun. The heavy mist lies over everything till almost eleven o'clock in the morning. While our luggage is being packed on the car, we watch the town of Badajoz awaken through what was at first an almost impenetrable fog. The children, ragged or patched, laughingly carrying water jars, milk cans, baskets of groceries; the old women always in black, and always carrying something, or performing some duty. The young women with touches of bright color if they are peasants, if not, again in plain black with pretty, little black veils loosely covering their heads. Old men with great black sombreros, young soldiers in khaki and vermilion berets.

Our next journey will be by car as far as Lisbon, and then one more voyage across the Atlantic on the Swedish liner *Gripsholm,* one of the few steamers still bringing Americans home as the war waxes hotter. The last picture that I carried away with me, as we waved "adios" to a serious little group, was of a Spanish youth in a loose brown coat with a fur collar, cut along the lines of Columbus' cloak in the painting "Our Lady of the Fair Winds."

EPILOGUE

Our longest voyage of the seven happy cruises that had occupied many years, had come to an end. During the quiescent twenty-five year period, between the upheavals of World War I and World War II, we made hay while the sun shone, and we acknowledged our blessings. It was Paul Hammond who had had the vision to make the most of those golden opportunities as they presented themselves along the way.

As I cast a backward glance down the vista of the past, described in *The Wake of Odysseus,* I feel that our crowning experience was the voyage with historical research for its purpose. Our leader, Samuel Eliot Morison, who conceived and carried out the expedition, whose intellectual powers and devotion to his objectives we were privileged to share, offered us the adventure of a search for the truth, and we eagerly accepted it. He opened windows for us on cosmographical lore, on the Renaissance in Europe, on Spain, on Portugal, and on ocean islands. All travels, all meetings of minds add to the sum of enjoyment and profit, and given a fair wind, "a man's reach should exceed his grasp."

My dedication at the beginning of this volume is to Greece—to her gifts and attainments, and to the Goddess of Memory who reminds us that we are, indeed, the children of the Graeco-Roman world. That great heritage, from which we draw inspiration, unfailingly encourages our desire for freedom and truth.

If you search the world over, you will return to your native land, I am sure, convinced that there is no cruising ground anywhere so beautiful as among the Ionian and Aegean Islands. To scholars and students, and even to such untutored people as ourselves, the fruits to be garnered can be savored with relish, and are balm to the spirit.

In 1959 after World War II, we once again returned to the eastern Mediterranean, this time in possession of our dream-ship, *Rara Avis*. It is about a hundred and fifty years since Byron wrote of Greece in *Don Juan* and *Childe Harold's Pilgrimage* on the eve of victory in her War of Independence. What other poet has so successfully given us the flavor of her immortal era and the beauty of her panorama?

> The Isles of Greece, the Isles of Greece!
> Where burning Sappho loved and sung.
> Where grew the arts of war and peace,
> Where Phoebus rose and Delos sprung . . .

Bibliography

ANDERSON, ISABEL. *A Yacht in Mediterranean Seas*. Boston: Marshall Jones, 1930.

APOLLONIUS OF RHODES. *The Voyage of Argo*. E. V. Rieu (trans.). Baltimore: Penguin, 1959.

BERENSON, BERNARD. *The Passionate Sightseer*. New York: Simon & Schuster, 1960.

COTTRELL, LEONARD. *The Bull of Minos*. New York: Holt, 1959.

FERMOR, PATRICK LEIGH. *Mani*. New York: Harper, 1958.

FORSDYKE, SIR JOHN. *Greece Before Homer*. London: Max Parrish, 1956.

Four Famous Greek Plays. Paul Landis (ed.). New York: Random House, 1929.

FRAZER, SIR JAMES. *Greece and Rome*. S. G. Owen (ed.). London: Macmillan, 1949.

Hachette World Guides, Greece. Paris: Hachette, 1955.

Hachette World Guides, Turkey. New York: Hastings Howe, 1960.

HAMILTON, EDITH. *Greek Way to Western Civilization*. New York: Mentor, 1962.

HERODOTUS. *The Persian Wars*. George Rawlinson (trans.). New York: Modern Library, 1942.

HOMER. *Iliad*. E. V. Rieu (trans.). Baltimore: Penguin, 1956.
———. *Odyssey*. E. V. Rieu (trans.). Baltimore: Penguin, 1956.

KITTO, H. D. F. *The Greeks*. London: Pelican, 1956.

KINROSS, LORD. *Europa Minor*. New York: Morrow, 1956.

LIVINGSTONE, R. W. *Legacy of Greece*. London: Oxford, 1922.

LOOMIS, ALFRED F. *Hotspur's Cruise in the Aegean*. New York: Jonathan Cape & Harrison Smith, 1931.

LUCAS, F. L. and PRUDENCE. *From Olympus to the Styx*. London: Cassell, 1949.

MORISON, SAMUEL E. *The Admiral of the Ocean Sea*. Boston: Little, Brown, 1942.

———. *Christopher Columbus*. London: Faber, 1956.

RAND, CHRISTOPHER. *Grecian Calendar*. New York: Oxford, 1962.

RICHTER, GISELA. *A Handbook of Greek Art*. London: Phaidon, 1959.

ROUSE, W. H. D. *Gods, Heroes and Men of Ancient Greece*. New York: Mentor, 1957.

SAND, GEORGE. *A Winter in Majorca*. Robert Graves (trans.). London: Cassell, 1956.

SCHILD, GÖRAN. *In the Wake of Odysseus*. London: Staple, 1953.

SMITH, SIR WILLIAM. *Everyman's Smaller Classical Dictionary*. London: Dent, 1951.

STARK, FREYA. *Ionia—A Quest*. New York: Harcourt, 1955.

———. *The Lycian Shore*. New York: Harcourt, 1956.

TOYNBEE, ARNOLD J. *Greek Civilization and Character*. New York: Mentor, 1950.

U.S. Coast and Geodetic Surveys, and Hydrographic Office Charts, U.S. Navy, may both be obtained from T. S. & J. D. Negus, 69 Pearl Street, New York 4, N.Y.

Yachting in Greece, a pamphlet, and charts giving yachting facilities, may be obtained from the Royal Greek Yacht Club, Piraeus, Greece; or from the Greek Press and Information Service, 69 East 79th Street, New York 21, N.Y.

ZIMMERN, ALFRED. *The Greek Commonwealth*. New York: Modern Library, 1956.

Index